The Hamlyn Guide to
Freshwater Fishes
of Britain and Europe

Peter S. Maitland B.Sc Ph.D

Illustrated by Keith Linsell

HAMLYN
London · New York · Sydney · Toronto

Preface

The main aim of this book is to provide a short popular account of the freshwater fishes of Europe, together with a means of identifying them. Because of the large number of species involved only the major features of the biology of each can be presented, and this is done in an entirely consistent manner among species in order to facilitate comparisons. It is hoped that this guide will stimulate interest in Europe's attractive and varied fish fauna not only among those directly concerned, such as anglers, conservationists and fishery biologists, but also among those indirectly involved, such as agriculturalists, industrialists and politicians, whose thoughts and decisions are among the main factors affecting the future nature of Europe's fish populations.

In creating this guide I have been greatly assisted and encouraged by colleagues and correspondents in many different countries. I am very grateful for all their help. The magnificent colour illustrations by Keith Linsell represent, I believe, the finest set of paintings of European freshwater fishes ever executed, and are an enormous asset to a guide of this kind. The line drawings by Jennifer Middleton maintain the same high standard. I would like to thank both artists for their care and interest in the work.

The help I have received throughout the development of the book from both Ian Jackson and Derek Hall of Hamlyn has greatly facilitated its production and I am grateful for their patience and advice. Finally, my wife Kathleen has been of continuous assistance to me during this work. She has typed all drafts of the manuscript and helped in numerous other ways.

Peter S. Maitland

Line drawings by Jennifer Middleton

Published by The Hamlyn Publishing Group Limited
London · New York · Sydney · Toronto
Astronaut House, Feltham, Middlesex, England

Text set in Univers by Filmtype Services Limited, Scarborough, Yorkshire
Printed in Italy by Officine Grafiche A. Mondadori, Verona

Contents

How to use this book

This guide covers the continent of Europe bordered by the Atlantic, the Mediterranean, the Bosphorus, the Black Sea, the Caucasus Mountains, the Caspian Sea, the Ural River and Mountains and the Arctic Ocean (see fig. 1). This whole area covers a land mass of more than 10 million km² (3,900,000 ml²) and includes a very wide range of freshwater habitats, from cold deep northern lakes and rivers, some of which are frozen for much of the year, to warm shallow ponds and streams in the Mediterranean area which are never frozen.

The book is divided into four broad sections. First there is a general account of fishes — their structure and physiology, behaviour and development, and ecology and distribution. This is concluded by a study of their value to man, not only commercially, but also from sporting, aesthetic, and scientific viewpoints. The second section is an identification key to the families of fishes found in fresh water in Europe. This is based on the standard dichotomous pattern found in many keys, where at each point in the key the reader who is trying to identify a fish is presented with two alternatives. The one followed is that which fits the specimen best. Having selected one alternative the reader is then led to another couplet, and this continues until the identity of the family is reached. This can generally then be confirmed by reference to the outline diagram provided for each family. The third section of the book is probably the most important, and is a guide to the individual species, family by family. Having identified the family from the first key, the reader then goes to a similar type of key within each family section to make the final identification. This can then be confirmed by the colour illustration and to some extent by the distribution map — where for each species inland distribution is shown in red, and coastal distribution is shown in black. The final section of the book is a list of useful references for further reading — usually these relate to particular aspects of fish biology or to accounts of the fish fauna of one particular country — an illustrated glossary, and a number of age:length curves (see pages 246—247).

Formal identification using the whole key is often not necessary, especially with the more unusual or obvious species. Thus if the reader wishes to identify an eel-like fish with one pair of fins it can be seen immediately from page 58, that this must be in the family Anguillidae. On looking up the relevant page in the species catalogue it will be found that if it is from fresh water in Europe it can really only be one species — the common eel (*Anguilla anguilla*).

The English names in this guide are those in most common use, and each is followed by the appropriate scientific name. This consists of two parts: the genus (equivalent to a surname in Europe), and the specific name (equivalent to a christian name). It should be noted, however, that the specific name is always placed second. Where no English names are available for a species, the most acceptable foreign name, or its English translation is given. For each species, the text, distribution map and illustration are placed together. The text has been standardized as much as possible to facilitate comparisons, and includes information on the size, habitat, distribution, breeding habits, growth, food and value of each European species. The maps show the freshwater distribution, and where applicable, also the saltwater distribution. It must be remembered that each species occurs only in suitable types of water within the areas shown, and not everywhere. There is normally only one illustration for each species, except where there are major differences between the sexes, for instance in the three-spined stickleback, or specific colour varieties, for instance in the orfe. Where both sexes are illustrated, ♂ denotes male, and ♀ denotes female.

Fig. 1 Map of Europe showing some important rivers and towns

Introduction

There are many books written on various aspects of the freshwater fishes of Europe, and the more important of these studies are included in the list at the end of this guide. Each of these may in turn contain useful references to specific topics. Identification of many species found in Europe is often possible using certain of these publications, simply by reference to, and comparison with, the various illustrations in them. This is often a slow and inaccurate method of identification and, moreover, most of the older works on the freshwater fishes of Europe do not include those species introduced relatively recently, for instance largemouth bass (*Micropterus salmoides*) and humpback salmon (*Oncorhynchus gorbuscha*). It is hoped that this guide will prove to be a relatively simple but accurate means of identifying any species of fish found regularly in fresh or brackish water in Europe.

This guide includes animals belonging to both cyclostomes and Pisces. Technically, since the cyclostomes belong to the Agnatha and have therefore no proper jaws, only the latter are true fishes. However, in this book the term 'fish' is understood to include both cyclostomes and Pisces.

Unfortunately we are still very ignorant about many European fishes, and indeed it is doubtful if a number of the species included here are proper species. It is more likely that they are simply local races of a more widespread species. However, until the groups concerned have been reviewed by competent taxonomists, most of these 'species' are dealt with individually.

In addition to those species of fish which are known to occur in fresh waters in Europe, a few other categories are also included in this guide. The most important among these are brackish water forms which, although basically marine, are also found regularly in brackish and sometimes in fresh waters. Marine species which occur only infrequently in brackish water are generally not included in the key, although mention is made of a few of these fishes where there may be confusion with true brackish water forms. Of necessity, the decision whether or not to include some of these species has been rather arbitrary. Native forms make up the bulk of the European freshwater fish fauna, but there are also several introduced species which have thrived and bred in this continent, sometimes establishing populations over quite a wide area. All such species are included in the keys that follow. Other species of freshwater fish of doubtful status in Europe have not been included: among these are various tropical species associated with heated effluents, like the guppy (*Lebistes reticulatus*) and odd records of temperate species for which there is no evidence of the existence of a population.

This guide is intended for use in the field, so it should be feasible to return fishes to the water alive after capture, examination and identification. During this process specimens should always be kept as cool and as damp as possible. The features used to differentiate between families and between species are mainly external; and in this book characters which are as objective and absolute as possible have been selected where feasible. Nevertheless, it is necessary in some instances to resort to features which involve killing and dissecting the specimen; the characters concerned here are mainly found in the region of the head — pharyngeal bones (in the Cyprinidae), vomer bones (in the Salmonidae) and gills (in the Clupeidae), etc.

As already mentioned, the keys given follow the dichotomous pattern common to many field guides. Where possible, several distinguishing characters have been used at each point in the key and these should be considered in combination with each other. Every species is illustrated, and both the text and the relevant illustration should be consulted. Due consideration must always be given to the possibility of any specimen being very young, malformed in some way, or a hybrid.

The most common numerical features used in the key are counts of fin rays and of scales. In all the fin ray counts mentioned, the number for each fin includes both the branched and the unbranched rays. The main scale counts are taken along the lateral line, starting at the first scale behind the operculum and ending at the last scale before the caudal fin. Some diagonal scale counts may also be used: these are normally counted from the lateral line up to the adipose fin (where present), and from the lateral line down to the anal fin. Occasionally, counts are made from the lateral line up to the dorsal fin, and down to the pelvic fin.

Where colours are used in the key they refer to the condition in the fresh fish and should be true irrespective of size (above the larva and fry stages), sex and condition, unless otherwise stated. With many species it is possible to determine the sex accurately only by dissection of the sex organs (this is especially true outside the breeding season); with others there are constant external sexual differences.

Various species of fish in Europe hybridize quite frequently with one another in the wild. Such hybrids are clearly rather difficult to identify with a key such as is found here, and normally their characters are intermediate between those of the two parent species. Unfortunately, due to the very nature of speciation it is often those species of fish which are most alike (and thus difficult to identify) which are most likely to hybridize. A very wide variety of hybrids has been recorded from Europe, mostly in the family Cyprinidae.

Fig. 2 Measurements given in the descriptive part of this book are metric, but the corresponding imperial units can be found by noting the metric measurement and reading directly across on to the imperial scale

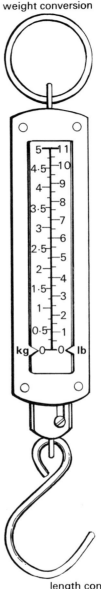

weight conversion

length conversion

cm	5	10	15	20	25	30	35	40	45	50
in	2	4	6	8	10	12	14	16	18	

Anatomy

The head

In fishes, most of the obvious external sense organs are located on the head: a pair of eyes, the nostrils (normally paired) and often barbels which may vary in number, size and position according to the species concerned. That part of the head anterior to the mouth is normally termed the snout. The position of the mouth itself can vary: it may be terminal, superior or inferior. In a few species of fish the mouth is modified to form a sucker. Associated with the mouth are several bones of taxonomic importance (see fig. 3); several of these sometimes carry teeth which may be long or short, permanent or deciduous. In adult lampreys oral discs are present which have supra-oral and infra-oral areas bearing teeth (see fig. 29). The mouth opens into the pharynx and in some fishes there are, at the back of this, bones specialized for chewing and crushing, known as pharyngeal bones; the structure of these is extremely important in the identification of the Cyprinidae (fig. 3). A diagrammatic representation of the form and positioning of the bones in the mouth of a fish is shown in fig. 4.

The alimentary canal

The pharynx leads into the oesophagus which opens, in turn, into the stomach. Food eaten by the fish is held for some time in the stomach before being passed into the intestine where it is digested; undigested materials continue into the rectum, from which they pass out through the anus as faeces. Most fishes are able to control their buoyancy in the water by means of a swim-bladder which is situated above the gut, and which in some groups is connected to the oesophagus by a duct.

The gills

Passing out from the sides of the pharynx are cavities leading past the main respiratory organs, the gills; together these form the branchial region (see fig. 5). Each gill consists essentially of a strong supporting arch, on one side of which is a set of comb-like rakers, whose function is

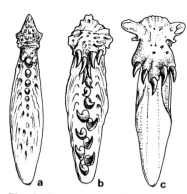

Fig. 3a Typical salmonid vomer bones: a = salmon; b = trout; c = charr

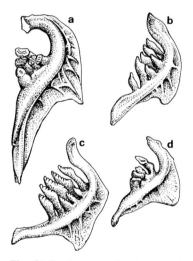

Fig. 3b Typical cyprinid pharyngeal bones: a = carp; b = silver bream; c = rudd; d = tench

to prevent material passing from the mouth into the delicate blood-filled respiratory lamellae, which are aligned on the other side of the gill arch. There are normally four gills on either side, the passages between them leading to the outside of the body through the gill openings. In most species these are protected by a single bony gill cover on either side, known as the operculum.

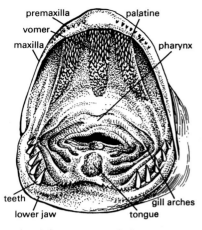

Fig. 4 Open mouth of pike showing major bones and teeth

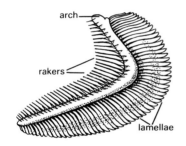

Fig. 5 Typical fish gill

The skin

The whole body is covered by skin; in most fishes small bony plates known as scales lie within this, forming a protective but extremely flexible covering over most areas except the head, where protection is afforded by the head bones themselves. The number and structure of the scales varies from species to species and they are often useful for identification purposes (see fig. 6). It should be noted, however, that in one species at least, *Cyprinus carpio*, there are cultivated varieties which have no scales (commonly called leather carp), or have a few very large scales (commonly called mirror carp). Some other species of fish

have no scales, and in others they are replaced by isolated bony scutes which project from the skin. Within the skin are pigment cells responsible for much of the coloration of the fish. Although colour patterning is a useful criterion for distinguishing various species of fish, it is one which should be regarded with caution, for even within a single species the colour can vary greatly with age, sex, season, time of day, emotional state, etc.

To the fish biologist scales present something more than just part of fish anatomy. Because of the structure of scales and the way they are laid down in the fish's skin, each represents a permanent record of the growth of its bearer in much the same way as the growth rings in the trunks of woodland trees (see fig. 7). Thus, given a single good scale from a mature fish, a competent biologist can often identify the species, give its age in years, and say how often it has spawned. In migratory fishes the biologist can often tell how long the specimen has spent in fresh water and how long in the sea, or how long in its nursery stream and how long in its present lake. In this way a detailed knowledge of scale anatomy is indispensable to any competent ichthyologist. Fig. 6 shows the general features of fish scales.

Only a few families of fish have no scales. In those which do there are normally differences between scales from different parts of the body — those from the head region, the lateral line and adjacent to the fins normally showing some modification of shape. Most keys refer to typical body scales (always the great majority) which are found above and below the lateral line between the head and the tail. The scales lie overlapping along the body of the fish like slates on a roof but, unlike slates, normally much less than half of each scale is exposed to view. The width of the circuli (ring-like ridges on fish scales), and the number laid down, is related to the growth of the fish: wide circuli indicate good (usually summer) growth, narrow circuli indicate poor (usually winter) growth. Groups of narrow circuli are normally formed each winter and are called annuli.

Fig. 6 Fish skin and scales: a = side view of scales near lateral line; b = section through lateral line showing its ducts passing through individual scales; c = individual scale; d = leather carp; e = mirror carp

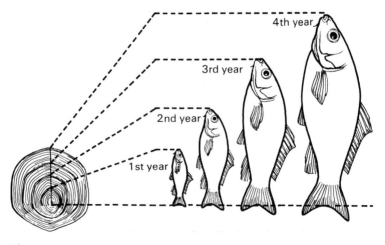

anterior field
circulus
lateral field
c
chromatophore
ctenii
posterior field

d

e

Apart from scales, other bony parts of the body can also be used for determining age: among the most important of these are the opercular bones and the otoliths.

Running along either side of the body in most fishes is the lateral line;

this is a long sensory canal just under the skin, but connected to the exterior by a series of pores. These often run through individual scales. The main function of the lateral line is sensory – the fine detection of various kinds of vibration through the water medium. Branches of the same system run on to the head region, where they terminate in sensory organs often found in grooves and cavities.

Fig. 7 Proportionate growth: the relationship between annual body length and size of scale in a cyprinid fish

4th year
3rd year
2nd year
1st year

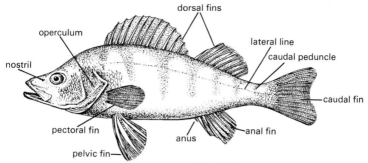

dorsal fins

operculum

lateral line

caudal peduncle

nostril

caudal fin

pectoral fin

anus

anal fin

pelvic fin

Fig. 8 Main external features of a typical fish (side view)

The fins

The typical arrangement of fins on a fish is shown in fig. 8. There are two sets of paired fins – the pectoral fins and the pelvic fins – both situated ventrally. These are equivalent to the fore and hind legs respectively of terrestrial vertebrates. On the back is a dorsal fin; this may occasionally consist of two distinct parts, or may be divided into two separate fins, or may have the anterior of these represented by several isolated spines. Behind the dorsal fin, in the Salmonidae and related families, is a small fleshy fin with no rays called the adipose fin. The portion of the body posterior to the anus is known as the caudal region. Ventrally, just behind the anus, this bears the anal fin, while posteriorly, behind where the body narrows to form the caudal peduncle, is the single caudal fin. The supporting structures of fins

are known as rays; these may be branched or unbranched (when they are usually referred to as spiny or bony), and are often useful taxonomic characters.

The skeleton and internal organs

Internally there are a number of important features which it is important to understand. As in other vertebrates the body of a fish is supported by a bony, but flexible, vertebral column. To this are linked the head and fins of the fish and the numerous blocks of muscle (often interspersed with fine bones) which run along either side of the body. This is that part of the body which gives propulsion, but it is also that most sought for food by man and other predators.

Below the vertebral column is the

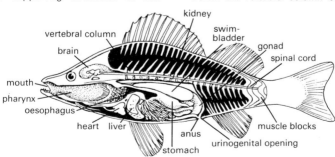

kidney

vertebral column

swim-bladder

brain

gonad

spinal cord

mouth

pharynx

oesophagus

heart   liver

anus

muscle blocks

urinogenital opening

stomach

Fig. 9 Main internal organs of a typical fish (side view)

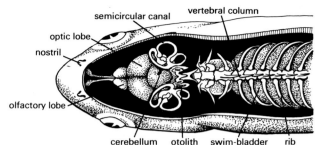

Fig. 10 Brain and balancing organs in a cyprinid fish (dorsal view)

major body cavity of the fish, containing many of its vital organs (see fig. 9); these can be examined properly only by dissection and are normally removed entirely during gutting. The gut has already been discussed. Associated with it is the liver, which is often used by man as food or as a source of rich oil. Above the gut on either side normally lie the sexual organs. These are relatively simple in most fishes and consist of two elongated bags opening to the exterior through a genital duct beside the anus. The sex of many fishes can be established only by examination of these organs: the ovaries normally contain what are obviously globular eggs — often yellowish or orange in colour, while the male testes are normally rather smooth and whitish in colour. Immediately below the vertebral column in most fishes lie the kidneys and the swim-bladder. The latter, by the adjustment of its volume through

gases being released from, or absorbed into, the blood of the fish, allows the maintenance of neutral buoyancy. This means that the fish has to expend no effort in maintaining its vertical position in the water.

Below the head and just posterior to the gills lies the muscular heart, which is responsible for pumping blood through the gills to be oxygenated, and then through the body of the fish.

The fish's brain is well protected inside a bony capsule and, although much simpler than the equivalent structure in birds and mammals, is none the less a complex lobed organ (see fig. 10). At the back of the head, also encased in bone, are the inner ears or semicircular canals which are particularly important in maintaining balance. Within a chamber inside them is secreted a loose piece of calcium carbonate, known as an otolith. This, like the scales, grows in proportion to the size of the fish.

Physiology

Digestion

Like all other animals fishes require food to live and grow. This food is always produced in the first instance by plants, but may come to the fish concerned indirectly via an invertebrate or a more complex food chain. By observation in the field and experiments in the laboratory, fish biologists have discovered much concerning the feeding behaviour and types of food eaten, as well as the nutritional value of different foods. Much of this work is very recent and related to developments in fish farming, which is discussed later.

A brief description has already been given of the mouth and gut of a fish. It is often not realized that not only is the mouth adapted to the type of food eaten but the gut also is often modified in this respect. Thus the oesophagus and stomach are very distensible in carnivorous fishes, allowing them to swallow whole fishes which are very large relative to their own size. The main purpose of the digestive system is to break down foods into soluble materials which can be absorbed through the gut wall and used by the fish for growth and metabolism. After food has been swallowed it is acted upon by various enzymes secreted by the gut and organs associated with it. Important among these is the liver which secretes bile, an important aid to digestion, and which also acts as a storage and processing organ for food after it has been absorbed.

Food material is moved down the gut by peristaltic waves of contraction of muscles in the gut wall. Although in some fishes a little absorption takes place in the stomach, it is in the intestine that most food material passes into the bloodstream as soluble fats, proteins and carbohydrates. Once food has been digested it can then be used to provide energy for movement, materials for replacing or regenerating old cells, or for growth. Since the body temperature of a fish is controlled by that of its environment, all these processes of metabolism are fast at high temperatures and slow at low temperatures. The efficiency of fishes in converting food is very variable but it is known in hatchery conditions, for instance, that rainbow trout have a conversion efficiency of about 3.5; i.e. for every 3.5 kg of food eaten they increase in weight by 1 kg.

Growth

The growth of fishes is closely concerned with the quality and quantity of food taken in, although many other factors (space, temperature, etc.) are involved too. One of the outstanding features of fishes is their phenomenal plasticity as far as growth is concerned. When food and other conditions are suitable many fishes are able to grow at very fast rates, but in adverse conditions, often with no food for long periods, they are able to maintain themselves with no growth at all. This is in considerable contrast to most birds and mammals which are much less flexible in this respect, and usually die after a relatively short period without food. Unlike birds and mammals, fishes continue to grow throughout their lives and do not stop on becoming sexually mature. Many small species of fish – especially in tropical zones, live for only 1 or 2 years, but some large species may live for up to 30 years.

The circulatory system

The circulatory system of a fish is one of the major aspects of its physiology, linking digestion, respiration and excretion. Its main function is to carry oxygen and carbon dioxide, cell wastes and products of excretion, and minerals and dissolved foods through the body. The blood of fishes, as in other vertebrates, consists of a fluid plasma in which are dissolved various materials, and in which the solid blood cells are carried. These blood cells are of two types: white lymphocytes and leucocytes, and red erythrocytes. The red haemoglobin in the latter greatly aids oxygen transport in the blood. The actual amount of blood present in the body of a fish is quite low, and is usually only about 2–3 per cent of the body weight (it is more than 6 per cent in mammals).

The circulatory system of fishes is relatively simple, consisting basically of a continuous tubular system of heart, arteries, capillaries and veins (see fig. 11). The heart (which contains one-way valves) pumps the blood forward into the gills where it passes through fine capillaries in close contact with the water outside. The blood then collects in vessels which transport it to the various tissues of the body where it again passes through capillary systems. The blood then passes into veins and back directly to the heart, although some flows through the liver and the kidneys where it passes through yet another capillary system before moving to the heart. Blood pressure is at its highest on leaving the heart, but drops considerably after passing through each capillary system and is quite low by the time it passes through the final major veins into the heart.

Respiration

Respiration in fishes, as in other animals, is concerned with the intake of oxygen and the elimination of waste carbon dioxide — one of the main products of internal cellular activity. The gills of fishes are equivalent to the lungs of many terrestrial animals, and represent the site where oxygen from the water in which the fish is living enters the bloodstream, and carbon dioxide leaves it. In a number of adult fishes and in many fish fry, some respiration takes place through the skin. It will be obvious that respiration in fishes is closely linked with the circulatory system — particularly in the area of the gills.

There are two main types of gills found among fishes. In the pouch-like gills of the lampreys (and other Agnatha) each pouch has an internal opening to the pharynx and an external opening to the water. The branchial gills of higher fishes, however, are carried on arches on either side of the oesophagus and connect individually to the outside through a series of gill slits (as in sharks and rays) or through a single opening protected and controlled by the gill cover or operculum. In a few unusual types of fish, particularly those which may have to withstand drought from

time to time, there are specialized organs of respiration involving the gut or swim-bladder. In all gill systems the main objective is the same: to allow maximum contact of the blood in the gill capillaries (enclosed in thin epithelial tissue) with the water moving past the gills.

The water moving over the gills is kept in constant unidirectional motion by the fish. When the fish's mouth opens, water is sucked inside and fills the whole of the mouth and buccal cavity, on either side of which are the gills. The mouth then closes and water is forced between the gills and out past the opercula which are opened at this point. Thus the mouth and opercula are in constant alternate motion at a rate dependent on the oxygen requirements of the fish. The flow of water is always one way, except in the case of lampreys where, when use of the sucker prevents entry of water, this passes both in and out of the gills by the pumping action of the buccal cavity. The respiratory system of fishes is made even more efficient by the fact that the flow of blood within the gills, and of water surrounding the gills, is in opposite directions, blood passing from the heart forwards, water passing from the mouth backwards. Counterflows of this nature are the most efficient methods of transferring materials from one solution to another.

Most of the oxygen taken up in the blood of fishes is carried in the red blood cells. This allows far larger amounts to be carried than are contained in the same volume of water. As oxygen is taken up, so carbon dioxide is released, and when the blood finally passes from the gills to the tissues it is rich in the former but deficient in the latter.

Excretion

A further function of the gills of fish which should not be forgotten is that concerned with the uptake and excretion of various salts. Fishes excrete their body wastes in various ways, partly through the gills, partly into the gut to pass out with the faeces, but mainly, as in other vertebrates, through the kidneys, from which the waste products pass to the exterior through special ducts. In fishes the kidneys have the dual function of eliminating body wastes and helping to control the water-salt balance. Fish blood is in a constant and dynamic equilibrium with its surroundings, in other words it can make changes in response to changing external salt concentration. This is a result of the process known as osmosis, in which water in solutions separated by a permeable membrane will pass from the more dilute solution into the more concentrated until they are at the same concentration. Thus in sea water, which is more concentrated than blood, water tends to pass out from the fish mainly through the gills, and fishes have to drink water regularly to compensate,

while in fresh water, water tends to pass in through the gills and must constantly be discharged via the kidneys to compensate. The ability to control the quality of the blood in relation to outside salt concentration is the main factor preventing fresh-water fishes from living in the sea and vice versa. Fishes which are able to pass from sea water to fresh and back have special excretory abilities.

The kidneys of fishes are made up of numerous small tubules. These act, under the pressure of the blood, as minute filters which take out various, mainly nitrogenous, salts from the blood and pass these, together with excess water, to the outside via the renal ducts. These open very close to the anus of the fish.

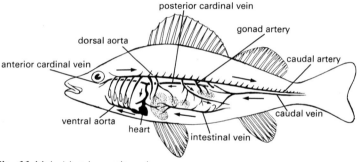

posterior cardinal vein

gonad artery

dorsal aorta

caudal artery

anterior cardinal vein

heart

caudal vein

ventral aorta

intestinal vein

Fig. 11 Main blood vessels and direction of flow in a typical fish (side view)

Behaviour

The behaviour of fishes, like that of other vertebrates, is made up of two components — instinct and learning. There can be no doubt that much of the life of the fish is dominated by the former, but the learning process should not be underrated, as a visit to a modern fish farm will show. Here, fish such as rainbow trout learn quickly to assemble at particular places to be fed, or even to feed themselves from automatic dispensers which release food when the fish presses on a lever.

Shoaling

One of the simplest kinds of behaviour is that shown by shoaling species. Many species of fish are solitary virtually all their lives, except to meet up with members of the opposite sex for spawning purposes, while others spend most of their lives in company with members of their own species, forming shoals which may often number many thousands. Most of the purely solitary species are predatory and often large: the pike is a good example. Other than on the spawning grounds members of this species are rarely found together in any numbers. One of the reasons for this is that large pike regularly eat smaller pike, and in certain situations where suitable food species are rare or absent they eat little else.

Shoaling species on the other hand tend to be smaller, herbivorous, or more commonly omnivorous, fishes which keep together in packs, the density of which usually depends on the activity in which they are engaged. Shoaling fishes often, but by no means always, tend to be silvery in colour, living in open areas of water. The roach is a good example of a shoaling species. Almost immediately after hatching the young start to congregate together and move about as one unit. This unit is at its most dispersed at night or sometimes when feeding, but when moving about — especially rapidly if danger threatens — a very tight pack is formed. These shoals may break up to form smaller units or join together to form larger ones, but many of the fishes may remain together most of

their lives. Spawning is likewise a shoaling activity, sometimes preceded by a very obvious migration in which enormous shoals move to one part of a lake or migrate upstream into rivers to lay their eggs.

The function of shoaling behaviour is usually thought to be one of mutual protection and advantage. It is much more difficult for predators to approach without being seen, while a new source of food discovered by one member of the shoal is very soon likely to be engaging the attention of most of its members. Sometimes fishes are found together in considerable numbers and are called shoals, but the congregation is one of chance and there is no interplay or reaction between fishes as in a true shoal. Thus during winter certain fishes, for instance sturgeon, may congregate in deep holes in lakes or rivers and remain together in a rather torpid state for many weeks.

Migration

This aspect of fish behaviour has received considerable attention from fish biologists and others. Many more fishes undertake migrations than is commonly supposed, but these are often of a local nature and do not involve the spectacular distances undertaken, or location problems solved by the better-known species. A good example of small-scale migration is found in the trout, populations of which are found in many thousands of lakes all over northern and highland Europe. The adult trout in these lakes are territorial and often occupy one small area of the lake for most of the year. In the autumn, however, they move to the mouths of streams entering the lake and migrate upstream to the spawning grounds. Normally trout only migrate into the actual stream in which they themselves were hatched.

In both Atlantic and Pacific salmon a similar pattern of migratory behaviour is exhibited, but the distances travelled and obstacles surmounted are spectacular. It is now known that many Atlantic salmon reach maturity in the seas off Greenland. In order to reach the European (or North American) coast these fishes have to migrate in a particular direction for many hundreds of kilometres and then locate the mouth of the river from which they migrated (see fig. 12). They then have to migrate through the estuary with its violent changes of salinity (and in modern times not insignificant pollution) and upstream to the headwaters, sometimes leaping waterfalls over 2m (6.5ft) in height. In contrast, the migration of the few adult fishes which live to return to the sea, or of the descending smolts, seems a much simpler and more passive affair, but in fact many of the same problems are involved. Although much studied, some of the patterns of behaviour responsible for the migratory abilities of these fishes are still not clearly understood. In general it is felt that orientation over long distances, say in the sea, is related to physical features such as water currents, but that in location and selection of parent rivers, chemistry is more important.

Migratory fish species such as salmon which move into fresh water to spawn but then pass down to the sea to grow to maturity are called *anadromous*. Sturgeon and several other species come into this category. *Catadromous* species, on the other hand, show the opposite type of behaviour, growing up in fresh water but migrating downstream to the sea to spawn. Eels and some populations of flounders are good examples of this category (see fig. 13).

Fig. 12 Life history of the Atlantic salmon

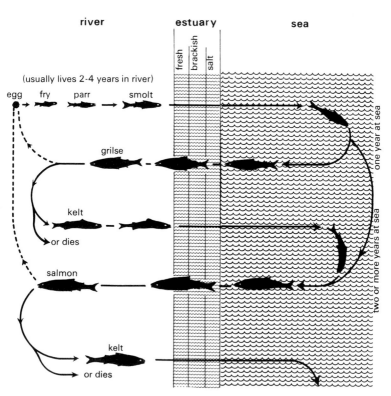

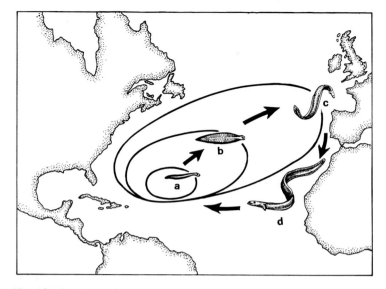

Fig. 13 Life history of the eel:
a = young larva leaving the
Sargasso area where it was
spawned; b = maturing larva
(leptocephalus) drifting across the
Atlantic; c = elver about to enter
fresh water on European coast;
d = adult eel returning to the
Sargasso to spawn

Breeding

The behavioural aspects of fish biology reach their most complicated
and bizarre at breeding time. In many
species only then is it possible to
distinguish externally between the
sexes, sometimes simply because the
female is very plump and swollen
with eggs, but more often because
the male has become brightly
coloured or has developed tubercles.
These are small white lumps which
appear on the head and sometimes
the fins and bodies of sexually mature
fishes during the spawning season.
They are most common among the
Cyprinidae, but occur in some other
families too (e.g. Coregonidae).
Many types of behaviour are shown
by a single species of fish during the
breeding season; apart from the
spawning act itself these range from
aggression towards males of the
same species, or predators of the

eggs and young, through complicated
nest-building activities, to fanning
the eggs in the nest and actively
'herding' the young fishes until they
can fend for themselves.

The Cyprinidae as a whole show
relatively little in the way of sophisticated spawning behaviour, although
a distinct exception to this is the
bitterling. This is a small, unobtrusive
fish which lives in ponds, canals and
slow-flowing rivers; for much of the
year the sexes are alike. At the be-
ginning of the breeding season in
late spring, however, the male becomes much more colourful and
exhibits beautiful blues and reds on
the body and fins. The female at this
time grows a long, thin, flexible tube
from the genital opening, which is in
fact an ovipositor. A pair of fishes
establish a territory in an area within
which is a freshwater mussel. After
preliminary courtship behaviour, the
pair approach the mussel and the
female, using her ovipositor, lays one
or more eggs actually inside the
mussel via its inhalent siphon; these
are fertilized instantly by the male
(see fig. 14). The process is repeated
until all the eggs are laid. Inside the
mussel via its inhalant siphon; these
oxygenated by the water currents
created by the mussel until they

hatch and the fry swim outside. After the spawning season the adults lose both their external sexual characteristics and their interest in mussels.

One of the best studied examples of sexual behaviour in the animal kingdom is that of the common three-spined stickleback. Outside the breeding season the sexes are very similar — usually a dull mottled grey-green — but in spring the male develops a bright red throat and belly, and iridescent blue-green eyes and sides. The female becomes silvery and very plump. Always a rather aggressive species, the male becomes particularly so at this time, establishing a territory and driving away intruders of all kinds. Within this area he starts nest building, clearing a shallow depression in which is built a tubular nest made up of fine pieces of plant material. Any ripe females

in the area are actively courted and led to the nest where they lay their eggs, which are then fertilized by the male. Usually the procedure is repeated with two or three females. These are driven away following spawning and the male defends the nest, keeping it clean and periodically fanning the eggs to keep them oxygenated. Even after the eggs have hatched the father protects the young for some days until they can swim well and fend for themselves. After the breeding season the fishes lose their colours and interest in territories.

Thorough and painstaking analyses of this apparently complex behaviour have shown that it is completely stereotyped and each part of it will only take place when the fish has been 'triggered' by some release mechanism. The spawning pattern

Fig. 14 Spawning behaviour in the bitterling

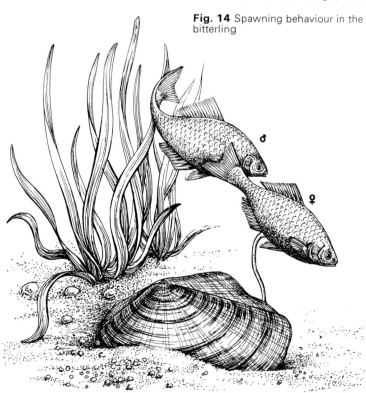

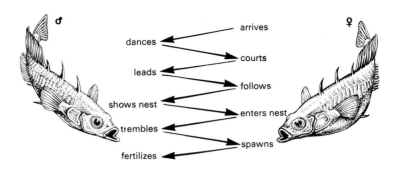

Fig. 15 Ritualized courtship behaviour of the three-spined stickleback (after Tinbergen)

is shown diagrammatically in fig. 15. The male will only perform the characteristic zig-zag dance in the presence of a ripe female. The two significant features of the female appear to be her silver colour and her plumpness, for the male can be persuaded to perform before a crude model as long as it is silver and has a large belly. Each display or movement by one sex releases the next movement in the other until the whole sequence is carried through or fails to develop through lack of appropriate response.

Feeding

The behaviour of fishes during feeding is also of extreme interest to biologists, anglers and others concerned with fishes. It is at this time that fishes exhibit their greatest potential for learning, and the opportunist nature of many species has led to their considerable success in some waters. The feeding patterns of some species, notably predators such as pikeperch on the one hand, and filter feeders such as lamprey larvae on the other, are very instinctive and stereotyped. Other fishes are more adaptable. Thus trout in a river may be feeding actively on benthic invertebrates on the bottom one day, but ignoring these completely the next day to feed on mayflies emerging near the edge. On the third day both these sources may not appear in the diet, and instead it will consist of terrestrial insects blown on to the water surface from nearby trees. In changing circumstances like these, opportunist fish species tend to choose the food source which is most easily available to them for the least expenditure of energy.

Development

Almost all European fishes are oviparous, i.e. the sperm and eggs are ejected close together in the water, and after fertilization the egg undergoes development quite independent of its parents, although they may protect it and keep it clean, etc. An exception to this system is the mosquito fish, where the anal fin of the male is modified to form an elongate penis. This is used to fertilize the eggs inside the female, where they remain protected until they hatch and the young are born alive. They do not, however, receive any food materials from the female subsequent to fertilization.

In all the other species in Europe the reproductive systems are essentially of one type, consisting of paired gonads (ovaries in the female, testes in the male) and their ducts leading to the exterior. In the testes a process known as spermatogenesis gives rise to the development of specialized sex cells known as sperm. These carry the hereditary characters of the father, and in order to ensure successful fertilization they are produced in huge numbers. Each sperm has a long whip-like tail which enables it to swim about in the seminal fluid secreted by the sperm ducts and subsequently in the water.

Oogenesis is the process in the female equivalent to spermatogenesis, and leads to the development of varying numbers of eggs within the ovary of the female. Like sperm, each egg carries hereditary characteristics of its parent but the cell itself is very much larger, having been provided during development with large quantities of yolk and fat. The number of eggs produced by a female fish generally increases with her size and varies tremendously among species. Thus small fishes like three-spined sticklebacks and bitterling, whose eggs and early fry are afforded considerable protection after laying, lay relatively few (50–100) eggs at each spawning. Larger species, however, whose eggs are shed into the water and given no further protection lay very large numbers each year (up to 1 million in the flounder). The number of eggs laid by a female is referred to as her fecundity.

Reproduction in almost all European fishes is a cyclic process, usually related to the seasons of the year. It is controlled by reproductive hormones whose secretions are in turn dependent on outside factors such as temperature and day length. The gonads, particularly the ovaries, may undergo tremendous changes in size and appearance during the year, starting at their smallest just after the spawning season and increasing to a maximum just before the next season, when the sexual products are shed (see fig. 16). Although the actual spawning period is normally relatively short for any population of a species (usually a few weeks) the time of year at which different species spawn can vary tremendously. Thus in Europe some fishes are spawning in each month of the year.

After spawning, the eggs of different fish species may find themselves in very varying situations. Many species construct a nest to give the eggs some protection during development. This 'nest' may be simply an open depression in the substrate, as in the rock bass; a similar hole in which the eggs are laid but then covered by additional substrate, as in the salmon and trout; a space cleared out underneath a rock, as in the bullhead; or a much more complicated structure created from pieces of weed, as in the three-spined stickleback. Some species protect the eggs and often the young fishes in these nests (for instance the rock bass), others leave them immediately after spawning (for instance the salmon).

Eggs which are spawned without the protection of a nest of some kind can be laid in various ways. A few species, perch for example, lay long strings of eggs which tangle up among vegetation. Many others lay adhesive eggs which may stick to stones (as in the sturgeon), to plants (as in the carp and pike), or to sand and plant roots (as in the gudgeon and spined loach). The spawning of the bitterling inside mussels has already been discussed in detail. Finally, other species spawn in the water, and the eggs may float (as in the golden mullet), or sink to the bottom and lie loose there (as in the cisco).

The time taken for egg development varies tremendously among species, and within species is very dependent on temperature. Usually the eggs of fishes which spawn in spring — and especially in summer — hatch quickly. The incubation period in carp lasts only 3—5 days. In fishes like the salmon which spawn in autumn and winter on the other hand, the eggs may take up to 150 days to hatch, or even longer.

During incubation the egg itself naturally undergoes profound changes. Most of its volume is occupied by the yolk; the cell resulting from the union of the sperm and the ovum being very small. This cell undergoes a process known as cleavage to give 2 cells, then 4, then 8, 16, 32 and so on, and each group of cells starts to grow and differentiate into a part of the embryo. The yolk is gradually used up during this process and eventually the egg consists of a spherical membrane, inside which is curled up a small embryo fish. The eyes and the constantly beating heart can be seen quite clearly at this stage.

After hatching, the young fish may start swimming immediately and continue to do so for more or less the rest of its life (for instance whitefish) or, more commonly, it will rest in a protected place for some time until

Fig. 16 Ventral view of dissections showing the typical cycle of ovary development in a fish

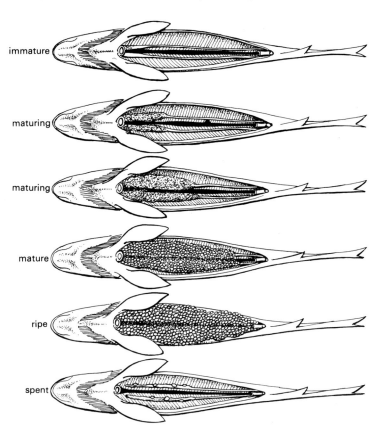

immature

maturing

maturing

mature

ripe

spent

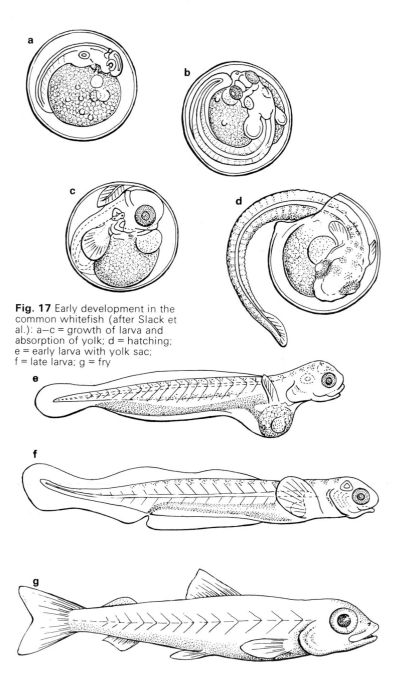

Fig. 17 Early development in the common whitefish (after Slack et al.): a–c = growth of larva and absorption of yolk; d = hatching; e = early larva with yolk sac; f = late larva; g = fry

23

the remains of the yolk sac are fully absorbed. Salmon remain among gravel in their nest during this period, while pike have a temporary adhesive organ by means of which they hang, resting, attached to vegetation. At some time during this period most species make a swift visit to the water surface to fill the swim-bladder initially.

The very young stages of fish are given a variety of names, the meaning of which is often rather imprecise. In general, the term larva is used to describe the stage from hatching until the fish is a miniature adult (see fig. 17). This may take only a few days in carp, but up to several years in eels and the sea lamprey. In some species, including the two just mentioned, the two forms are so different that they were originally described by scientists as different species. The larval stage itself is sometimes divided into prolarval, where the yolk sac is present, and postlarval, when it has disappeared. In general, larvae are characterized by transparency, absence of scales, presence of large pigment cells and embryonic, undifferentiated fins. Beyond the larval stage fishes tend to look very much more like the adults although many features, particularly coloration and sexual differences, are not evident until full maturity is reached. As indicated elsewhere, most identification keys, including the one in this book, refer to mature specimens of the species concerned and some diffi-

culty may be met if only young fishes are available. If it is necessary to identify larval specimens, specialist keys must be used.

The age at which fishes become mature (i.e. are able to reproduce) varies very much among different species and even among different populations of the same species. In general, sexual maturity is related to size, which in turn is dependent on growth. Thus fishes in fast-growing populations tend to become mature earlier than those in slow-growing populations. Both food and temperature affect growth; fishes at higher latitudes mature later than those at lower ones. In Finland, roach do not mature until they are 5—6 years old, whereas in southern Europe the same species may be mature at 2—3 years.

Small species tend to mature and die early. The stellate tadpole goby, for instance, matures and dies within 1 year, whereas the beluga does not mature until it is 15—20 years old and may live for 10 or more years beyond that. Some fishes spawn only once; the Atlantic salmon spends 2—6 years in fresh water and a further 1—2 years in the sea before it is mature, but very few fishes live beyond this to spawn a second time. In the case of the humpback salmon and the eel there appears to be complete mortality after the first spawning. Other species, such as trout, may spawn several times during their lives.

As previously mentioned, the growth of most European fish species takes place in annual spurts — usually during the warmer months of the year. These seasonal variations lead to physical differences in scales and various bones, which are of great value to fishery biologists in determining age and growth. Growth itself is controlled by many factors, among which the most important are food, temperature and genetic constitution of the population, and the individual concerned. An understanding of these and other factors is essential to the successful management of fish stocks, particularly in fish farms and small closed sport

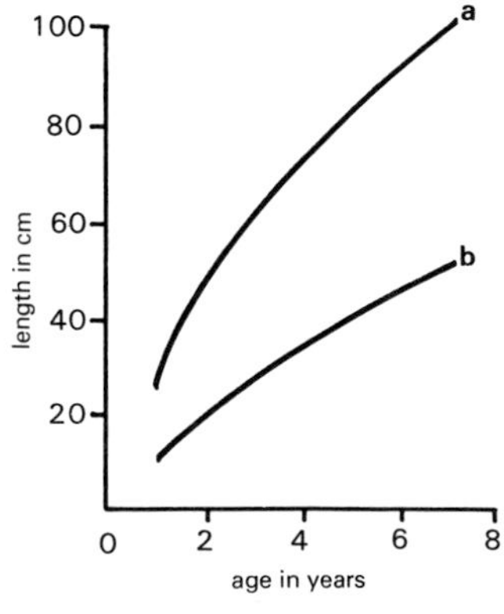

Fig. 18 Fast and slow growth in the pike: a = Lough Rea, Ireland; b = Dubh Lochan, Scotland

fisheries where success may be determined by the ability of the fish stock to achieve optimum growth (see fig. 18).

It has been shown that in both benthic and pelagic feeding fishes growth is related to the amount of food available. Thus populations of carp in ponds with high densities of invertebrates grow faster than those in ponds with low densities. The growth of the latter fishes may be improved either by decreasing the number of fishes, or increasing the density of the benthos (the animals and plants living in, or on, the bottom of the habitat). Changes in the quality and quantity of food can very quickly affect growth rates. In Atlantic salmon, for instance, a dramatic increase in growth takes place immediately after migration from fresh water to the sea. For their first few years sea trout and brown trout may live together in streams and grow at identical rates. As soon as sea trout move into salt water, however, they start to grow at a very much faster rate than brown trout which have remained in fresh water. Growth is usually measured by increase in weight or in length. There are three different ways of measuring length in fishes (see fig. 19), fork length being the measure in commonest use.

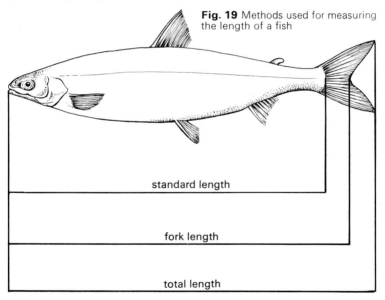

Fig. 19 Methods used for measuring the length of a fish

standard length

fork length

total length

Ecology

Ecology is the study of animals and plants in relation to their environment. In the case of any particular species of fish this means understanding not only its physical and chemical surroundings, but also its biological surroundings—vegetation, predators and prey. The whole basis of speciation in the biological world is related to the fact that over generations species of animals and plants develop differently from one another as a result of one type being particularly successful in at least one environment. This implies that, although living together in the same body of water, different species often tend to exploit different parts of it.

Physically, fresh waters may be divided into two major categories—running and standing waters. The obvious primary distinction between these is the constant unidirectional flow of water in the former, and its absence in the latter. Each has different size categories. Running waters, for instance, range from small trickles and burns through streams to large rivers. Canals are an important type of man-made running water. Standing waters range from small (often temporary) pools, through ponds to large lakes (see fig. 20). The most important type of man-made systems in this category are reservoirs, which in some areas are the dominant type of water body.

Superimposed on the size and other physical attributes of a water (its altitude, geology, etc.) is its chemistry. Apart from the influence of salinity in waters in coastal areas, the chemical nature of a water depends basically on the geology of its catchment. Broadly speaking, base-rich rocks and soils (limestones, some sandstones, etc.) give rise to chemically rich water while base-poor rocks (granites and other igneous rocks) are associated with poor waters. Often the former are found in lowland areas and the latter in highland areas. The influence of man is important here, and the forms of agriculture carried out in a catchment can substantially affect the chemical quality of the water there. Lowland waters tend to be affected more than highland waters in this way.

Biologically speaking, two major types of water are recognized by freshwater biologists. *Eutrophic* waters are usually rather turbid, with chemically rich water characterized by high pH and alkalinity. The invertebrate fauna is made up of large numbers of worms, leeches, snails, mussels and shrimps, while coarse fishes, especially Cyprinidae, are the dominant vertebrates. In *oligotrophic* waters on the other hand, the clear water is low in chemicals and is typically acid with a low pH. The invertebrate fauna is dominated by insects, especially stoneflies, mayflies and midge larvae, while Salmonidae are the major fishes found. A third type of water, known as *dystrophic*, is found in some areas. This is characterized by high quantities of humic acids derived from peat which stain the water brownish.

Although waters can be classified into these various types there are often intermediate categories, and indeed a single system may be divided in several different ways according to which part is examined. This is particularly true in the case of large rivers (see fig. 21). In the upper reaches of a typical river the main substrate is often near the source, followed by bare rock and boulders farther downstream. The river is very small (often not more than a trickle in dry weather) and the gradient is steep. The dissolved salt content of the water and the average temperature are low, and higher plants are represented by mosses. The dominant invertebrates are stoneflies and very few fishes occur. Those that do occur are usually only trout, but sometimes bullheads and a few other highland species also occur.

In the middle reaches of the river the volume increases and the main substrate gradually changes from boulders to stones, and thereafter from stones to gravel. The gradient is now much less steep, and the dissolved salt content of the water is higher than upstream. A number of

Fig. 20 Typical highland lake showing the main fish habitats: the shallow weedy or stony *littoral zone;* the *pelagic zone* of open water; and the deep *profundal zone*

higher plants occur here, and a variety of invertebrates, particularly mayflies and caddisflies. A wider variety of fishes occurs, often including trout, bullhead, grayling, minnows and loach. In the lower reaches of the river the substrate of coarse gravel gives way to sand and eventually to fine silt near the mouth. Here the river is large, and the gradient slight, while the dissolved salt content is relatively high. The river is flowing at low altitudes and the average water temperature is much higher than near the source. A wide variety of invertebrates and plants occurs here, some typical of rivers, others commonly also found in ponds and lakes. The fish fauna is varied and includes many cyprinid fishes such as bream, tench, roach and carp, as well as perch, pike, eels and many others.

Near the sea the river opens out into a broad estuary and the ecolo-

Fig. 21 Typical river starting in an upland area where the current is fast and the bed stony, and finishing in the lowlands where the current is slow and the bottom silty or weedy.

gical situation is dominated by the regular presence of salt, or at least brackish, water. Many of the fishes found upstream are immediately restricted here, but a few are tolerant (e.g. sticklebacks and dace), and many others pass through as they migrate to or from fresh water. Such fishes include lampreys, eels, salmon and flounders. Typical estuarine species are shads, smelt and mullets.

Zones characterized by different fish species must not be treated too seriously for they are obviously dependent on the species concerned being present in the river system. Thus most rivers in the north of Scotland have only two non-migratory freshwater species (trout and sticklebacks), whereas rivers in the south of Europe may have twenty to thirty species. Schemes of classification developed by ecologists for one area are often transplanted to others with most curious effects.

The food available to fishes is obviously a very important part of their environment, and indeed one on which the survival of each population depends (see fig. 22). Many fishes are much more opportunist in their feeding behaviour than fisher-

men or scientists give them credit for, and although their diet may be virtually 100 per cent one type of food on one day it may be quite different the next. In broad terms, however, fishes may be divided into categories according to the type of food they eat, although it must always be remembered that the diet of young fishes often differs from adults'.

A few fishes feed on fine organic detritus and microscopic organisms on the beds of rivers. Lamprey larvae feed wholly on such material which is carried into the mouth by currents and filtered off in the pharynx. Zooplankton, those small transparent invertebrates which spend all their lives floating free in the water, are an important source of food to many young fishes and some adults, notably charr and whitefish. Benthic invertebrates are a major source of food for fishes and many species are highly modified (in the possession of barbels, etc.) for locating these small animals and grubbing them out of the bottom. Good examples of these are sturgeon, carp, and loach. Plants are eaten in large quantities by very few fishes in Europe, although rudd and a few others eat them as part of

an omnivorous diet. A number of fishes are piscivorous and feed on various other species. Good examples of these are pike and pikeperch. Such fishes are often cannibalistic and can indeed survive perfectly well in the absence of any other fish species. Thus several cases of pure pike populations are known, where the young fishes feed on invertebrates, while they themselves form the food of the adult fishes.

The transfer of material in this way from one type of organism to another, which is then eaten by a third, is called a food chain or food web. The amount of organic material accumulated at each stage is referred to as *production*, and is most often measured as weight, or less commonly, but more precisely, as units of energy (such as calories or joules). At each stage in the chain there is considerable loss of energy due to metabolism and other processes, and usually only between 10 and 30 per cent is transferred to the next level.

The basis of most food chains in nature is the energy supplied by the sun. This is utilized by green plants (during the process known as photo-

synthesis) to elaborate more plant tissue from carbon dioxide, nutrient salts and water. These plants (called the primary producers) are then eaten by herbivorous animals (called the secondary producers) such as insect larvae, which in turn become the food of carnivorous fishes (the tertiary producers) such as trout. Food chains may be quite simple, for example diatom — rudd — pike, or more complex, for example diatom — water flea — water beetle — trout — pike — osprey.

Fig. 22 Diet of five common fishes in a stream community (River Endrick, Scotland)

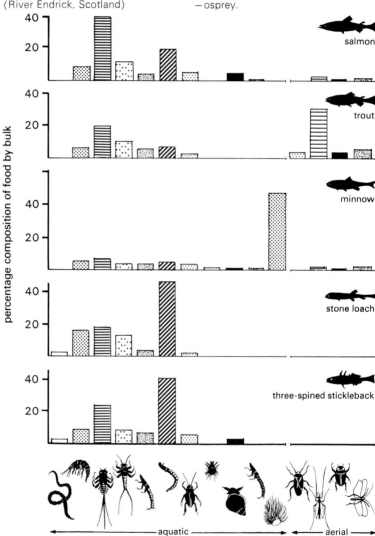

percentage composition of food by bulk

aquatic — aerial

principal food items

Distribution

The distribution of fish species within a given geographic area can be considered at two levels: their general occurrence or absence throughout the area, and their detailed presence and abundance in specific waters there. The reasons for the general spatial distribution of any species are mainly historical while specific sites where the species is successful are usually determined by ecological factors.

Although the status of a few of the species and subspecies mentioned in this book is in some doubt, roughly 215 species can be listed for Europe (*c.* 10 million km²) as a whole. These are contained within 29 different families. This is a far less rich fish fauna than that of any other continent and the reasons for this are of considerable interest. For instance, North America (*c.* 24 million km²) has 687 species in 34 families, and Africa (*c.* 30 million km²) has 1,425 species in 50 families. Many of the reasons for this are found by a study of the history of the area, and in particular the impact of the Ice Ages.

During the last Ice Age, which came to an end approximately 10,000 years ago, almost the whole of the British Isles and much of northern and central Europe were completely covered by ice. This meant that at that time the fish fauna of Europe was made up partly of cold-tolerant forms which were able to survive in the lakes and rivers associated with the ice cap, partly of marine fishes, and partly of fishes living in southern Europe beyond the limit of the ice cap. It is likely that most of the indigenous species now making up Europe's fish fauna occurred in its southern waters at that time. In modern times there is very little permanent ice cover in Europe and many species of fish have moved into waters in the northern areas in particular. The European fish fauna as a whole can be considered as having originated from four different elements over the last 10,000 years: **1** Indigenous species which have gradually moved north from southern Europe. **2** Species with marine affinities which have colonized the area from the sea. **3** Species native to continents adjacent to Europe which have managed to invade European waters by natural means. **4** Foreign species (mainly from North America) which have been introduced by man.

Indigenous species have moved about within Europe at different rates, and some fishes obviously have much better powers of dispersal than others. This is an aspect of fish biology about which we know very little, and although various ideas have been put forward about the possibility of fish eggs being transported on the feet of waterfowl, of fishes moving from one catchment to another via adjacent head waters, and of fishes swimming from the mouth of one river to that of an adjacent one via stretches of fresh or brackish water along the coast, there is really very little firm evidence to support any of these suggestions. In general, the fish fauna of Europe becomes more impoverished as one moves from south to north or from the mainland on to adjacent islands, and it seems likely that an active, but very slow, process of natural dispersal is still taking place.

Many European fishes are anadromous or catadromous, or at least able to tolerate fairly high salinities for considerable periods. It is quite easy to envisage these fishes spreading rather rapidly as the ice cap disappeared, and indeed such fishes are among the most widespread in Europe today, including trout, eel and sticklebacks. Some species which are purely freshwater at the southern end of their distribution have migratory races further north. The charr is a good example of this, with many isolated freshwater populations in the British Isles and highland Europe, but anadromous stocks in Iceland and northern Norway.

Invasion of fishes from adjacent continents is probably the least likely source of new species because Europe is separated from most other continents by considerable seas. The major land connection is to Asia in the east, north of the Caspian Sea. However, the high mountain ranges here, and the fact that northern Asia itself was similarly impoverished by the ice cap, has meant that there is little likelihood of fishes entering in

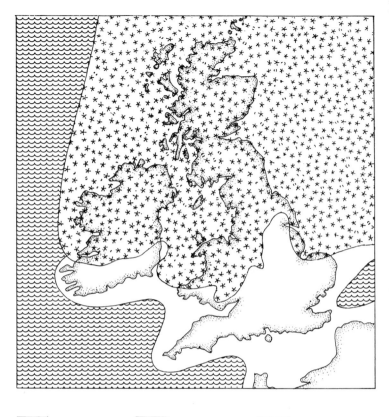

$\boxed{\text{ice}}$ ice $\qquad$ $\approx$ sea $\qquad$ $\square$ land

Fig. 23 Maximum extent of the ice cap over the British Isles during the last Ice Age, 10,000 years ago

this way. The main movement of species has probably been in the Transcaucasian area, where a number of species occur which are found nowhere else in Europe.

Man has moved fishes from place to place for many hundreds of years, but it is probably within the last 200 years that large numbers of significant introductions have been made in all parts of the world. Most introductions in Europe have come from North America, and of the list of species now established here several of the Salmonidae, and all the Ictaluridae and Centrarchidae, as well as various other species, have come from across the Atlantic. Changes like these, together with those caused by pollution and various fishery and land use practices, mean that most future distribution trends will be due to man's activities and not to natural agencies. This makes it essential for individual countries to consider the status of their native fish populations most carefully if the rarer endemic species are to be preserved. The fact that we are still very ignorant about the basic biology and distribution of many of the less common European species of freshwater fishes means that a great deal remains to be done in this field.

Commercial fishing

It is very likely that man has eaten fishes from early in his history, and evidence of this is available from prehistoric times in the form of cave paintings and certain types of stone traps. More recently, history has shown the importance of fishes to man in abundant literary references, coats-of-arms, drawings, etc. Almost all sizes and types of fish are eaten, (except those which are actually distasteful or poisonous) ranging from several small species cooked and eaten whole as 'whitebait' to very large fishes such as sturgeon and sharks. Fishes may be eaten raw, or after preservation in various ways such as drying, smoking, salting, canning or freezing, although most fish is cooked before being eaten.

Methods

There are many different ways of catching fishes and the methods used in fresh water are essentially similar to those used in the sea, although usually on a smaller scale (see accompanying tables). Spears were one of the earliest methods of catching fishes, and were very successful for flatfishes like flounders in shallow water or large fishes like salmon in small streams. Today spearing is carried out in Europe only as a form of sport — usually for flounders or for other species by scuba divers.

Baited hooks were also used very early in the history of fishing, originally being made of carved bone or thorns, but more recently mainly of metal. The size of the hook (like the size of the mesh in a net) is closely related to the size of the fish to be caught. In commercial fisheries long lines containing hundreds or even thousands of hooks, baited in various ways, but usually with pieces of fish or mollusc, are set for short periods (normally overnight) in suitable waters. Freshwater species caught in this way include eels, wels, burbot and, in the sea, salmon. The method is of relatively little importance in commercial freshwater fisheries, however.

In addition to spears and hooks, simple traps were among early methods of catching fishes and many, much more sophisticated types are in use today. Almost all of these traps are based on some kind of funnel attached to an enclosure. The fishes swim into the middle of the enclosure from which they have difficulty in swimming out. This is mainly because they swim round the outside of the enclosure and rarely near the centre where the small exit hole is sited. The earliest traps in Europe were made from stone or from wicker work. These were used to capture salmon, eels and other fishes which tend to follow distinct routes (in which the traps were sited), especially during migrations. Most

Quantity and percentage of total world catch of fishes per continent (average catch for 1955–57)

Continent or region	Million metric tons	%
Asia	12.13	42.0
Europe	7.78	27.0
North America	4.09	13.0
Soviet Union	2.55	9.0
Africa	1.76	6.0
South America	0.85	2.5
Oceania	0.12	0.5
	29.28	100.0

The catch of freshwater fishes in various regions for 1938 and 1956

Region	1938 (1,000 metric tons)	%	1956 (1,000 metric tons)	%
Asia	1,270	55	1,780	58
Soviet Union	610	26	660	22
Africa	180	8	380	12
Europe	130	6	90	3
North America	70	3	120	4
South America	40	2	40	1

modern traps are made of netting, supported by stakes, weights and floats. Many of them are quite complex and include a long lead net which guides fishes towards the entrance, and two funnel traps, one leading into the other. There is very little chance indeed of fishes escaping from the innermost of these. Traps are still of considerable importance in many countries of Europe, such as Scotland and Ireland, for the capture of various fish species such as salmon and eel.

The bulk of modern commercial fishing, however, is based on various types of fixed or moving nets (see fig. 24). Originally these were made from natural fibres such as wool and cotton, which were liable to rot, but most nets are now made from synthetic materials like nylon and terylene which are light, strong and much less likely to deteriorate. The manufacture of fishing nets is a skilled business and an important light industry in many countries such as Norway and Sweden. Three main types of net are in general use today in both freshwater and marine commercial fisheries. These are gill, seine and trawl nets.

Gill nets are sheets of netting hung in the water by means of an arrangement of floats, leaded lines and anchors. Since such nets depend on fishes actually moving into them, they are normally made of very fine materials, often in a colour appropriate to the water in which they are being used. Many of them are most successful in poor visibility (i.e. in turbid waters) or in the dark. Gill nets depend on the fishes swimming partly through an individual hole in the mesh and then becoming trapped by the meshes slipping behind the gill covers so that the fishes can move neither backwards nor forwards. In other cases the fish may continue to swim forwards so that its body becomes securely wedged in the meshes. The size of the meshes used is critical in relation to the size of the fish caught.

Seine nets function on the principle of paying out a wall of netting from a boat so as to surround a certain area of water and enclose the fishes therein; the method is a very popular and successful one. In shore seining, the net is set in a semicircle from a small boat and hauled to the shore by two groups of men. Shore seine nets may, or may not, have a bag in the centre of the net to help to retain the catch. Most open water seines do have such a bag, and the net is set from a boat in a full circle before hauling. Two boats are often necessary in the operation. A rather specialized type of seine is that known as the purse seine or ring net: this is not, like the open water seine net, cast in a full circle. It is normally much deeper than other seines and along the bottom of the net, running through large rings, is the purse line; as the net is hauled in, this line is tightened to close the bottom of the net.

Trawl nets are essentially open bags of netting hauled through the water at constant speed, normally from a powered boat. The main features of such nets are the shape and length of the bag, and the method used to hold the mouth of the net open. Two main types of trawl are commonly used in fresh waters: beam trawls, where one or more rigid poles keep the mouth of the net open; and otter trawls, where planing surfaces known as otter boards are used to keep the net open at either side while floats and a weighted line keep it open in the middle. The bags of such nets must be sufficiently long to ensure that the catch, having been overtaken by the mouth and moved back into the net, find it difficult to make their way out again.

Fish products

A high percentage of the body weight of fishes (usually more than 50 per cent) is made up of muscle, or fish flesh as it is more commonly called. The most popular species for human consumption have a light-coloured flesh (usually white or pink) with few bones and a fairly mild taste or smell. Many less popular species are extremely bony or have powerful oily smells. The food value of fish flesh is high, comparing favourably with high quality beef or other meats. The main constituents of fish flesh are water, protein and fats, (very approximately in the ratio of 70:20:10) and a

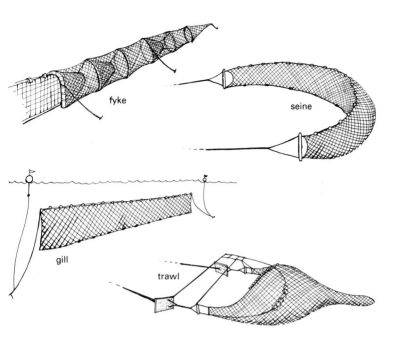

fyke

seine

gill

trawl

Fig. 24 Four types of commercial fishing net commonly used today

number of important vitamins. The fat content of many fishes varies very much on a seasonal basis according to their condition, and the fats—unlike those of mammals—are unsaturated and therefore better suited for human consumption.

Since most European countries are adjacent to the sea, much of the fish eaten is of marine origin; it is really only in central Europe and one or two other areas that freshwater fishes feature largely in man's diet. The number of species eaten in most countries is few, largely due to conservatism or prejudice against eating fish from local lakes and rivers. A few species are highly valued and may be classed as luxury foods. The most important among these is the Atlantic salmon.

Fishes provide man with useful products other than flesh; oil is an important product from many species —particularly in the Clupeidae and Gadidae—as are fish meals and fertilizers. These are obtained either from fish-processing factories where, after filleting, the waste parts of the fishes are ground to make meal, or direct from fisheries where the fishes are too small or of insufficient value to be sold for food. The meal is fed to poultry, pigs and cattle in combination with carbohydrates to give a balanced diet. The skin of some fishes is used to make glue, while the swim-bladders of many freshwater species (for instance sturgeon and carp) are an important source of isinglass. This is used mainly for clearing wines and beers. The scales of the bleak are processed to produce an iridescent pigment used in the manufacture of artificial pearls.

Fish farming

The main aim of fish farming is the production, in large numbers, of one or more species of fish for usually one of two purposes: either to stock waters for sport or commercial fishing, or for direct sale as food. In the former case, large numbers of small fishes (sometimes even just eggs) are produced and sold for stocking. Occasionally adult fishes are reared, placed in natural waters and then caught almost immediately by anglers. With table fishes the final objective is the size and quality of the individual fish produced for sale. The intensive nature of fish farming means that fishes are often kept under extremely unnatural conditions and fed on unusual substances. This has led to many problems in fish farming and combined with the fact that, although some types of fish farming are of very great antiquity, its science is very much behind that of most other agricultural sciences. This is because most meat comes from farmed sources, while most fish is still caught in the wild. Fish farming is rapidly becoming a very important industry, however, and significant advances are being made every year in such fields as genetics, disease and feeding.

The Chinese and the Egyptians reared fishes many hundreds of years ago, and the Romans also regarded this as an important aspect of agriculture. In Europe in the Middle Ages most fish farming was carried out by religious orders in monasteries, carp being the most important single species. Within the last hundred years, and particularly in the last ten years, fish farming in Europe has increased greatly, as has the number of different species which are now farmed. There are a number of reasons for this expansion: the shortage of food, especially protein, has meant that more land and water must be used for its production; the availability of fertilizers and new types of food for improving growth; and the increasing demand for luxury foods in many countries. (The present drive towards salmonid production for the table is a good example of this.)

The wide variety of freshwater species now reared in Europe is shown in the table on page 37. It can be seen that many of the fishes involved are not native species, but have been imported from North America and Asia especially for rearing. There is no doubt that further introduction will still be made, and that fish genetics will play an increasing part in fish husbandry, just as it has with other domestic animals. Not only will strains of particular species be selected which show especially desirable qualities of growth, resistance to disease, etc., but hybrids of many species will be produced in an attempt to produce fishes ideally suited to intensive farming.

Three of the species listed in the table on page 37 are not wild in Europe, but have been introduced and are only maintained in fish farms, mainly in central Europe. They are: Grass Carp, *Ctenopharyngodon idella* (Valenciennes) originally from China; Silver Carp, *Hypophthalmichthys molitrix* (Valenciennes) from China and Bighead Carp, *Hypophthalmichthys nobilis* (Richardson), also from China.

Most fish farming is carried out in artificial ponds, and often in cages in ponds. Sometimes natural waters (usually small lakes) are used, and occasionally cages or large enclosures are placed in lakes, but rarely in rivers or in the sea. Ponds, especially those specifically designed for fish farming, have overwhelming advantages over other types of water. They can be emptied or filled easily. Fishes can be caught without difficulty by netting or emptying, and feeding is simple. Predators such as herons and gulls, and diseases (including parasites), are much easier to control. Ponds used in fish farming can vary in size from a fraction of a hectare (1 hectare is equivalent to 2.47 acres) to hundreds of hectares; the majority in Europe are between $\frac{1}{10}$ and 1 hectare in surface area.

Two major points must be remembered when a fish farm is being planned: the ground and the water. Economically, sandy, marshy or other poor quality (agriculturally speaking) ground is often best, but is not always appropriate. Soil which is too porous is often unsuitable, and the best sites lie on ground which is impermeable, or which is permanently waterlogged (but not subject to flooding). The slope of the ground is also important. Ideally, the ground should be sufficiently low at some point – preferably near a river or some other watercourse for the ponds to be able to be drained without pumping. Ideally either the water supply available should also have pressure, or the source of water to the fish farm should be sufficiently high above it to provide a reasonable flow.

The actual water used for the farm should be free from pollution and adequate in quantity and quality for the type of fish farming being carried out. Broadly speaking, the fish species being reared fall into two ecological categories: salmonids and related forms which require large amounts of cool (lower than 20°C or 68°F), pure water with a high oxygen content, and cyprinids and similar fishes which are much less exacting in the amount and quality of water, including oxygen, needed. They also require far higher temperatures (preferably higher than 20°C) for much of the year if adequate growth is to be attained. There is a tendency for salmonid culture to predominate in fish farms in the highland and northern areas of Europe, and cyprinid culture to be of greatest importance in lowland and southern Europe.

As well as matching the environment of the fish farm to that required

The principal species of freshwater fishes cultured in Europe

Common name	Scientific name	Purpose of culture
Sterlet	*Acipenser ruthenus*	food
Sturgeon	*Acipenser sturio*	food
Allis Shad	*Alosa alosa*	food
Chum Salmon	*Oncorhynchus keta*	food
Humpback Salmon	*Oncorhynchus gorbuscha*	food
Atlantic Salmon	*Salmo salar*	food/sport/farming
Trout	*Salmo trutta*	food/sport/farming
Rainbow Trout	*Salmo gairdneri*	food/sport/farming
Charr	*Salvelinus alpinus*	sport
Brook Charr	*Salvelinus fontinalis*	sport
American Lake Charr	*Salvelinus namaycush*	sport
Cisco	*Coregonus albula*	food/farming
Common Whitefish	*Coregonus lavaretus*	food/farming
Grayling	*Thymallus thymallus*	sport
Pike	*Esox lucius*	food/sport
Roach	*Rutilus rutilus*	sport
Belica	*Leucaspius delineatus*	bait species
Orfe	*Leuciscus idus*	ornamental pond fish
Minnow	*Phoxinus phoxinus*	bait species
Rudd	*Scardinius erythrophthalmus*	sport
Tench	*Tinca tinca*	sport
Bleak	*Alburnus alburnus*	bait species/artificial pearls
Crucian Carp	*Carassius carassius*	food/farming
Goldfish	*Carassius auratus*	ornamental pond fish
Carp	*Cyprinus carpio*	food/sport/farming
Grass Carp	*Ctenopharyngodon idella*	farming/weed control
Silver Carp	*Hypophthalmichthys molitrix*	farming/algal control
Bighead Carp	*Hypophthalmichthys nobilis*	farming
Wels	*Silurus glanis*	food/sport
Eel	*Anguilla anguilla*	food/farming
Striped Mullet	*Mugil cephalus*	food
Thinlipped Mullet	*Mugil capito*	food
Perch	*Perca fluviatilis*	food/sport
Pikeperch	*Stizostedion lucioperca*	food/sport

by the species reared, the farming procedure must also be geared to the biology of the fishes. The rearing process is normally carried out in three stages: incubation, rearing of fry, and rearing of adults. Although the eggs used on fish farms are sometimes obtained by natural spawning in ponds, or even in the wild, most species are captured at spawning time and stripped of their eggs and sperm. These are mixed together in a container and left for a few minutes before being washed and placed in containers for incubation.

Most incubation takes place indoors where precise conditions of water flow and quality (especially temperature, oxygen and silt content) can be maintained. Eggs are placed, usually in thousands or even millions, in shallow troughs or open jars in which a flow of water is maintained throughout incubation. In addition to maintaining appropriate conditions for the species being reared, each batch of eggs must be examined regularly to check that development is taking place and to remove dead eggs which can rapidly rot and kill off other members of the batch. After hatching, which may take from 5–10 days in carp but up to 100–150 days or longer in trout and salmon, the larvae are normally removed to another part of the farm.

The larvae may not require feeding for several days if the yolk sac is large after hatching, as is usually the case with salmonids. As soon as feeding commences, however, adequate quantities of food must be supplied regularly, usually several times a day. This must be adequate for the stimulation of good growth in the larvae without causing deoxygenation. Old decaying food combined with fish faeces quickly rob water of its dissolved oxygen, leading to high fish mortalities. Adequate supplies of water which bring in oxygen and carry off wastes are most important at this stage. Having changed from larvae to fry, which may vary in size from 3–10 cm (1–4 in) or more, fishes are removed for the next stage of the rearing process.

It is at this point that most fishes used for stocking are taken and liberated in natural waters. This is usually carried out by lorries loaded with special tanks and oxygen supplies, but it is not uncommon for remote waters to be stocked from aeroplanes or helicopters. Many fish-stocking programmes are correctly criticized by fishery biologists, and considerable research is still required on this subject. It is known, for instance, that for many days after being released, hatchery fishes find difficulty in adapting to natural surroundings and are much more vulnerable to predators and less able to find food than wild stock.

The final phase in fish farming is that of rearing the fry until they are large enough to be sold for the table, or are of a catchable size for selling to angling syndicates for 'put and take' fisheries. This stage is the most expensive of the rearing process for it requires the greatest input of the two most valuable commodities — food and manpower. Almost all species require to be fed regularly, usually two or more times a day. The food varies according to species but is often very expensive — particularly for salmonids, which require a protein-rich diet. This food, usually in pellet form, is often based on fish meal obtained either as waste from fish-filleting plants or directly from species harvested for the purpose. During the final rearing stage the fishes are regularly graded for size so that only those of similar size are kept together. A constant watch is kept for parasites and disease, and many ponds are cleaned or drained regularly to keep these troubles to a minimum.

Fish farming in Europe is still expanding, but much of it will not answer the world's food shortage, for the systems concerned are based on high-quality protein diets, much of which is wasted in the conversion to fish flesh. These systems in times of shortage can only lead to luxury foods and can never be considered as a source of cheap protein. The few herbivorous fishes at present being reared in Europe can convert vegetable (often waste) material to high-quality protein, and it is these systems which should be encouraged if the principal search is for cheap food.

Sport fishing

No outdoor sport has more active participants than angling. The most recent survey indicated that more than 3 million people went fishing at least once a year in Britain alone, and France is said to have 5 million anglers. A huge industry has developed to meet their needs, with most of the tackle being produced in Britain, France and Sweden, and nearly all the nylon monofilament line being manufactured in Germany. So vast is the business associated in one way or another with angling that if the sport suddenly ceased it would affect the livelihoods of a great many people. Such a disaster would not only affect fishing tackle manufacturers, but all levels of the fishing industry from the breeder of maggot bait to the owner of a top salmon beat who charges £1,000 or more for a week's sport.

The sport of freshwater angling is divided into two basic kinds — coarse fishing and game fishing — and both kinds subdivide into various separate interests. Within coarse fishing there are match anglers who fish against each other purely for the competitive element, or for money or both, so-called 'pleasure anglers' who fish for anything they can catch, and specimen hunters who concentrate upon the capture of exceptionally big fishes. Sometimes they will even concentrate on one single species, and there are clubs for specialists in the pursuit of pike, carp, tench and eel, for instance.

Game fishing is rather less fragmented, but there are those who specialize in migratory fishes such as sea trout and salmon, and others who find their paradise in river fishing for brown and rainbow trout. The most recent developments in game fishing are trout fishing in reservoirs, and small-water fishing for very big fishes — rainbow trout reared to record breaking proportions by fishery and fish farm owners with an eye for publicity.

A comprehensive description of the tackle that anglers need, and the many methods employed by them, would fill a large book. The following is intended to be no more than a brief summary of fishing tackle and how it is used. The most universal item of tackle is the rod, which is now made almost exclusively of fibre glass, although carbon fibre is also making an impact, especially in the reservoir angling field. Formerly rods were made from various types of wood, and the best rod in that material was hollow-built split bamboo. Many game fishermen still need convincing that hand-built cane rods are inferior to glass, but they pay dearly for their principles. Rods have three main functions. The first is to deliver the bait to the fish, the second is to allow a 'strike' to be made, thus hooking the fish, and the third is to absorb the strain exerted on the line when playing a fish. Since the anglers' quarry varies in size from a few grams to 90 kg (40 lbs) or more, and their baits vary in weight from almost nothing to 100 g or more, it follows that rods must vary greatly in length, weight, strength and taper. A 4 m (13 ft) feather-light match rod capable of casting a toothpick-sized float when fishing for tiny gudgeon, would never land a salmon. Equally a salmon rod would be no use to an angler after gudgeon, so it must be clearly understood that there is a rod for every purpose. Although many anglers use one rod for the majority of their fishing, there is really no such thing as a general-purpose rod. In coarse fishing an angler might need a rod up to 4 m (13 ft) for match fishing, a medium-powered 3 m (10 ft) rod for chub, tench and barbel fishing, and a stronger version of the same length for bigger fishes like carp and pike. He would also need shorter rods for specialized purposes such as spinning, to be mentioned later.

Every rod is capable of handling a limited range of line. Line which is too weak for a rod will break on striking a fish, and there is little point in using line strong enough to bend a rod double. A match rod will satisfactorily take reel line up to 1.35 kg (3 lbs) breaking strain, a carp rod 6.3 kg (14 lbs) and a pike rod for waters where large specimens are found would be capable of handing 11 kg (25 lb) line. In almost all cases the line is nylon monofilament, although braided terylene is used on a limited scale for pike fishing. In fly fishing for game fishes, in which the angler seeks to deceive his quarry with an imitation of an aquatic insect, the line is quite different. Each rod is made to cast a given size of line, and it is the weight of the line itself which flexes the rod and gives it casting power. These lines, usually 30 metres (about 100ft) in length, are plastic coated and they are made to perform particular functions once they reach the water. There are lead-cored lines which sink down to deep-feeding fishes; lines with built-in bubbles to make them float; and lines which float but which have two or three metres of sinking tip. To facilitate certain types of casting the lines also vary in shape.

Casting with fly tackle is a precision business best learned from an expert tutor, but it is easy enough to summarize the aim of the fly fisherman. It is to present a recognizable imitation of natural food as near as possible to the nose of a feeding fish or to provoke a fish into snapping at an offering which intrudes into its domain. Sometimes trout and salmon will attack the gaudiest of artificial flies, often resembling little more than a bunch of feathers and tinsel, but at other times they appear extremely fickle.

The casting weight, which helps carry the bait to the quarry, and hold it in position, is usually lead in the case of bait fishing, but it could also be a live or dead fish if the angler is after predatory species such as pike. For the same species he might also use metal spinners or wooden lures which are designed to travel through the water as imitations of live fishes or other aquatic animals. Ingenious anglers have even been known to use imitation water rats, with some success.

Clearly, if the angler has to make his lures behave in such a manner he needs a high degree of versatility from the second most important item of tackle — the reel. They are available in a variety of shapes and sizes, but easily the most popular is the fixed spool reel — a reel so easy to operate that even a novice can master it in just a few minutes. The fixed spool has almost completely replaced the

older centre pin reel, with which anglers can exercise perfect control over their tackle, but cannot cast as far. The fixed spool outcasts it easily, but offers less control. The newer closed face reels offer better control than the fixed spool, but they, too, will not cast quite as far. The longest caster of all is the multiplier, sometimes used for deadbaiting and heavy-bait spinning, but basically a sea fishing reel for long casting from beaches. Highly geared versions of the multiplier are used for big game fishing at sea.

The angler who fly fishes, or who seeks his quarry with artificial lures, or live or dead fishes, can travel very much lighter than the angler who fishes with bait. The bait fisherman must carry a holdall filled with rods, an umbrella, landing net handle and a variety of metal poles for supporting the rod, and a basket which contains boxes of floats, lead weights, reels, groundbait, hook bait and many other accessories, too numerous to mention. The basket doubles as a seat, and the canvas bag he also carries usually transports a keepnet for retaining his catch, and the head of the landing net to scoop the bigger fishes out of the water. The angler's bait is also varied — usually a large tin of maggots or casters (pupae of the maggot) and worms, although the complete list of edibles capable of catching fishes is endless. Some of the most popular are bread in various forms, hempseed, tares, wheat, cheese, luncheon meat, sausages and elder berries.

The bait fisherman has two basic ways of fishing — suspending the bait under a float which is weighted down so that only the tip shows above the water, or fishing hard on the bottom with a lead weight. This second method is known as legering, and bites are signalled by movement on the tip of the rod. To emphasize the movement anglers sometimes use thin, screw-in extensions to their rods called quiver-tips, or an ingenious device which hangs from the rod tip. This is called the swing-tip, and it moves either forward or backward in response to a bite. Generally speaking, quiver-tips are used in rivers which have a fair amount of flow, and the swing-tip is for still waters or slow-moving rivers. The float angler relies on his float either disappearing or lifting to signal the bite, and complete books have been written about the types of floats to use in different conditions. Floats are made from bird quills, peacock quills, porcupine quills, balsa wood, cane, reed, polystyrene — in fact almost anything sufficiently buoyant to support the weight of lead shots and bait. Tiny floats are used at close range, and large floats are employed for long-distance angling. About 36 m (120 ft) is the optimum range of the float angler. Beyond that he will usually resort to the leger.

Very much bound up with the employment of either method is careful preparation of, and attention to, the swim (the area of water where fishes are expected to be caught). This is done primarily to attract and hold fishes in one area, and then to get them feeding avidly on the bait which is offered on the hook. One reason for the immense popularity of maggot and caster baits is that they are easily 'loose' fed into the water by hand or catapult. Sometimes they have to be introduced in groundbait — finely ground bread crumb mixed with water. There are times when groundbait itself is attractive to the fishes, but it is also used when distance, depth or speed of flow defeats 'loose' feeding. The texture of the bread crumbs, and the amount of water added to the mix, dictate whether it sinks through the water in a milky cloud or whether it goes down in a solid lump to the bottom of a fast-flowing river.

Groundbaiting is an exact science as far as the top competition angler is concerned, but that is true of every single aspect of angling. The reality of the game is far removed from its peaceful public image. Successful anglers, whatever branch of the sport they follow, are deep thinking people who devote many hours to maintaining and improving their tackle, ensuring that their bait is of the highest quality, and plotting the downfall of

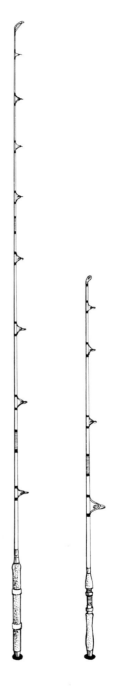

Fig. 25a Bottom-fishing rod (left); spinning rod (right)

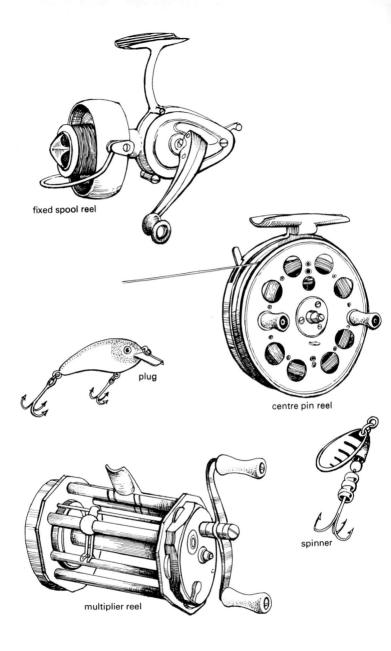

fixed spool reel

plug

centre pin reel

spinner

multiplier reel

Fig. 25b More important items of angling equipment

42

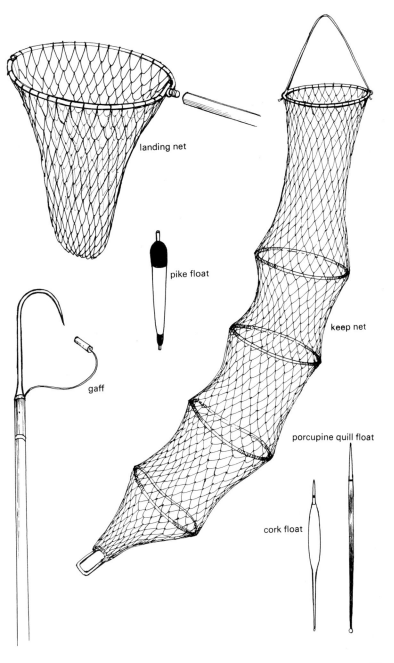

landing net

pike float

keep net

gaff

porcupine quill float

cork float

43

their quarry. They will examine every factor involved in the capture of their quarry, right down to the exact size and design of the hook. To meet the particular needs of anglers literally thousands of hook types and sizes have become available, and factories in many parts of Europe have machines manufacturing them at the rate of hundreds per minute. They range from sizes so small that it is hard to see them, to much larger versions for use in fishing for big sea fishes. Hooks are numbered, and the higher a hook number the smaller the hook. A no. 24 is about the smallest ever used in fresh water, and specimen hunters might use one as big as no. 2 for carp. (Sea fishing hooks are much bigger, and the sizes of these are expressed differently.)

It will be seen from what has been said about sport fishing that it can be an involved and exciting sport, depending not only on the angler's tackle and how it is used, but on weather, the water and the mood of the fish. It has the capacity to exercise the mind of a chess master, and yet it can be simple enough to absorb the smallest of children. It is because pleasure can be derived from angling at so many levels that the sport is so popular. It is claimed, perhaps with some truth, that man goes fishing because he has not entirely forgotten the hunting instincts his ancestors once needed in order to survive. If this is so then his motive has certainly changed, for very few anglers actually fish for food. Coarse fishermen rarely eat what they catch. They retain their fishes in nets and release them at the end of the day or after the match. Game fishermen certainly do eat at least some of what they catch, but it cannot be said that they fish simply for food, for this would result in very expensive meals due to the high cost of a day's trout fishing on a good reservoir, and one fish is about the average catch per rod per day on the reservoirs of Britain. The more skilful anglers probably average about six fishes per day over a good season, but they give most of them away or sell them to defray expenses. At the top end of the scale, in salmon fishing, an angler could pay hundreds of pounds for a week's fishing and catch nothing at all. Even so, such holidays must be booked well in advance, and if the weather has been dry for some weeks there will be no salmon running up from the sea. Again, financial rewards cannot be the motive.

Man is still a hunter, and in those where the hunting instinct remains deeply buried, there is still a spark of interest in what the hunter catches. Witness the crowds which gather on the harbour wall when the fishing boats come home. But the anglers' hunting instinct is now converted into a sport, and because of man's penchant for organizing almost anything, it is inevitable that angling is organized. Thus there are small clubs, large clubs, national associations and federations, and in turn there are links between the national bodies of various countries and their counterparts in other parts of Europe.

Aquaria

To many people the word 'aquarium' conjures up little more than the idea of a sterile goldfish bowl and its prisoner, or a brightly lit tank in a restaurant with multi-coloured plastic gravel, plastic plants and sometimes even plastic fishes! Aquaria mean much more than this, however, and to many thousands of people in Europe and elsewhere form the basis of an absorbing hobby. In other spheres aquaria offer a valuable educational tool, or the basis for exciting work on processes ranging from animal behaviour to the growth of cancers. With modern technology it is possible to successfully keep almost all species of fish alive in aquaria, with the exception perhaps of those which live in very deep water.

Aquaria are employed in two main ways: firstly, simply as containers for keeping alive fishes which are required for some purpose such as food or experimentation. Secondly, as small isolated habitats replicating those found in nature and including not only fishes, but also aquatic plants and invertebrates. Such aquaria can be both educational and aesthetically pleasing, as can many types of outdoor pond (see fig. 26).

The object of experimental aquaria is to test the performance of fish under various, often extreme conditions. Thus light, temperature, water flow and quality (including oxygen content), are all variables which may be altered during experimentation. Some of the work in this field is of a very theoretical nature, but much of it is totally applied and relevant to man's needs. The study of fish genetics and the value of various types of foodstuffs are two examples of research related to priorities in fish farming at the moment. One of the obvious impacts of pollution on fresh waters is the death of fishes — often in very large numbers. Indeed, were it not for the death of fishes many people would not know (or even care) that a stream was suffering from severe toxic pollution. Attempts are being made at the moment with various species of fish in aquaria to develop a 'standard fish', whose precise reactions to various polluting substances, and to combinations of these, are known. This will allow the possibility of biological assay of effluents, etc. by introducing them to fishes in aquaria, or suspending fishes in cages in the effluent channel. Such tests have a number of advantages over existing, purely chemical methods of detecting pollution, mainly in the ways in which they act as integrators both of time, and of several different pollutants which may be present.

The main attraction of the indoor aquarium is that it represents an easily observed microcosm, with conditions similar to those found in nature. The object of keeping such aquaria is to achieve a balance between the various components, so that something equivalent to natural recycling can be attained. It is rare for this to happen completely, and normally some material is added to the system in the form of fish food and some removed in the form of fish droppings and decaying or excessively growing plants. Nevertheless something near a balance can be achieved.

The plants in an aquarium are normally rooted in gravel and are able to use up quantities of waste salts and carbon dioxide produced by the fishes. Under the action of light the plants photosynthesize and produce oxygen (much of this also comes through the surface of the water) which is respired by the fishes. Certain fishes eat parts of the plants and also algae, which grows on all surfaces in the aquarium, and the ecosystem is often made more complex by adding invertebrates such as molluscs and sometimes crustaceans, which may help to prevent excessive plant growth and whose eggs and young form a source of food for the fishes. Many very useful books have been written about aquaria, and some of these are listed in the bibliography. In addition there are many hundreds of aquarium societies all over Europe and anyone with an interest in this subject is recommended to join one.

The educational value of fishes in aquaria is something which should not be underestimated, for if appropriate species are kept in the right

Fig. 26 Formal garden pond; a suitable habitat for many of the small species of fish found in Europe's ponds and canals

conditions they may be persuaded to go through their full life cycle in one year and to demonstrate a wide range of biological principles which are relevant to the theory being taught in the classroom. This may include many aspects of behaviour, reproduction, ecology, anatomy and physiology. Common European species which are of great value as educational aids since they may be kept and bred in aquaria include the mudminnow, minnow, bitterling, goldfish, stickleback, mosquito fish, rock bass, pumpkinseed, sunfish, chanchito and bullhead.

The value of aquaria in teaching is well known, and they are a com-mon feature of many educational establishments. Their value to the general public is less appreciated and it is a lamentable fact that most in-habitants of European countries have seen only a few of their native fishes, and these only too often on a fish-monger's slab. Fishes are among the most difficult of animals to observe in nature and can only be fully appre-ciated when observed in aquaria of sufficient size, set up according to their ecological requirements. The few really good public aquaria in the world today (for instance in Van-couver and Amsterdam) show that it is quite possible to display the range of mature species found in a country and that these are often more attrac-tive and exciting than the standard brightly coloured exotic species so commonly featured in other public aquaria.

Collection and preservation

Depending on the species concerned, fishes may be caught by a wide variety of methods. In a country such as the British Isles, among the commonest methods of capture are angling for large fishes, and the use of a hand net for smaller fishes. There are many other methods of capture (some of them much more efficient, but illegal in most situations) which can be used. These include gill nets, seine nets, trawl nets, and traps, which are described in detail elsewhere. Most methods of fishing are highly selective and may often capture only one size group of one species, and sometimes even only one sex. In carrying out any detailed study of a mixed fish population in a habitat, it is normally advisable to use several different methods of capture.

As noted elsewhere, the major key in this book will not serve to identify the very small specimens of most species. For a short time after hatching the young of most fishes are changing very rapidly in form, and features characteristic of the species do not appear for some time. Unlike many invertebrates, adult fishes, because of their large size, can in most cases be identified in the field, and so there is no need to take them to the laboratory. Thus in very many instances, it is possible to identify specimens correctly immediately after capture and then return them alive to the water. There is little point in killing such fishes unless they are required for food, research or some other legitimate purpose. In the case of species which are difficult to identify accurately in the field it may be necessary to take them away for detailed examination. It is preferable that they be kept alive for this purpose, but this is often not possible, especially with large or delicate specimens, and most of these fishes have to be killed. Clearly all specimens must be killed where dissection is essential for their accurate identification.

Killing

Apart from asphyxiation, one of the best methods of killing fishes without damaging them is to use a liquid anaesthetic, a suitable one being the chemical known as MS222. Specimens dropped into a 0.1 per cent solution are narcotized very quickly and can then either be frozen or transferred to a suitable fixative. Ideally, fishes should be examined as fresh as possible.

Freezing and fixing

Frozen fishes retain their colours much better than fixed specimens; the best procedure for freezing is to place each specimen in a polythene bag with a little water and a suitable label and freeze in its entirety as quickly as possible. The specimen should be kept straight during this process and care must be taken not to damage its fins.

Even frozen fishes will not keep indefinitely, however, especially if they have to be subjected to periodic thawing for examination purposes, and normally specimens to be stored must be fixed in some way. The most useful fixative is 4 per cent formaldehyde. Each fish should be preserved by placing it flat on its side in a shallow dish with its fins spread as much as possible, and then pouring enough of this solution over it to cover it completely. Specimens should be left for several days to ensure complete fixation. With fishes more than 30cm (1ft) in length, it is normally advisable to make a small slit in the ventral body wall, or to inject the body cavity with a small amount of 40 per cent formaldehyde. This ensures complete fixation internally, after which the fishes can be stored temporarily in polythene bags or permanently in suitable jars, either in 4 per cent formaldehyde or in less offensive preservatives such as 70 per cent alcohol or 1 per cent propylene phenoxetol. Each jar should have inside it a label, written in pencil or indelible ink, with a note of the species concerned, the water where it was collected, the date and the name of the collector.

In situations where the suggested preservations are not available, quite good results can be obtained by using other materials which are normally easily obtained. For example, reasonable preservation can be obtained with: **1** Methylated

Spirits, diluted 7 parts of spirits to 3 parts of water, **2** Salt, diluted 1 part of salt to 2 parts of water, **3** Vinegar (acetic acid), as used as a condiment. Preservation can be carried out satisfactorily in polythene bags, again keeping the fish straight.

Eggs or larvae can be preserved and stored in small tubes containing either 4 per cent formaldehyde or 70 per cent alcohol. Labels with relevant data (species, locality, date, colour of eggs when fresh, exact habitat, name of collector, etc.) should be placed inside each tube. In the case of eggs, a reasonable number should be taken where possible, especially if the eggs are adhering to each other, for the form of attachment may be important in identification. This type of material is exceedingly scarce, and the author would be very glad to receive samples of the eggs or larvae of any of the less common species.

Some species of fish can be identified from their scales alone, and in addition it is often possible with several good scales taken from the side of the body to establish the specimen's age, and certain features of its history. When scales are available from specimens they should be placed inside a small envelope which is flattened and then allowed to dry; they will keep indefinitely in this way. The envelope should bear on the outside the following data: species, locality, date, name of collector, length, weight and sex of the specimen concerned. For identification, the scales should be cleaned and mounted on glass slides, either dry or in glycerine jelly. The length of a fish can be read in a number of different ways; the most useful method is to record the exact distance between the tip of the snout and the tip of the middle ray of the tail fin.

As with other vertebrates, bones are often very useful in the identification of fishes, and in some cases (e.g. with the pharyngeal bones of Cyprinidae and the vomer bones of Salmonidae) they may be essential for accurate identification. Certain bones are also of major importance in providing information on the age and growth of some species (e.g. the opercular bones of Percidae and Esocidae). Preparation of all such bones for examination and subsequent preservation is a relatively simple task; fresh or frozen material should be used – not material which has previously been fixed. The relevant bones should be dissected out from the fish concerned, along with their attached tissues. Each bone should then be dropped into very hot water for a few minutes and then scrubbed gently with a small stiff brush to clean away soft tissue. The process should be repeated until the bone is completely clean; it can then be placed on clean paper and allowed to dry out slowly in a *warm* atmosphere. Details concerning the fish from which the bone was removed (species, locality, date, name of collector, length, weight and sex), should be written either on a small stiff label attached to the bone by strong thread, or on the outside of an envelope or small box in which the bone is kept. Bones cleaned and dried in this manner will keep more or less indefinitely.

Although it is possible with the aid of this key to identify down to species all fishes known to occur in fresh water in Europe, a few species are rather difficult to identify accurately without experience, and there is also the possibility of the occurrence of a hybrid, or of a species new to a country. In cases of doubt one or more specimens of the species concerned should be killed and preserved as described above, and then sent together with relevant details to a competent ichthyologist for examination. It is not normally advisable to send fresh specimens by post, as they deteriorate too rapidly. When sending preserved specimens they should be drained of preservative, wrapped in damp muslin and then sealed inside a polythene bag. If this is finally placed in a box with packing, and then parcelled, the fish will travel for several days in perfect condition. The author would be extremely interested to receive any such difficult specimens for examination and verification, which should be sent to: Dr Peter S. Maitland, Institute of Terrestrial Ecology, Wetlands Research Group, 12 Hope Terrace, Edinburgh EH9 2AS, Scotland.

Conservation

The maps included in this book show the present distribution of each species of freshwater fish in Europe. Several species are increasing their range of distribution, whereas others are decreasing in this respect. A few are in danger of extinction — mainly as a result of stresses imposed by man. There is a considerable amount of fundamental research still required, especially on the less common species, if all interests in the resource are to be protected and the extinction of rare species is to be prevented.

The conservation of freshwater fishes means a number of quite separate things to different people. Most of the discussion on fish conservation in the past has centred around species which are of direct importance to man either commercially or for sporting purposes. The number of people involved in these activities is very large (about 3 million in the British Isles alone), and forms a significant proportion of the population.

In considering the conservation of fish populations, there are a number of other important aspects which have received far less attention — presumably because they appear to have no economic importance or, if it is admitted that they have such importance, because it is too difficult to assess in terms of 'cash value'. Amenity is one such reason. The amenity value of water bodies is an accepted fact now, and one of the attractions of being near them is to see fishes swimming and leaping in clear water. For many people it is psychologically satisfying to know (without necessarily seeing) that a water body contains healthy, stable fish populations. As already mentioned, fishes are excellent indicators of the degree of pollution of a water body: fish deaths are often one of the first obvious indications of sudden pollution, and waters which are fishless owing to pollution are generally considered to be unsatisfactory — regardless of their visual condition. Usually among the top consumers in food-chains in aquatic systems, fishes often provide a very sensitive measure of pollution of the environment by insecticides and other insidious poisons.

The recreational value of fish populations is often equated solely with their use for sport fishing, whereas this is often far from the case. The economic element and adult participation in sport fishing often mask the fact that large numbers of children (and their parents!) gain very great recreational pleasure from catching small fishes and later keeping them in ponds or aquaria. The range of important species in this context is far wider than that which is appropriate to sport fishing. Related to this activity is the educational value of these species to schools and universities — especially from behavioural and anatomical viewpoints. The ecological relationships within waters can also be important as far as fishes are concerned. Thus, for example, they often form the main food supply for interesting or rare predatory birds.

In the scientific context, fish populations have a number of uses, and are widely employed in a variety of research studies. One important aspect of this field is the maintenance of populations of rare species or isolated populations of common species which may possess unique gene pools.

Fish populations have concerned man for many thousands of years, and it is often difficult to separate the effect of his impact from changes due to more natural processes. Over the last hundred years, particularly the last decade, many new and intense pressures have been applied, and in most cases these have been detrimental to fish conservation as a whole. Inevitably, many of these are interlinked, the final combination often resulting in a complex and unpredictable situation.

Fisheries

The impact of fisheries (both commercial and sport) on the populations which they exploit can range from total extinction of the populations to the more or less stable relationship of recruitment and cropping which exists in many old-established fisheries. The essence of success in fisheries is to have a well-regulated fishery where statistics on the catch are monitored continuously and used as a basis for future management of the stock. It is clearly in their own interests for those concerned with fisheries to adopt sound policies in relation to the close season, the type of gear used, and the numbers and sizes of fish caught, etc., so that the stocks will survive. Although there are considerable gaps in our knowledge of the population dynamics of many fish species, we have sufficient information to suppose that well-regulated fisheries, whose management is based on existing scientific information, should prove successful for the species of fish concerned. Yet all too often freshwater fishery management is still not based on sound ecological information.

Stocking was once considered by many (and is still thought by some) to be the main management tool to be used in fisheries; a large number of derelict fish hatcheries and ponds in various countries provide evidence of the faith of past generations in this procedure. There is no doubt that stocking is a valuable part of the management policy of some fisheries, but it is only necessary in waters where spawning and nursery areas are absent or inadequate to provide recruitment for the losses due to the angling pressure involved. The numbers of waters where this is true are in the minority, and are likely to remain so except where 'put and take' fisheries are developing. Fish-food production in them is largely irrelevant, as the fishes introduced are of a catchable size and likely to be caught before they starve. There are very few aquatic ecosystems into which a species of fish could be introduced and established without some major alteration within the system itself. This being the case, all proposed introductions of fishes, either as species that do not occur in Europe or that would be new to a water system within it, should be given the most careful consideration.

With native species of restricted distribution, or foreign species already well established in Europe, careful consideration should be given to any proposals to introduce them outside their present areas of occurrence. Many native species appear to be gradually distributing themselves by natural means, for example perch and pike, but even in these instances the effect may be drastic. Thus several cases are known of pike gaining access to waters containing populations of trout, and completely eliminating them. Many species, too, have been dispersed by man. The introduction of dace and roach to Ireland, and their influence on other fishes there, have been carefully documented, while recently the barbel has been moved well beyond its former area of occurrence. Many hundreds of lesser introductions take place annually, but mostly within the existing distribution boundaries of the species involved.

In the case of fish species that are new to Europe, there are several points which should be taken into account before introduction is contemplated: **1** It should be quite clear that there is some real purpose behind the introduction, such as sport management, or diversification of certain fish communities. **2** It is undesirable to introduce species which are likely to have a major influence on ecosystems by predation, competition, or feeding habits (such as destruction of vegetation). **3** Consideration should be given as to whether or not the species could be controlled readily. Some species may not breed because of climatic conditions, while others may have very specialized requirements for spawning, etc.

There are without doubt some circumstances in which translocation of a native species may be justifiable. Obvious cases include introduction into clean waters fishes whose former populations have been destroyed by pollution of some kind, and the establishment of suitable species in newly created waters such as reservoirs. Some natural waters contain no fish species, and while it is scientifically desirable that some of these remain like this, a case could be made for the introduction of certain suitable fishes into others. It is particularly undesirable, on the other hand, that any new species be introduced to waters containing rare native species. Rare native species may well be moved to other waters as a conservation measure, however.

Pollution

Pollution of fresh waters is a subject which is widely discussed nowadays and will not be dealt with in detail here. Suffice to say that most pollution comes from domestic, agricultural, or industrial wastes and that it can be either toxic, thereby eliminating all the fish species present, or selective, killing off only a few sensitive species or altering the environment so that some species are favoured and others are not. (Eutrophication is sometimes thought of as mild pollution.)

Because of the large numbers of rivers and the proximity to the sea, there is less direct pollution of standing waters in Europe. Most effluents are directed into running waters and estuaries (or the sea), and it is the species concerned with such systems which are mostly influenced by pollution. Species with marine affinities are especially affected, for it is normally the lowest reaches of rivers and their estuaries that are most seriously polluted, but through which such fishes must pass at one stage in their life history. Thus one extreme belt of pollution in a river system can affect the fish population of that whole system by acting as a barrier to these fishes.

The process of eutrophication in a wide array of waters is now receiving considerable attention in many parts of the world. Essentially, the phenomenon is due to increasing amounts of nutrients entering the water from geological, domestic, industrial and agricultural processes. The general changes which take place in a body of water that is undergoing eutrophication will not be discussed here, except to mention that they involve large increases in the abundance of algae (associated with this is a change in the species composition, and subsequent changes in the benthos and fish populations).

As far as fishes are concerned, one common response to increased eutrophication is a marked increase in growth rate. There appears also to be a direct relationship between accelerated eutrophication and an increased rate of parasitism in fishes. With the change from clean oxygenated substrates to silted, sometimes poorly oxygenated, substrates in waters undergoing eutrophication, many fishes lose valuable areas of spawning ground. This has a serious effect on species which spawn in deep water, such as whitefish. In lakes that are undergoing normal eutrophication in nature, there appears to be a succession of species and dominance from salmonines (for instance charr) to coregonines (for instance whitefish) to percids (for instance perch) to cyprinids (for instance carp). This succession, usually considered undesirable from game angling points of view, is considerably accelerated by artificial eutrophication. The mechanisms which bring about these changes are still rather poorly understood.

Land use

The impact of different forms of land use can be important to fish populations in various parts of Europe. The creation of reservoirs for hydro-electricity or water supply is an obvious example, where shallow streams or small ponds are transformed to large, often deep, reservoirs. In some cases these reservoirs have highly fluctuating water-levels, and this can have a significant influence on littoral populations, including fishes, which either live or spawn in shallow water or inundated tributaries. The dams of such reservoirs normally act as barriers to migratory fishes, and in Scotland for instance, most remedial measures in such situations are directed towards the conservation of anadromous species. Such measures include a guarantee of minimum river flow, the provision of freshets, construction of fish passes, erection of smolt screens, creation of artificial spawning gravels, use of hatcheries, and the opening up of previously unused natural spawning gravels. Although some impoundments may improve the quality of sport fishing, practically never is thought given to species other than those of sporting or commercial value.

One serious problem related to land use is the widespread destruction by draining or filling of many thousands of small ponds, ox-bow lakes, and other minor waters in all parts of Europe—particularly in the lowland areas. Such habitats are of major importance to populations of smaller fish species (as well as being important aquatic communities in their own right), but rarely is there any outcry about their destruction. The economic and social claims of those destroying them are well known (cheap dumping grounds for garbage, reclamation of land for agriculture or industry, and removal of a potential 'nuisance' and danger to children), and apparently outweigh all else in the minds of those concerned. In a few areas the trend is the reverse, where new waters are dug out for water storage, for agriculture or the winning of gravel. Although the original aim is an economic one, such waters can be important in conservation terms if constructed and managed intelligently, and they are becoming an increasingly important amenity in some areas.

Fig. 27 Layout of a typical fish farm pond: a = longitudinal section; b = cross section; c = ground plan (after Maier and Hofman)

Future trends

The pressures described above are likely to continue and to be supplemented by other complications as the demand for water by industrial, domestic, and recreational concerns increases. The main impact would seem to be in favour of angled species in most cases, and extremely detrimental to non-sport fishes—especially rare species. Generalizations are difficult to make, but the main trends appear to be as follows. **1** Natural, stable mixed fish communities are likely to be changed through poisoning (or shocking) followed by stocking with unstable, virtual monoculture populations of introduced sport species such as rainbow trout. **2** Eutrophication processes are likely to continue and to speed up the succession in natural waters towards conditions which favour coarse species. The fishes which will be most successful here are likely to be coarse species of sporting value, such as bream. **3** Pollution has eradicated certain populations of estuarine and migratory species but seems likely to lessen in future years, so that there is the possibility of re-establishing many of these fishes. In some cases,

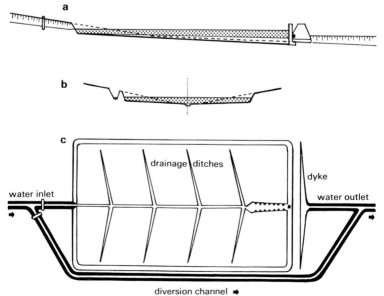

water inlet

drainage ditches

dyke

water outlet

diversion channel ➡

e.g.: the River Thames in England, parts of the fish fauna are recolonizing naturally. Where pollution is a continuing or increasing problem, sensitive and game species, such as salmon, will disappear before coarse species, such as roach. **4** Obliteration of small water bodies will continue, with consequent destruction of populations of small species such as sticklebacks. **5** Haphazard introductions of various kinds will continue, mainly involving sport species or small species used as bait; but regardless of the ecological effects of such introductions the value of the gene-pools within the species concerned must deteriorate as a result of indiscriminate mixing and dominance by the commoner types. **6** The general impact of increased land use, further connections between catchments, etc., is likely to favour the distribution and abundance of the more adaptable species, to the disadvantage of the more sensitive forms with poor powers of dispersal. Examples of the former are roach and dace, and of the latter, cisco and charr.

Although there may be an increase in the abundance of sport species throughout Europe, from most other points of view there will be a loss within the resource as a whole. Among sport species this is likely to involve loss of genetic material, increased incidence to disease and parasites, and loss of stability within the ecosystems involved. Among other, non-sport, species these same changes may be expected, along with the loss of many small local populations; in extreme cases, unique taxa may disappear.

————————————

The main hope for the future would seem to lie in persuading those concerned in sport fishery management to adopt a more responsible attitude towards our native fish stocks, and in stimulating those concerned with all aspects of water use to take account of the value of this resource in their planning. In particular, the following lines of action would seem to be worth developing.

Firstly, increasing the awareness, among those concerned, of the conservation value of fish species and populations in their geographic area or region of control. Secondly, slowing down the obliteration of small aquatic systems and indeed increasing the number available by the creation of new ponds within country parks, nature reserves, etc. Such new ponds, and indeed all new reservoirs, should be designed so that the ecosystem developing within them is suitable for various fish species. Thirdly, there should be more stringent control of poisoning of waters and of the movement of fish stocks (even of common species) from one catchment to another Lastly, there should be further active work on the conservation of rare species, and of valuable stocks of common species, by protecting the ecosystems in which they occur at present and by transferring selected stock to appropriate waters in the same area. Even with common species, there should be action to reintroduce species to waters (including estuaries) from which they have disappeared, if conditions there currently appear suitable, and to establish appropriate mixed communities in new water bodies. The stocks used for such introductions should be chosen carefully.

Also, it should not be thought necessary that every body of water has a fish population. It is highly desirable that, among the diversity of water bodies in Europe, there should remain a number which have no fish species, thus allowing for the development there of the interesting natural communities which exist in the absence of fishes.

Classification

The classification and naming of living creatures has always appeared something of a mystery to the layman. Much of the misunderstanding and difficulty has arisen over the fact that biologists have used Latin or Greek derivations for the scientific names chosen. This, together with ignorance over the status of specific, generic, and other higher rank names, has led to a division between scientists who only recognize the two-worded scientific name for a species wherever it occurs, and laymen who may use different names for the same species in different countries, and even in different parts of the same country.

A good example of the complexity of naming fishes is found in the pike, which is widespread in Europe, Asia, and North America. Biologists clearly recognize this fish by the scientific name *Esox lucius*. In Europe alone, however, the following common names are used in different countries (and even within these countries various other local dialect names are found): **Czechoslovakia** Stika obecna; **Denmark** Gedde; **Germany** Hecht; **Great Britain** Pike; **Spain** Lucio; **France** Brochet; **Ireland** Lius; **Yugoslavia** Stuka; **Italy** Luccio; **Hungary** Csuka; **Netherlands** Snoek; **Norway** Gjedde; **Poland** Szczupak; **Romania** Stiuca; **Russia** Shtschuk; **Finland** Hauki; **Sweden** Gadda; **Turkey** Turna baligi.

The value of a single international name for each species is quite clear in this context!

The two-worded scientific name for a species is equivalent to the names given to many individual humans, with the first, generic, name (e.g. *Esox*) equivalent to the surname, and the second, specific, name (e.g. *lucius*) equivalent to the christian name. Although of course they are used in reverse here. A species name is often followed by the name of the scientific authority who first described it, and the year the description was published (viz. *Esox lucius*, Linnaeus, 1758). The scientific name chosen for each species usually refers to some character of shape or habit, but occasionally species are named after particular people or places.

The naming of species is not, however, merely a haphazard process subject to the whim of each scientist discovering a new species. The whole basis of the way in which names are grouped together is founded on belief in the theory of evolution which

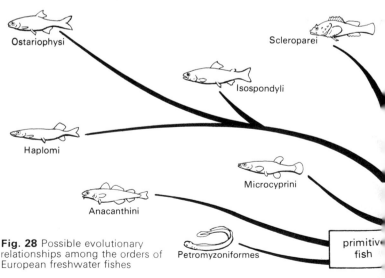

Fig. 28 Possible evolutionary relationships among the orders of European freshwater fishes

Ostariophysi

Scleroparei

Isospondyli

Haplomi

Microcyprini

Anacanthini

Petromyzoniformes

primitive fish

suggests that living things are continually changing to meet the demands of their environment (see fig. 28). Thus a single species, subjected to differing stresses in two different waters can, over a long period of time, evolve into two new species which are distinctly different from the original stock, and eventually so different from each other that they are incapable of interbreeding.

Different though they are, however, these two species will be more closely related to each other than to any other fish and it is likely that they would be placed in the same genus. Thus in North America there is a second species of pike known as the muskellunge. Its scientific name is *Esox masquinongy*. (European pike anglers will be interested to know that this fish grows up to 1.8m (6ft) long and over 50kg (110lb) in weight). Together with several other species, these two species of *Esox* make up the family Esocidae. This family and another related one, the Umbridae, make up a small order known as Haplomi. There are many other, mostly larger, orders of fish which are united with the Haplomi in the Class Osteichthyes. All members of this class possess a bony skeleton, in contrast to members of

the only other class of fish found in European fresh waters, the Marsipobranchii. Here the skeleton consists only of soft cartilage.

It will be seen, therefore, that different fish species are classified together in increasingly larger groups, the relationships within each group being believed to be due to common ancestry. The classification covering European freshwater fishes is given in the check list below, and as a final example the status of pike and man — both vertebrates — is given here in terms of their classification.

	PIKE	MAN
Sub-phylum	Vertebrata	
Class	Osteichthyes	Mammalia
Order	Haplomi	Anthropoidea
Family	Esocidae	Hominidae
Genus	*Esox*	*Homo*
Species	*lucius*	*sapiens*

Some of the important characters of the various European fishes are indicated in the identification keys and description of families, genera and species which are given later in this book.

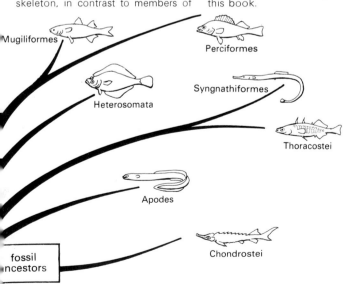

Mugiliformes

Perciformes

Heterosomata

Syngnathiformes

Thoracostei

Apodes

Chondrostei

fossil ancestors

Key to families of European freshwater fishes

1 No paired fins; 7 pairs of gill openings; no lower jaw, mouth in adults a sucking disc; a single median nostril between the eyes
PETROMYZONIDAE (page 66)

   1 or 2 paired fins; 1 pair of gill openings, each protected by an operculum; lower jaw present, mouth never a sucking disc; paired nostrils anterior to eyes **2**

2 Body covered with bony rings; snout tubular; caudal fin absent or very small
SYNGNATHIDAE (page 190)

   Body not covered with bony rings; snout not tubular; caudal fin always present and more or less normal **3**

3 Upper lobe of caudal fin much longer than lower (heterocercal); 5 longitudinal rows of large bony plates on body; snout greatly elongated
ACIPENSERIDAE (page 74)

   Caudal fin more or less symmetrical (holocercal); no large bony plates on body; snout normal **4**

4 Small fleshy protuberance over eye; single dorsal fin extending from head almost to tail fin
BLENNIIDAE (page 224)

   No fleshy protuberance over eye; dorsal fin or fins shorter **5**

5 1 dorsal fin, or if 2, then posterior (adipose) fin small and fleshy, without rays; pelvic fins, where present, approximately midway between pectoral fins and anus, or nearer anus; pneumatic duct present between swim-bladder and oesophagus **6**

   2 dorsal fins, or if 1, then either this is divided into 2 distinct parts, the anterior part being very spiny or replaced by isolated spines, or the body is greatly flattened with both eyes on one side of the head; pelvic fins just below, or slightly posterior to, pectoral fins; pneumatic duct absent between swim-bladder and oesophagus **19**

6 Barbels present on head, largest pair longer than pectoral fins, dorsal fin with less than 8 rays; scales absent **7**

   Barbels either absent on head, or if present then much shorter than pectoral fins; dorsal fin with more than 8 rays; scales present (although very small in 2 families)

7 4 or 6 barbels, the dorsal pair very long, reaching back to the dorsal fin; anal fin very long with about 90—92 rays   SILURIDAE (page 180)

8 barbels, the dorsal pair short, not reaching back beyond the operculum; anal fin short with only 20—22 rays   ICTALURIDAE (page 182)

8 2 dorsal fins, posterior (adipose) fin fleshy without rays   **9**

    1 dorsal fin   **12**

9 Scales relatively small, more than 100 along lateral line; red pigment often present in skin   SALMONIDAE (page 88)

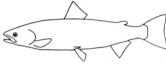

Scales relatively large, less than 100 along lateral line; red pigment rarely present in skin   **10**

10 Lateral line complete almost to caudal fin; teeth absent or poorly developed; pelvic axillary process present   **11**

Lateral line present only for about first 10—20 scales; teeth well developed; pelvic axillary process absent   OSMERIDAE (page 106)

11 Dorsal fin large, depressed length of which is much greater than that of head, and with more than 20 rays; large black pigment spots normally present in skin; small teeth present   THYMALLIDAE (page 106)

Dorsal fin normal, depressed length of which is never greater than that of head, and with less than 20 rays; large black pigment spots never in skin although small black chromatophores may be common
    COREGONIDAE (page 100)

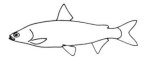

12 Dorsal fin distinct from caudal fin; pelvic fins present; body not extremely elongate **13**

Dorsal fin continuous with caudal and anal fins; pelvic fins absent; body extremely elongate   ANGUILLIDAE (page 184)

13 Scales on ventral surface keeled; lateral line absent; large elongate scales over inner part of caudal fin   CLUPEIDAE (page 80)

Scales on ventral surface not keeled; lateral line present; no elongate scales over inner part of caudal fin **14**

14 Dorsal fin mostly posterior to anus; teeth present **15**

Dorsal fin entirely or mostly anterior to anus; teeth absent **18**

15 Head elongate, mouth very large with well-developed canine teeth; lateral line present   ESOCIDAE (page 108)

Head and mouth normal with small teeth; no lateral line **16**

16 Anal fin with less than 8 rays; more than 32 scales along side of body
                UMBRIDAE (page 108)

Anal fin with more than 8 rays; less than 32 scales along side of body **17**

17 Anal fin in male normal; oviparous; dorsal fin with more than 9 rays; adult teeth trifid at tip   CYPRINODONTIDAE (page 194)

Anal fin in male produced to form copulatory organ; viviparous; dorsal fin with less than 9 rays; adult teeth conic at tip

                POECILIIDAE (page 196)

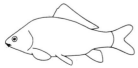

18 Less than 5 barbels on head; mouth normal; scales usually distinct on body   CYPRINIDAE (page 110)

More than 5 barbels on head; mouth small; scales on body indistinct
COBITIDAE (page 170)

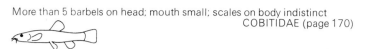

19 2 dorsal fins, or if 1, then divided into 2 distinct parts, the anterior part being very spiny; body never greatly flattened or with isolated spines **20**

1 dorsal fin; body greatly flattened or with a row of dorsal spines **28**

20 Head with single barbel below mouth and 1 small barbel beside each nostril; anal fin with more than 60 rays GADIDAE (page 184)

Head without barbels; anal fin with less than 60 rays **21**

21 Well-developed scales over most of body; anterior dorsal fin rays rigid **22**

Scales absent over most of body; anterior dorsal fin rays flexible
COTTIDAE (page 242)

22 Lateral line absent; less than 5 spiny rays in anterior dorsal fin; dorsal fins widely separated, distance between them always exceeding length of longest dorsal ray **23**

Lateral line present; more than 5 spiny rays in anterior dorsal fin; dorsal fins continuous or close together, distance between them never exceeding length of longest dorsal ray **24**

23 Head flattened dorso-ventrally, scaled dorsally; anal fin with less than 10 rays MUGILIDAE (page 198)

Head compressed laterally, not scaled dorsally; anal fin with more than 10 rays ATHERINIDAE (page 204)

24 1 nostril on each side of head; less than 30 scales along lateral line
CICHLIDAE (page 224)

2 nostrils on each side of head; more than 30 scales along lateral line **25**

25 2 or fewer anal spines present; either less than, or more than, 9 or 10 spiny rays in first dorsal fin **26**

3 or more anal spines present; 9 or 10 spiny rays in first dorsal fin **27**

26 2 anal spines present; tail fin forked; more than 10 spiny rays in first dorsal fin; pelvic fins not joined medially   PERCIDAE (page 208)

Anal spines absent; tail fin rounded; less than 9 spiny rays in first dorsal fin; pelvic fins joined medially   GOBIIDAE (page 226)

27 Second dorsal fin jointed to first anteriorly; less than 70 scales along lateral line; anal fin convex   CENTRARCHIDAE (page 218)

Second dorsal fin separated from first anteriorly; more than 70 scales along lateral line; anal fin concave   SERRANIDAE (page 206)

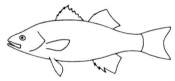

28 3 or more strong spines anterior to dorsal fin; body not flattened; eyes on either side of head; pelvic fins with less than 3 rays
GASTEROSTEIDAE (page 186)

No spines anterior to dorsal fin; body extremely flattened with both eyes on one side of the head (usually the right); pelvic fins with more than 3 rays   PLEURONECTIDAE (page 244)

Check list of European freshwater fishes

Class MARSIPOBRANCHII
Order PETROMYZONIFORMES
Family PETROMYZONIDAE
Sea Lamprey *Petromyzon marinus* Linnaeus 1758
Caspian Lamprey *Caspiomyzon wagneri* (Kessler 1870)
Danube Lamprey *Eudontomyzon danfordi* (Regan 1911)
Vladykov's Lamprey *Eudontomyzon vladykovi* Zanandrea 1959
Ukrainian Lamprey *Eudontomyzon mariae* Berg 1931
Arctic Lamprey *Lampetra japonica* (Martens 1868)
River Lamprey *Lampetra fluviatilis* (Linnaeus 1758)
Brook Lamprey *Lampetra planeri* (Bloch 1784)

Class OSTEICHTHYES
Order CHONDROSTEI
Family ACIPENSERIDAE
Beluga *Huso huso* (Linnaeus 1758)
Ship Sturgeon *Acipenser nudiventris* Lovetsky 1828
Sterlet *Acipenser ruthenus* Linnaeus 1758
Russian Sturgeon *Acipenser guldenstadti* Brandt 1833
Adriatic Sturgeon *Acipenser naccari* Bonaparte 1841
Sturgeon *Acipenser sturio* Linnaeus 1758
Stellate Sturgeon *Acipenser stellatus* Pallas 1771

Order ISOSPONDYLI
Family CLUPEIDAE
Allis Shad *Alosa alosa* (Linnaeus 1758)
Twaite Shad *Alosa fallax* (Lacepede 1800)
Dolginka Shad *Caspialosa brashnikovi* Borodin 1904
Kizilagach Shad *Caspialosa curensis* Surowow 1904
Bigeye Shad *Caspialosa saposhnikovi* Grimm 1901
Suworow's Shad *Caspialosa suworowi* (Berg 1913)
Black Sea Shad *Caspialosa pontica* Eichwald 1838
Caspian Shad *Caspialosa caspia* Eichwald 1838
Tyulka Sardelle *Clupeonella delicatula* (Nordmann 1840)
Abrau Sardelle *Clupeonella abrau* (Maliatski 1931)

Family SALMONIDAE
Chum Salmon *Oncorhynchus keta* (Walbaum 1792)
Humpback Salmon *Oncorhynchus gorbuscha* (Walbaum 1792)
Atlantic Salmon *Salmo salar* Linnaeus 1758
Trout *Salmo trutta* Linnaeus 1758
Rainbow Trout *Salmo gairdneri* Richardson 1836
Charr *Salvelinus alpinus* (Linnaeus 1758)
Brook Charr *Salvelinus fontinalis* (Mitchill 1815)
American Lake Charr *Salvelinus namaycush* (Walbaum 1792)
Huchen *Hucho hucho* (Linnaeus 1758)
Taimen *Hucho taimen* (Pallas 1811)
Adriatic Salmon *Salmothymus obtusirostris* (Heckel 1851)

Family COREGONIDAE
Inconnu *Stenodus leucichthys* (Guldenstadt 1772)
Cisco *Coregonus albula* (Linnaeus 1758)
Peled *Coregonus peled* (Gmelin 1758)

Arctic Whitefish *Coregonus pidschian* (Gmelin 1758)
Broad Whitefish *Coregonus nasus* (Pallas 1776)
Common Whitefish *Coregonus lavaretus* (Linnaeus 1758)
Houting *Coregonus oxyrinchus* (Linnaeus 1758)

Family THYMALLIDAE
Grayling *Thymallus thymallus* (Linnaeus 1758)

Family OSMERIDAE
Smelt *Osmerus eperlanus* (Linnaeus 1758)

Order HAPLOMI
Family UMBRIDAE
Mudminnow *Umbra krameri* Walbaum 1792
Eastern Mudminnow *Umbra pygmaea* (De Kay 1842)

Family ESOCIDAE
Pike *Esox lucius* Linnaeus 1758

Order OSTARIOPHYSI
Family CYPRINIDAE
Roach *Rutilus rutilus* (Linnaeus 1758)
Danube Roach *Rutilus pigus* (Lacepede 1804)
Adriatic Roach *Rutilus rubilio* (Bonaparte 1837)
Portuguese Roach *Rutilus macrolepidotus* (Steindachner 1866)
Pardilla Roach *Rutilus lemmingii* (Steindachner 1866)
Macedonian Roach *Rutilus macedonicus* (Steindachner 1892)
Pearl Roach *Rutilus frisii* (Nordmann 1840)
Calandino Roach *Rutilus alburnoides* (Steindachner 1866)
Moranec *Pachychilon pictum* (Heckel & Kner 1858)
Greek Minnowcarp *Phoxinellus minutus* (Karaman 1824)
Spanish Minnowcarp *Phoxinellus hispanicus* (Steindachner 1866)
Adriatic Minnow *Paraphoxinus alepidotus* (Heckel 1843)
Croatian Minnow *Paraphoxinus croaticus* (Steindachner 1865)
Dalmatian Minnow *Paraphoxinus ghethaldii* Steindachner 1882
South Dalmatian Minnow *Paraphoxinus pstrossi* Steindachner 1882
Greek Minnow *Paraphoxinus epiroticus* Steindachner 1896
Spotted Minnow *Paraphoxinus adspersus* (Heckel 1843)
Belica *Leucaspius delineatus* (Heckel 1843)
Tsima *Leucaspius marathonicus* Vinciguerra 1920
Marida *Leucaspius stymphalicus* (Valenciennes 1844)
Dace *Leuciscus leuciscus* (Linnaeus 1758)
Danilewskii's Dace *Leuciscus danilewskii* (Kessler 1877)
Adriatic Dace *Leuciscus svallize* (Heckel & Kner 1858)
Yugoslavian Dace *Leuciscus illyricus* (Heckel & Kner 1858)
Chub *Leuciscus cephalus* (Linnaeus 1758)
Black Sea Chub *Leuciscus borysthenicus* (Kessler 1859)
Caucasian Chub *Leuciscus aphipsi* Aleksandrov 1927
Blageon *Leuciscus souffia* Risso 1826
Croatian Dace *Leuciscus polylepsis* (Steindachner 1866)
Ukliva Dace *Leuciscus ukliva* (Heckel 1843)
Makal Dace *Leuciscus microlepsis* Heckel 1843
Turskyi Dace *Leuciscus turskyi* (Heckel 1843)
Orfe *Leuciscus idus* (Linnaeus 1758)
Swamp Minnow *Phoxinus percnurus* (Pallas 1811)
Minnow *Phoxinus phoxinus* (Linnaeus 1758)
Poznàn Minnow *Phoxinus czekanowskii* Dybowski 1869
Rudd *Scardinius erythrophthalmus* (Linnaeus 1758)
Greek Rudd *Scardinius graecus* Stephanidis 1937
Asp *Aspius aspius* (Linnaeus 1758)
Tench *Tinca tinca* (Linnaeus 1758)
Nase *Chondrostoma nasus* (Linnaeus 1758)

Italian Nase *Chondrostoma soetta* Bonaparte 1841
Caucasian Nase *Chondrostoma colchicum* Kessler 1899
Iberian Nase *Chondrostoma polylepis* Steindachner 1866
Terek Nase *Chondrostoma oxyrhynchum* Kessler 1877
Laska Nase *Chondrostoma genei* Bonaparte 1841
French Nase *Chondrostoma toxostoma* Vallot 1837
Dalmatian Nase *Chondrostoma kneri* Heckel 1841
Minnow Nase *Chondrostoma phoxinus* Heckel 1843
Gudgeon *Gobio gobio* (Linnaeus 1758)
Kessler's Gudgeon *Gobio kessleri* Dybowski 1862
Danube Gudgeon *Gobio uranoscopus* (Agassiz 1828)
Whitefin Gudgeon *Gobio albipinnatus* Lukasch 1933
Caucasian Gudgeon *Gobio ciscaucasicus* Berg 1932
Dalmatian Barbelgudgeon *Aulopyge hugeli* Heckel 1841
Barbel *Barbus barbus* (Linnaeus 1758)
Turkish Barbel *Barbus cyclolepis* Heckel 1840
Macedonian Barbel *Barbus prespensis* Karaman 1924
Caucasian Barbel *Barbus ciscaucasicus* Kessler 1877
Greek Barbel *Barbus graecus* Steindachner 1896
Albanian Barbel *Barbus albanicus* Steindachner 1895
Mediterranean Barbel *Barbus meridionalis* Risso 1826
Bulatmai Barbel *Barbus capito* Guldenstadt 1773
Aral Barbel *Barbus brachycephalus* Berg 1914
Iberian Barbel *Barbus comiza* Steindachner 1866
Bleak *Alburnus alburnus* (Linnaeus 1758)
White Bleak *Alburnus albidus* (Costa 1838)
Caucasian Bleak *Alburnus charusini* Herzenstein 1889
Shemaya *Chalcalburnus chalcoides* (Guldenstadt 1772)
Schneider *Alburnoides bipunctatus* (Bloch 1782)
White Bream *Blicca bjoerkna* (Linnaeus 1758)
Bream *Abramis brama* (Linnaeus 1758)
Whiteye Bream *Abramis sapa* (Pallas 1811)
Blue Bream *Abramis ballerus* (Linnaeus 1758)
Vimba *Vimba vimba* (Linnaeus 1758)
Chekhon *Pelecus cultratus* (Linnaeus 1758)
Bitterling *Rhodeus sericeus* (Bloch 1782)
Crucian Carp *Carassius carassius* (Linnaeus 1758)
Goldfish *Carassius auratus* (Linnaeus 1758)
Carp *Cyprinus carpio* Linnaeus 1758

Family COBITIDAE
Stone Loach *Noemacheilus barbatulus* (Linnaeus 1758)
Angora Loach *Noemacheilus angorae* Steindachner 1897
Terek Loach *Noemacheilus merga* (Krynicki 1840)
Weather Loach *Misgurnis fossilis* (Linnaeus 1758)
Spined Loach *Cobitis taenia* Linnaeus 1758
Golden Loach *Cobitis aurata* (De Filippi 1865)
Caspian Loach *Cobitis caspia* Eichwald 1838
Caucasian Loach *Cobitis caucasica* Berg 1906
Venetian Loach *Cobitis conspersa* (Cantoni 1882)
Balkan Loach *Cobitis elongata* Heckel & Kner 1858
Italian Loach *Cobitis larvata* De Filippi 1859
Rumanian Loach *Cobitis romanica* Bacescu 1943

Family SILURIDAE
Wels *Silurus glanis* Linnaeus 1758
Aristotle's Catfish *Silurus aristotelis* Garman 1840

Family ICTALURIDAE
Black Bullhead *Ictalurus melas* (Rafinesque 1820)
Brown Bullhead *Ictalurus nebulosus* Le Sueur 1919

Order APODES
Family ANGUILLIDAE
Eel *Anguilla anguilla* (Linnaeus 1758)

Order ANACANTHINI
Family GADIDAE
Burbot *Lota lota* (Linnaeus 1758)

Order THORACOSTEI
Family GASTEROSTEIDAE
Three-spined Stickleback *Gasterosteus aculeatus* Linnaeus 1758
Ten-spined Stickeback *Pungitius pungitius* (Linnaeus 1758)
Ukrainian Stickleback *Pungitius platygaster* (Kessler 1859)

Order SYNGNATHIFORMES
Family SYNGNATHIDAE
Black Sea Pipefish *Syngnathus nigrolineatus* Eichwald 1831
Mediterranean Pipefish *Syngnathus acus* Linnaeus 1758
Broadnose Pipefish *Syphonostoma typhle* Linnaeus 1758
Straightnose Pipefish *Nerophis ophidion* (Linnaeus 1758)

Order MICROCYPRINI
Family CYPRINODONTIDAE
Mediterranean Toothcarp *Aphanius fasciatus*
   (Humboldt & Valenciennes 1821)
Iberian Toothcarp *Aphanius iberus* (Cuvier & Valenciennes 1846)
Valencia Toothcarp *Valencia hispanica* (Cuvier & Valenciennes 1846)

Family POECILIIDAE
Mosquito Fish *Gambusia affinis* Baird & Girard 1853

Order MUGILIFORMES
Family MUGILIDAE
Striped Mullet *Mugil cephalus* Linnaeus 1758
Golden Mullet *Mugil auratus* Risso 1810
Thinlipped Mullet *Mugil capito* Cuvier 1828
Grey Mullet *Mugil labeo* Cuvier 1828
Thicklipped Mullet *Mugil labrosus* Risso 1826
Sharpnose Mullet *Mugil saliens* Risso 1810

Family ATHERINIDAE
Sandsmelt *Atherina hepsetus* Linnaeus 1758
Mediterranean Sandsmelt *Atherina mochon* Valenciennes 1835
Atlantic Sandsmelt *Atherina presbyter* Cuvier 1829

Order PERCIFORMES
Family SERRANIDAE
Sea Bass *Dicentrarchus labrax* (Linnaeus 1758)
Spotted Bass *Dicentrarchus punctatus* Bloch 1797

Family PERCIDAE
Perch *Perca fluviatilis* Linnaeus 1758
Pikeperch *Stizostedion lucioperca* (Linnaeus 1758)
Sea Pikeperch *Stizostedion marina* (Cuvier & Valenciennes 1828)
Volga Pikeperch *Stizostedion volgensis* (Gmelin 1785)
Don Ruffe *Gymnocephalus acerina* (Guldenstadt 1775)
Ruffe *Gymnocephalus cernua* (Linnaeus 1758)
Striped Ruffe *Gymnocephalus schraetzer* (Linnaeus 1758)
Asper *Aspro asper* (Linnaeus 1758)
Streber *Aspro streber* Siebold 1763
Zingel *Aspro zingel* (Linnaeus 1766)
Percarina *Percarina demidoffi* Nordmann 1840

Asprete *Romanichthys valsanicola* Dumitrescu, Baranescu & Stoica 1957

Family CENTRARCHIDAE
Largemouth Bass *Micropterus salmoides* (Lacepede 1802)
Smallmouth Bass *Micropterus dolomieu* Lacepede 1802
Rock Bass *Ambloplites rupestris* (Lacepede 1802)
Pumpkinseed *Lepomis gibbosus* (Linnaeus 1758)
Redbreast Sunfish *Lepomis auritis* (Linnaeus 1758)
Green Sunfish *Lepomis cyanellus* (Rafinesque 1819)

Family CICHLIDAE
Chanchito *Cichlasoma facetum* Jenyns 1842

Family BLENNIIDAE
Freshwater Blenny *Blennius fluviatilis* Asso 1801

Family GOBIIDAE
Bighead Goby *Gobius kessleri* Gunther 1861
Ginger Goby *Gobius cephalarges* Pallas 1811
Syrman Goby *Gobius syrman* Nordmann 1840
Racer Goby *Gobius gymnotrachelus* Kessler 1857
Toad Goby *Gobius batracocephalus* (Pallas 1811)
Sand Goby *Gobius fluviatilis* Pallas 1811
Round Goby *Gobius melanostomus* Pallas 1811
Grass Goby *Gobius ophiocephalus* (Pallas 1811)
Canestrini's Goby *Pomatoschistus canestrini* (Ninni 1882)
Caucasian Goby *Pomatoschistus caucasicus* (Kawrajsky 1899)
Longtail Goby *Pomatoschistus longicaudatus* (Kessler 1877)
Common Goby *Pomatoschistus microps* (Kroyer 1840)
Berg's Coby *Hyrcanogobius bergi* Iljin 1928
Relict Goby *Relictogobius kryzanovskii* Ptschelina 1939
Tubenose Goby *Proterhorinus marmoratus* (Pallas 1811)
Panizza's Goby *Padogobius panizzai* (Verga 1841)
Italian Goby *Padogobius nigricans* (Canestrini 1876)
Caspian Goby *Caspiosoma caspium* (Kessler 1877)
Caspian Tadpole Goby *Benthophilus macrocephalus* (Pallas 1787)
Stellate Tadpole Goby *Benthophilus stellatus* (Sauvage 1874)
Banded Tadpole Goby *Benthophilus brauneri* Beling & Iljin 1927
Rough Tadpole Goby *Benthophilus granulosus* Kessler 1877

Order SCLEROPAREI
Family COTTIDAE
Bullhead *Cottus gobio* Linnaeus 1758
Siberian Bullhead *Cottus poecilopus* Heckel 1836
Fourhorn Bullhead *Myoxocephalus quadricornis* (Linnaeus 1758)

Order HETEROSOMATA
Family PLEURONECTIDAE
Flounder *Platichthys flesus* (Linnaeus 1758)
Arctic Flounder *Liopsetta glacialis* Pallas 1776

Family PETRO-MYZONIDAE

The Petromyzonidae, or lampreys, belong to a small but important group known as Agnatha — literally 'jawless' fishes. Thus they are quite distinct from all the other fishes described in this guide which have upper jaws fixed closely to the skull and hinged lower jaws which oppose them. The lampreys, in contrast, have no lower jaws and the whole mouth is surrounded by a round sucker-like disc within which, in the adults, are developed horny rasping teeth. These vary in position and number among the species, and are an important aid to identification.

Lampreys also have a number of other very characteristic features: they are always very eel like in shape, but have no paired fins or scales on the body. They have no bones — all the skeletal structures are made up of stiff but flexible cartilage. There is a single nostril, situated on top of the head, just in front of the eyes. (The latter may not be functional or even visible in the young.) The gills open directly to the sides of the head (i.e. there is no operculum), so that there is a row of gill pores immediately behind each eye. The adults have two dorsal fins which are often more or less continuous with the elongate tail fin.

Most lampreys have a similar sort of life cycle, which involves the migration of adults to special spawning areas — normally stony or gravelly stretches of running water. There they spawn in pairs or groups, and the eggs are laid in crude nests created by the adults lifting small stones with their suckered mouths. These stones are used to surround, and sometimes to cover and protect, the eggs, while the nest itself may often be under a large stone, log, or clump of vegetation. After hatching, the young elongate larvae, known as *ammocoetes*, swim or are washed by the current to areas of sandy silt in still water where they burrow and spend the next few years in tunnels. They are blind, the sucker is incomplete around the mouth and the teeth are undeveloped. The ammocoete larvae feed by creating a current which draws loose organic particles (coated with bacteria), and minute plants such as diatoms, into the pharynx. They there become entwined on a slimy mucous string which is swallowed regularly by the animal. The change from larval to adult form is a

Fig. 29 Oral disc of an adult lamprey, showing main mouthparts

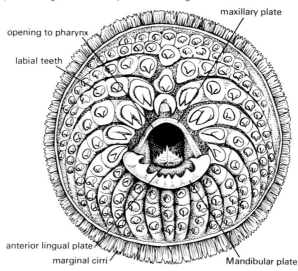

opening to pharynx

labial teeth

maxillary plate

anterior lingual plate

marginal cirri

Mandibular plate

fairly dramatic metamorphosis which takes place within a relatively short time — usually just a few weeks. The mouth develops into a full sucker inside which are rasping teeth. The skin becomes much more silvery and opaque except over the eyes where it clears to give the animal proper vision for the first time. The adults then migrate, usually downstream, away from the nursery areas.

Some species of lampreys never feed as adults — these spawn and die soon after metamorphosis — but most are parasitic on various species of fish which they attack either in large freshwater lakes or in the sea where most of the adult life is spent. They attach themselves to the side of a fish and rasp away the skin, eating both it and the body fluids and muscle beneath. The prey often never recovers from such an attack (especially if the body cavity is pene-trated) and in some waters lampreys are a serious pest of commercial fish stocks. (The most famous example of this is in North America, where canalization gave the marine lamprey access, for the first time, to the Great Lakes. Various commercial fish stocks there were soon seriously depleted, particularly the American lake charr whose population collapsed in a dramatic way.) On reaching sexual maturity, the adult lampreys migrate back again to the spawning areas.

Lampreys are still caught commercially in a number of countries, and in some are regarded as a great delicacy. River lampreys, for instance, smoked or soaked in oil were formerly highly prized, and King Henry I of England is supposed to have died from a surfeit of them. There are 8 species of Petromyzonidae in fresh water in Europe, and a number of subspecies.

Key to European Petromyzonidae

1 Maxillary plate narrow, bearing 1 or 2 teeth **2**

Maxillary plate wide, bearing 1 tooth on each side **3**

2 2 teeth on maxillary plate; 7—8 teeth on mandibular plate; teeth strong, sharp; anterior lingual plate with median depression
Petromyzon marinus

Normally 1 tooth on maxillary plate; 5 teeth on mandibular plate; teeth weak, blunt, rounded; anterior lingual plate without median depression
Caspiomyzon wagneri

3 Outer and inner labial teeth; lower labial teeth present; mediolateral labial teeth bifid **4**

Outer lateral labial teeth absent; mediolateral labial teeth bifid or trifid **6**

4 Body thickest near middle; lingual plate with 9—13 teeth
Eudontomyzon danfordi

Body thickest anteriorly; lingual plate with 9 or less teeth **5**

5 Lingual plate with 5—9 teeth *Eudontomyzon vladykovi*

Lingual plate with 5 teeth *Eudontomyzon mariae*

6 Lower labial teeth well developed; mediolateral teeth bifid
Lampetra japonica

Lower labial teeth absent; mediolateral labial teeth trifid **7**

7 Mandibular plate with 7—10 teeth, all of them strong and sharp; dorsal fins separate *Lampetra fluviatilis*

Mandibular plate with 5—9 teeth, all of them weak and blunt; dorsal fins connected *Lampetra planeri*

Sea Lamprey *Petromyzon marinus*

Size 50−70 cm; maximum 86 cm; a 53 cm specimen weighs about 360 g. **Distinctive features** characteristic tooth pattern; adults with very mottled colour; the largest European lamprey. **Distribution** a native anadromous species common in most of the Atlantic coastal area of western Europe and eastern North America and in estuaries and easily accessible rivers there. **Reproduction** March−May. Clear eggs, laid in nests among stones in running water, hatch into elongated blind ammocoete larvae which live buried in silt in quiet waters for 2−5 years. They then metamorphose and migrate to the sea where they mature, returning to fresh water to spawn after 3−4 years. 34,000−240,000 eggs per female. **Food** filtered organic material (diatoms, bacteria, etc.) when larvae, fishes when adult. **Value** formerly more popular than now, it is still trapped or netted in some European rivers when ascending to spawn. Never angled for. A serious pest to commercial and sport fisheries in some areas.

Caspian Lamprey
Caspiomyzon wagneri

Size 20−40 cm; maximum 55 cm − this fish weighed 205 g. **Distinctive features** characteristic tooth pattern; adults of uniform (usually grey) colour. **Distribution** a native anadromous species widespread in the Caspian Sea and its larger easily accessible rivers, especially the Volga. **Reproduction** March−May. Eggs laid in nests among stones and gravel in flowing water. The ammocoete larvae, which live buried in sand and silt, metamorphose after about 3 years and descend to the sea. 20,000−32,000 eggs per female. **Food** filtered organic material (algae and detritus) when larvae. The adults probably feed on other fishes, but some have been found to contain vegetable material. **Value** an important commercial species caught in nets and traps, mainly during spawning migrations (e.g. in the Volga). Early this century, 15−30 million fishes were caught annually in the lower Volga and used as food. Of no sporting significance.

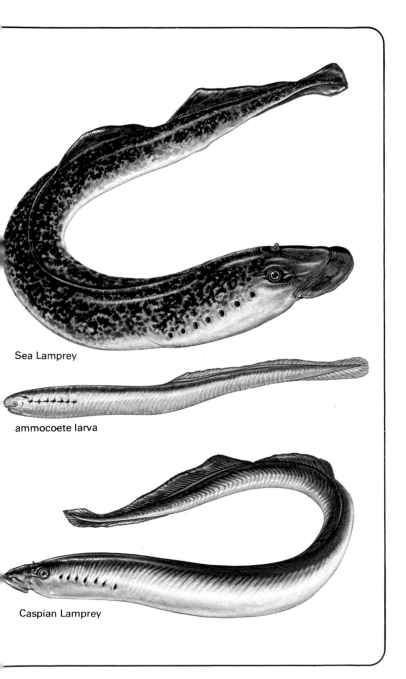

Sea Lamprey

ammocoete larva

Caspian Lamprey

69

Danube Lamprey
Eudontomyzon danfordi

Size 15—25cm; maximum 30cm. **Distinctive features** thickest part of body near middle; 9—13 teeth on lingual plate. **Distribution** found only in the Danube basin or waters closely associated with it. A purely freshwater species. **Reproduction** April—May, mostly in the smaller tributaries of the Danube. Larvae live in silted sandy beds for 3—4 years before metamorphosing into adults which move down into the larger rivers. The adults mature after about 1 year. **Food** small organic particles filtered by larvae. The adults feed on various other stream fishes. **Value** of no commercial or sporting value.

Vladykov's Lamprey
Eudontomyzon vladykovi

Size 15—20cm; maximum 21cm. **Distinctive features** body thickest anteriorly; 5—9 teeth on lingual plate; innermost lateral teeth usually with 2—4 points. **Distribution** a purely freshwater species found only in parts of the Danube basin. **Reproduction** April—May, mainly in small tributaries. Larvae live in silted areas of streams for 4—6 years before metamorphosing into adults which spawn soon afterwards. **Food** fine filtered organic particles when larvae. The adults do not feed. **Value** of no commercial or sporting value.

Ukrainian Lamprey
Eudontomyzon mariae

Size 15—20cm; maximum 21cm. **Distinctive features** numerous small outer labial teeth along the margin of the disc, usually in several rows; lower labial teeth present but rarely forming a continuous patch. **Distribution** occurring only in fresh water, in rivers entering the northern shore of the Black Sea (e.g. Don, Dnieper and Dniester). **Reproduction** March—May, mainly in smaller streams among stones and gravel. Larvae live in silt beds of streams and rivers for 4—6 years before metamorphosing to adults which spawn soon afterwards. 2,429 eggs were found in a female 14.7cm long. **Food** larvae filter fine organic particles from their surroundings. The adults do not feed. **Value** of no commercial or sporting value.

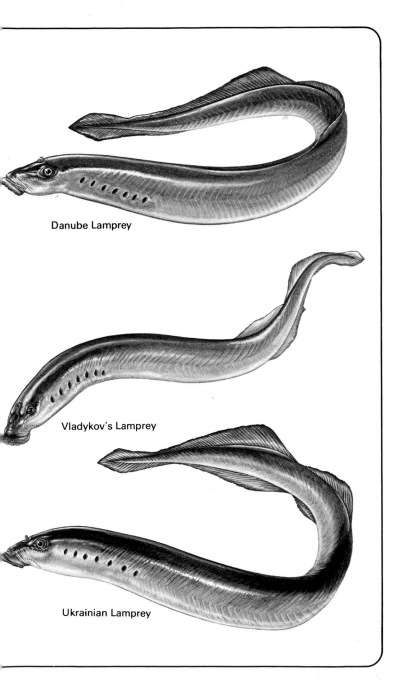

Danube Lamprey

Vladykov's Lamprey

Ukrainian Lamprey

Arctic Lamprey *Lampetra japonica*

Size 40–60cm; maximum 63cm; lampreys with a mean length of 54cm weigh about 146g. **Distinctive features** a wide maxillary plate with well-developed lower labial teeth. **Distribution** northern Europe and Asia in rivers associated with the Arctic and Pacific basins. **Reproduction** May–June, in rivers easily accessible from the sea. Larvae live in silted river beds for 3–4 years before metamorphosing and migrating to the sea where they grow to maturity. 80,000–107,000 eggs per female. **Food** fine organic particles when larvae, fishes (including anadromous species, e.g. *Oncorhynchus gorbuscha*) when adult. **Value** little used commercially and of no sporting value.

River Lamprey *Lampetra fluviatilis*

Size 30–35cm; maximum 41cm; the mean weight of females 32–34cm long is about 62g. **Distinctive features** maxillary plate wide, but no lower labial teeth; 7–10 teeth on mandibular plate. **Distribution** occurs over much of western Europe from southern Norway to the western Mediterranean. In the sea and in accessible rivers. There is a number of non-migratory populations isolated from the sea. **Reproduction** April–May. Eggs laid in nests among stones in running water. The ammocoete larvae live in silted stream beds for 3–5 years, then metamorphose into adults which migrate to the sea (or a large lake in isolated populations). The mature adults migrate upstream again in winter and spring. 19,000–20,000 eggs per female. **Food** filtered organic material when larvae, fishes when adult. **Value** an important commercial species, the adults being caught in nets and traps as they migrate upstream. Many are smoked. Of no angling value except that the larvae are occasionally used as bait for angling.

Brook Lamprey *Lampetra planeri*

Size 12–15cm; maximum 21cm. **Distinctive fearures** wide maxillary plate present but no lower labial teeth; 5–9 teeth in mandibular plate. **Distribution** a purely freshwater species occurring in streams in much of western Europe, especially in basins associated with the Baltic and North Seas. **Reproduction** April–June. Eggs laid in nests in stones in running water. Larvae live in silt in streams and rivers, metamorphosing after 3–5 years to adults which spawn and die soon afterwards. 854–1,400 eggs per female. **Food** filtered organic material when larvae. The adults do not feed. **Value** of no commercial value, but the larvae are occasionally used as bait for angling.

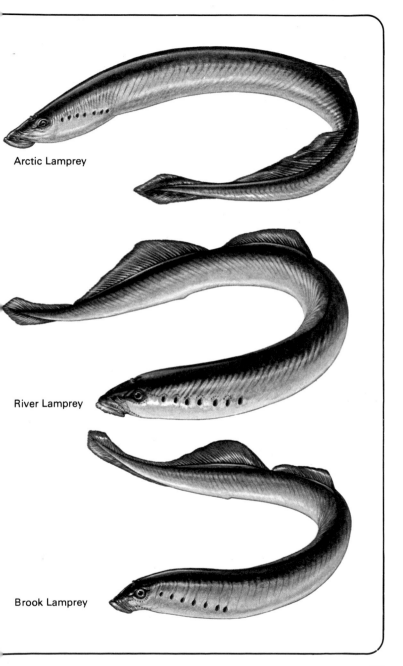

Arctic Lamprey

River Lamprey

Brook Lamprey

Family ACIPENSERIDAE

The Acipenseridae, or sturgeons, are an extremely interesting family of large primitive fishes which are quite distinct from all other living bony fishes. They occur in the Northern Hemisphere, and the family contains about 23 species. The elongate body has no scales, but has several rows of characteristic bony plates which are often an important aid to identification. These plates become smoother with age and in some cases disappear altogether in old specimens. The tail is upturned into the dorsal lobe of the tail fin (a condition known as heterocercal) and forms its main support. The snout is elongate and projects well in front of the ventral mouth, in front of which are four barbels, the exact form of which varies among the different species. The mouth itself is unusual in being a protrusible tube, well adapted for its mode of feeding, which is mainly on benthic invertebrates.

Sturgeons usually spawn in twos or threes in suitable stretches of large rivers or sometimes in lakes. The adults, which are often extremely large, are not particularly efficient swimmers; they are rarely found in fast-flowing, or small bodies of water. The eggs, which are rather unusual in being very dark in colour, are mostly scattered loosely on to the bottom where, being adhesive, they stick to stones and logs. After hatching, the young migrate gradually into their nursery areas — usually large lakes, the lower reaches of large rivers or, in many species, the sea. There, growth is very slow and it may be up to 15 years before maturity is reached and the fishes migrate back to the spawning areas.

Sturgeons have been valued as a commercial species for hundreds, if not thousands, of years. Their large size, ease of capture, and tasty flesh and eggs have led to the development of important fisheries in almost all parts of the world where they occur. However, their slow rate of growth has rendered them very susceptible to overfishing, and a number of populations have become extinct because of this. Others have disappeared due to major pollution in the lower reaches of rivers which they once

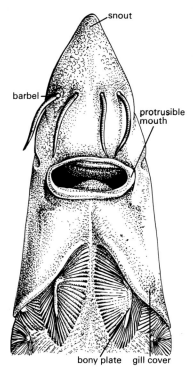

Fig. 30 Ventral view of head and mouth of the ship sturgeon

frequented. The flesh is eaten fresh or smoked, and in some areas is dried. The roe is eaten as caviar. To prepare this the ovaries are removed from ripe females, cleaned carefully and then packed in brine.

Depleted stocks in some areas have led to experimental fish farming with a number of species. The fact that several of these interbreed to produce hybrids has helped make the industry quite successful. Several of these hybrids occur in nature, the most common of these being: *Huso huso* x *Acipenser stellatus; Huso huso* x *Acipenser nudiventris; Huso huso* x *Acipenser guldenstadti; Acipenser nudiventris* x *Acipenser stellatus; Acipenser ruthenus* x *Acipenser sturio; Acipenser ruthenus* x *Acipenser stellatus; Acipenser guldenstadti* x *Acipenser stellatus.*

The anadromous sturgeons have

two seasonal forms: a spring form which ascends rivers in spring and spawns in spring or early summer of the same year; and a winter form which ascends rivers in late summer or autumn and spawns the following year, having spent the winter in the river. Seven species occur in Europe.

Key to European Acipenseridae

1 Mouth large, crescentic; branchiostegal membranes coalesced, forming a free fold below isthmus *Huso huso*

Mouth small, transverse; branchiostegal membranes attached to isthmus, not forming a fold underneath **2**

2 Lower lip continuous, not interrupted medially; barbels fimbriate *Acipenser nudiventris*

Lower lip with a median space **3**

3 Snout short, usually less than 60 per cent of head length **4**

Snout elongate, usually more than 60 per cent of head length; lateral scutes 26—43 *Acipenser stellatus*

4 More than 50 lateral scutes; barbels with distinct fimbria *Acipenser ruthenus*

Less than 50 lateral scutes; barbels with no, or small, fimbria **5**

5 Snout shorter and rounded; lateral scutes 21—50 *Acipenser guldenstadti*

Snout longer and pointed **6**

6 Lateral scutes less than twice as high as broad; snout less rounded when viewed from above *Acipenser sturio*

Lateral scutes more than twice as high as broad; snout more rounded when viewed from above *Acipenser naccari*

Beluga *Huso huso*

Size 1.5–3m; maximum 4.24m; maximum weight 1220kg. **Distinctive features** adults very large with large crescentic mouth. **Distribution** the Black, Caspian and Adriatic Seas and easily accessible rivers (e.g. Volga, Danube and Don). **Reproduction** May. The spawning grounds occur mainly in the lower and middle reaches of the rivers concerned. The young migrate downstream to the sea during their first year. They may take 15–20 years before maturing and entering the rivers again to spawn. Specimens as old as 60 years have been recorded. **Food** invertebrates when young, but mostly small species of fishes (e.g. gobies and anchovies) when in the sea. **Value** of major commercial importance in the seas and rivers concerned. Adults of over 1000 kg are not uncommon,and very heavy total catches are taken each year by the fisheries concerned. The females are especially valuable since they provide not only flesh, but their eggs are used as caviar.

Ship Sturgeon *Acipenser nudiventris*

Size 1–1.25m; maximum 2m; specimens with a mean length of 1.5m weigh 20kg. **Distinctive features** a small mouth with a continuous lower lip. **Distribution** common in the Black, Caspian and Aral Seas, and the larger rivers entering them (e.g. Kura and Syr-Darya). **Reproduction** April–May, in the middle and lower reaches of the rivers concerned. The young move down to the sea where they take 10–15 years to mature. Some individuals may live up to 30 years, spawning several times during their lives. 216,000–1,002,000 eggs per female. **Food** invertebrates when young, invertebrates and some fish when adult. **Value** an important commercial species netted in very large numbers in the seas and rivers concerned. The eggs are used as caviar.

Sterlet *Acipenser ruthenus*

Size 25–50cm; maximum 92cm – this fish weighed 19kg. **Distinctive features** small mouth with median space in lower lip; more than 50 lateral scutes. **Distribution** river basins entering the north of the Black Sea and east of the Caspian Sea and the western Baltic. This is mainly a freshwater species found in rivers and large lakes, but it is sometimes found in salt water. **Reproduction** April–June in fast flowing rivers over a gravel bottom. The adhesive eggs hatch in 6–9 days and the young gradually disperse downstream. Adults mature and start to spawn after 4–5 years, but may live up to 25 years. 7,800–76,400 eggs per female. **Food** mainly bottom-dwelling invertebrates – especially the larvae of insects such as blackfly, caddis fly and midge. **Value** important commercially and caught in nets or traps.

Beluga

Ship Sturgeon

Sterlet

Russian Sturgeon
Acipenser guldenstadti

Size 1–2 m; maximum 2.3 m; maximum weight over 100 kg. **Distinctive features** short rounded snout with less than 50 lateral scutes. **Distribution** Black and Caspian Seas and their large rivers (e.g. Volga). **Reproduction** May–June, in lower reaches of rivers. After 3 years young descend to the sea, but a few stay in fresh water all their lives. Adults mature in 10–15 years and live up to 50 years. **Food** invertebrates (mainly insect larvae and molluscs) and some fishes when in the sea. **Value** caught in large numbers during migration. The roe is eaten as caviar.

Adriatic Sturgeon *Acipenser naccari*

Size 1–1.5 m; maximum 2 m. **Distinctive features** snout short and pointed; lateral scutes more than twice as high as broad. **Distribution** Adriatic Sea and inflowing rivers (e.g. Po). **Reproduction** April–May in the middle reaches of rivers. The young then move down to the sea where they mature and migrate upstream again to spawn. **Food** bottom-dwelling invertebrates when young, invertebrates and fishes when adult. **Value** commercially important in the Adriatic area.

Sturgeon *Acipenser sturio*

Size 1.5–2.5 m; maximum 3.45 m – this fish weighed 320 kg. **Distinctive features** snout pointed; lateral scutes less than twice as high as broad. **Distribution** the coast of western Europe, including the Black Sea, and large accessible rivers. **Reproduction** April–July in middle reaches of rivers. The eggs adhere to stones and hatch after 3–5 days. The young move to the sea after 2 years, except for purely freshwater populations (e.g. in Lake Ladoga). Adults mature after 7–15 years. 800,000–2,400,000 eggs per female. **Food** benthic invertebrates and, when adult, some fish. **Value** formerly important commercially and caught for flesh and caviar; still netted in some areas but numbers taken now are far less than 100 years ago.

Stellate Sturgeon *Acipenser stellatus*

Size 1–1.5 m; maximum 190 cm. **Distinctive features** elongate snout with 26–43 lateral scutes. **Distribution** the northern Caspian Sea, Black Sea, Sea of Azov, and associated rivers. Sometimes in the eastern Mediterranean. **Reproduction** April–June, in the middle reaches of rivers. The young move gradually down to the sea and mature in 8–12 years. **Food** when young, invertebrates; when adult, invertebrates and small fishes. **Value** caught commercially during migration. The flesh and roe (caviar) are both of importance.

Russian Sturgeon

Adriatic Sturgeon

Sturgeon

Stellate Sturgeon

Family CLUPEIDAE

The Clupeidae, many of which are known as herrings or shads, is a large family of pelagic fishes which are found in oceans all over the world. Most species are marine, but some are anadromous and a few live permanently in fresh waters. There are several genera including a total of more than 190 species.

The herrings are mainly small to medium-sized fishes with a stream-lined laterally compressed body covered by large, circular cycloid scales. These are unusual in that the circuli are arched across the scale rather than arranged in concentric rings as in most cycloid scales. The ventral edge of the belly is armed with scute-like scales, forming a very characteristic toothed edge when viewed in profile. The head has large eyes with characteristic fleshy eyelids. The mouth is usually terminal, and teeth are either small or absent. The many gill rakers lining the back of the pharynx are long and thin, and their number is an important character in identification. There is no lateral line.

Most members of the family are pelagic in habit and swim around in large shoals. These may often reach enormous numbers—sometimes comprising many thousands of individuals. The main foods of these shoals are the abundant masses of zooplankton which thrive in the richer parts of the sea. Feeding on the invertebrates is facilitated by the comb-like gill rakers, which help to separate the food from the water— the former being swallowed, the latter passing out through the gills.

The herrings themselves form a major source of food for many larger fishes, and for enormous colonies of sea-birds in some parts of the world.

Because of the large size of the shoals, and the ease with which they may be captured, this is one of the most important families of commercial fish species in the world. They are caught mainly in gill nets, ring nets and trawls, and the total world catch is about 30 per cent of all fishes caught by man. The flesh is particularly rich in fats and oils. Fishes which cannot be marketed fresh are frozen, pickled or smoked. Fishes which are too small for individual consumption are processed in bulk to make fish meal (for feeding to domestic mammals and birds) or for oil extraction.

Since they are very dependent on the local abundance of zooplankton, the success of various populations of Clupeidae is closely linked with the fate of zooplankton, and in turn the phytoplankton, on which these small animals feed. The phytoplankton itself is dependent on an effective supply of nutrients washed up to the surface of the sea by up-welling currents. Thus the researches of hydrologists who study and plot the ocean currents are of great assistance in helping to understand the fluctuations in abundance of populations of Clupeidae.

European Clupeidae are mainly marine, but a few species are found in fresh water throughout their lives, and a number of others enter fresh water, either casually, or regularly at some time during their lives.

Altogether 10 species in Europe may be considered in these categories.

Fig. 31 Gills of two common Clupeidae

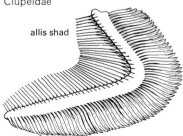

allis shad

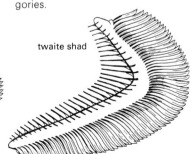

twaite shad

Key to European freshwater Clupeidae

1   Upper jaw with a marked median notch; lower jaw articulating behind posterior margin of eye   **2**

Upper jaw with no, or only a small, median notch; lower jaw articulating anterior to posterior margin of eye   **9**

2   Vomerine teeth absent   **3**

Vomerine teeth present   **4**

3   More than 90 gill rakers on 1st arch; more than 70 lateral scales
Alosa alosa

Less than 60 gill rakers on 1st arch; less than 70 lateral scales
Alosa fallax

4   More than 90 gill rakers on 1st arch; teeth small or absent
Caspialosa caspia

Less than 90 gill rakers on 1st arch; teeth present   **5**

5   Less than 45 gill rakers   **6**

More than 50 gill rakers   **8**

6   Upper and lower profiles of head straight; gill rakers less than gill filaments in length   **7**

Upper and lower profiles of head rounded; gill rakers longer than gill filaments   *Caspialosa curensis*

7   Eye large, its diameter more than 6 per cent of fish length; body depth more than 24 per cent of length   *Caspialosa saposhnikovi*

Eye small, its diameter less than 6 per cent of fish length; body depth less than 24 per cent of length   *Caspialosa brashnikovi*

8   Usually 50—55 gill rakers; gill arches slender and weak; gill rakers half as long again as filaments   *Caspialosa suworowi*

Usually 60—90 gill rakers; gill arches thick and strong; gill rakers not exceeding filaments in length   *Caspialosa pontica*

9   Body deep, more than 20 per cent of length; 52—64 gill rakers
Clupeonella delicatula

Body shallow, less than 20 per cent of length; 38—52 gill rakers
Clupeonella abrau

Allis Shad *Alosa alosa*

Size 30—50 cm; maximum 70 cm; British rod record 1.488 kg. **Distinctive features** well-developed median notch in upper jaw; no vomerine teeth; more than 70 lateral scales. **Distribution** the coasts of western Europe from southern Norway to Spain and in the Mediterranean eastward to northern Italy. Migrates into the lower reaches of large accessible rivers along these coasts. **Reproduction** May—June, the clear eggs are laid in the lower rivers or near estuarine waters. The eggs hatch after 6—8 days and the young move downstream to the sea after a few months. The adults mature after 3—4 years when they migrate, often in large numbers, back to the parent rivers. **Food** mainly invertebrates, especially pelagic crustaceans. **Value** formerly more important commercially than now, it is still netted in some estuaries and large rivers.

Twaite Shad *Alosa fallax*

Size 25—40 cm; maximum 55 cm; British rod record 1.417 kg. **Distinctive features** marked median notch in upper jaw; no vomerine teeth; less than 70 lateral scales. **Distribution** along most of the western European coast from southern Norway to the eastern Mediterranean, and in large accessible rivers along these coasts. **Reproduction** May—June, in the lower reaches and estuaries of these rivers. The eggs hatch after 5—8 days and the young migrate downstream to the sea, except in purely freshwater populations where the young move into large lakes (e.g. Killarney, Como, Lugano and Maggiore). The adults mature after 3—4 years. 75,000—200,000 eggs per female. **Food** mainly invertebrates especially pelagic crustaceans. **Value** though less common than formerly, it is still netted commercially in some areas. Considerable numbers are also angled for in various rivers such as the Severn.

Dolginka Shad *Caspialosa brashnikovi*

Size 30—45 cm; maximum 49 cm. **Distinctive features** marked median notch on upper jaw; vomerine teeth present; eye small. **Distribution** the Caspian Sea and the Sea of Azov. Found near the mouths of some rivers, but occasionally in freshwater. **Reproduction** April—June, the young mature after 3 years and live up to about 8 years. **Food** invertebrates when young, invertebrates (especially crustaceans) and fishes (e.g. gobies) when adult. **Value** of considerable commercial importance, large numbers being netted in various parts of the Caspian Sea.

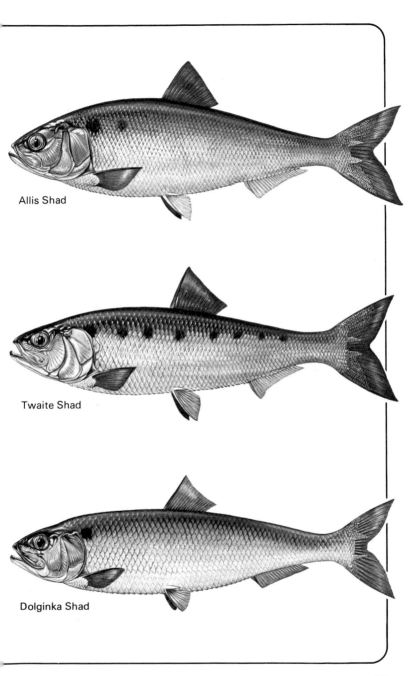

Allis Shad

Twaite Shad

Dolginka Shad

Kizilagach Shad
Caspialosa curensis

Size 14—16cm; maximum 19cm. **Distinctive features** no notch on upper jaw; distinct teeth and large eyes. **Distribution** Caspian Sea, especially the Kizilagach Bay. **Reproduction** April—May in the sea. Relatively little is known of the biology of this species. The young mature at 3—4 years. **Food** invertebrates, especially crustaceans. **Value** of commercial importance, especially in the Kizilagach area where it is netted in some numbers.

Bigeye Shad *Caspialosa saposhnikovi*

Size 20—30cm; maximum 36cm; fishes with a mean length of 18cm weight 84g. **Distinctive features** upper jaw with marked notch; teeth strong; eyes large. **Distribution** mainly the northern Caspian Sea and the delta of the River Volga, although it never enters the river proper. **Reproduction** April, in estuarine waters in the north-eastern part of the sea. The young mature after 3—4 years and live 6—7 years. **Food** invertebrates, especially crustaceans. **Value** netted commercially (e.g. off the coast of Daghestan), but not as important as other *Caspialosa* species.

Suworow's Shad *Caspialosa suworowi*

Size 15—20cm; maximum 27cm. **Distinctive features** median notch in upper jaw; vomerine teeth present; gill rakers usually 50—55. **Distribution** Caspian Sea, particularly the northern areas; regularly enters the delta of the Volga. **Reproduction** May. Spawning takes place in the sea, off the Volga delta. **Food** mainly invertebrates. **Value** netted commercially in considerable numbers in the northern Caspian Sea.

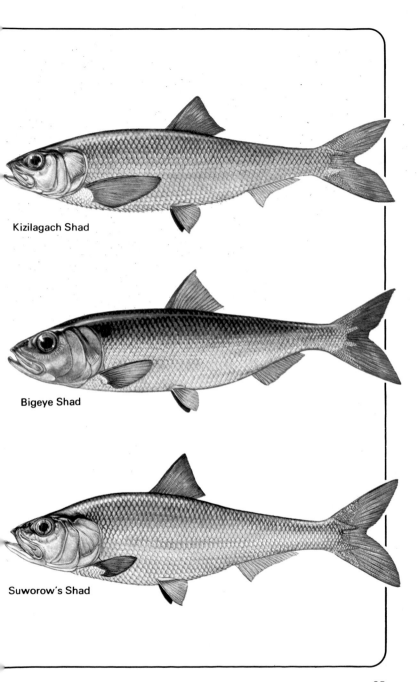

Kizilagach Shad

Bigeye Shad

Suworow's Shad

Black Sea Shad *Caspialosa pontica*

Size 15—20 cm; maximum 41 cm; average weight about 69 g. **Distinctive features** marked median notch in upper jaw; 60—90 gill rakers. **Distribution** Black and Caspian Seas and the Sea of Azov. Enters large rivers (e.g. Dneiper, Danube, Volga) in spring and migrates upstream **Reproduction** April—July, in the middle reaches of rivers, spawning over sand and gravel. Fry migrate downstream in a few months and mature in the sea at 2—3 years. They live for a maximum of 7 years. **Food** invertebrates when young, invertebrates and small fishes when adult. **Value** an important commercial species.

Caspian Shad *Caspialosa caspia*

Size 12—20 cm; maximum 32 cm; mean weight about 100 g. **Distinctive features** upper jaw with median notch, but teeth small or absent; more than 90 gill rakers. **Distribution** Black and Caspian Seas, and Sea of Azov. Migrates into large rivers (e.g. Danube, Don) in spring. **Reproduction** May—June. Spawns in the lower reaches of rivers and their estuaries. The semipelagic eggs hatch after 2—3 days, and the young move to the sea, maturing in 2—3 years. 400,000—700,000 eggs per female. **Food** mainly invertebrates and small fishes. **Value** an important commercial species, netted in large numbers in the Caspian Sea.

Tyulka Sardelle *Clupeonella delicatula*

Size 9—12 cm; maximum 17 cm; mean weight about 5 g. **Distictive features** no notch in upper jaw; more than 52 gill rakers. **Distribution** Black and Caspian Seas and the lower reaches of their large rivers (e.g. Danube, Bug). One isolated population in Chorkhal Lake (Ural basin). **Reproduction** April—May, spawning in the lower reaches of rivers and in estuaries. The semipelagic eggs hatch in 3—4 days, the young moving to the sea where eggs and larvae are occasionally found. Adults mature at 2—3 years and live up to 5 years. About 30,000 eggs per female. **Food** mainly invertebrates. **Value** an important commercial species, netted in the sea. Used for canning.

Abrau Sardelle *Clupeonella abrau*

Size 6—7 cm; maximum 8.5 cm. **Distinctive features** no notch in upper jaw; less than 53 gill rakers. **Distribution** found only in fresh water; Lake Abrau near Novorossiisk and Abulional Lake near Bursa (Asia Minor). **Reproduction** June—October, the pelagic eggs hatching in about 12 hours. Adults mature after 2 years. **Food** invertebrates, especially opossum shrimps. **Value** of little commercial or sporting value.

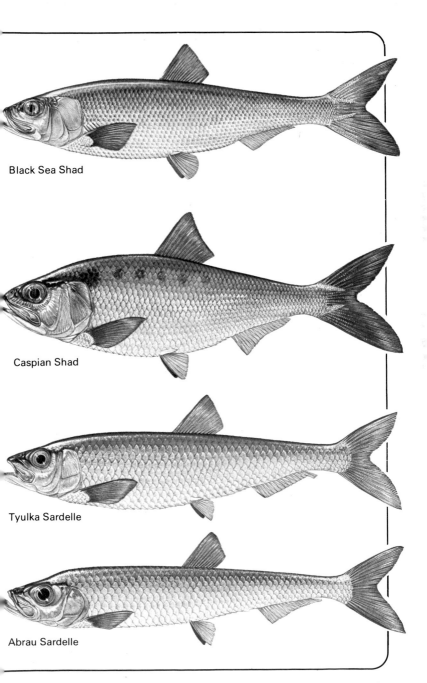

Black Sea Shad

Caspian Shad

Tyulka Sardelle

Abrau Sardelle

87

Family SALMONIDAE

The Salmonidae includes several groups of fishes known commonly as salmon, trout and charr. None of this important family is entirely marine, all its members being either anadromous or purely freshwater. Members are native to Europe, north-west Africa, northern Asia and North America, but have been introduced to many other parts of the world, including South America, India, Australia and New Zealand. Much of the original stock for these introductions came from Europe.

All Salmonidae possess an adipose fin, and the body is covered with well-developed cycloid scales. Spots of various kinds are a common feature of coloration, and the young stages of many species are characterized by dark parr marks along the sides. Teeth are usually present and well developed in some species, and there are often marked differences between the sexes at spawning time.

The biology of all species in the family presents many common features. All of them spawn in fresh, usually running, water, but sometimes on clean areas of lake bottoms. No matter which part of the world is concerned, they are found only in cool water (i.e. only highland areas in the tropics), and spawn during the coldest months of the year. Spawning usually takes place in pairs: after a sexual display, the female digs out a nest, or redd, from the gravelly substrate, and in this they spawn. After the eggs have been laid they are covered over with gravel by the female.

Members of the family Salmonidae are prized by anglers and commercial fishermen in many countries, and good populations of salmon and trout in particular are a valuable natural resource. The Pacific salmon (*Oncorhynchus*) are of major importance in western North America and north-eastern Asia. The 5 species occurring here form the basis of many huge fisheries which have been operating for more than 100 years. Competition for the stock among Pacific nations (especially the U.S.S.R., Japan, Canada and the U.S.A.) became so great that it was necessary to set up an international commission to regulate the fishery and carry out research on the biology of the species concerned. The results of this research have led to many valuable discoveries about *Oncorhynchus* and other fishes, including information on fish navigation (both in the sea and in fresh water), the physiology of adjustment to fresh or salt water, and factors controlling the abundance of stocks.

Major canning industries have been established on many rivers in which there are runs of Pacific salmon, and both canned and smoked fishes are exported to all parts of the world. Attempts to introduce these fishes to other parts of the world have been less successful than with trout, but populations of two species are now apparently established in northern Europe and in New Zealand.

Eleven species occur in Europe.

Fig. 32 Cycloid scale from a trout, showing annual rings

Key to European Salmonidae

1 Postorbital bones reaching preopercular; 10–16 branched rays in anal
fin   **2**

Postorbital bones not reaching preopercular; 7–10 branched rays in anal
fin   **3**

2 Scales large, 150–160 along lateral line; 19–25 gill rakers
Oncorhynchus keta

Scales small, 177–240 along lateral line; 26–33 gill rakers
Oncorhynchus gorbuscha

3 Vomer elongate, always toothed posteriorly in young specimens   **4**

Vomer short and wide, toothless posteriorly even in young specimens   **7**

4 More than 130 scales along lateral line; no red spots on body, but a
broad pink band along sides; numerous black spots on body and fins,
including adipose and tail fins   *Salmo gairdneri*

Less than 130 scales along lateral line; the body may be completely silver,
but normally has many black and some red spots; black spots on the
adipose and tail fins are ill defined or absent; no broad pink band along
side   **5**

5 Less than 110 scales along lateral line   *Salmothymus obtusirostris.*
More than 110 scales along lateral line   **6**

6 Head of vomer toothless, the shaft poorly toothed with deciduous teeth;
10–12 rays in dorsal fin; 10–13 scales between adipose fin and lateral
line   *Salmo salar*

Head of vomer toothed, the shaft also well toothed with persistent teeth;
8–10 rays in dorsal fin; 13–16 scales between adipose fin and lateral line
Salmo trutta

7 Well-developed space between vomerine and palatine teeth; no dark
spots on body   **8**

Vomerine and palatine teeth forming a continuous horseshoe-shaped
patch; dark spots present on body   **10**

8 Caudal fin deeply forked; body and fins covered with small, oval light
spots, never orange or red on body; more than 90 pyloric caeca
Salvelinus namaycush

Caudal fin not, or only slightly, forked; body and fins with pink or red
spots and usually dark lines and marks; less than 75 pyloric caeca

9 Hyoid teeth present; premaxillary not toothed on right side; back uni-
formly coloured with pale spots; black stripe absent on anal fin
Salvelinus alpinus

Hyoid teeth absent; premaxillary toothed on right side; back strongly
vermiculated; black stripes present on anal fin   *Salvelinus fontinalis*

10 16 gill rakers on 1st arch; 180–200 scales along lateral line
Hucho hucho

11–12 gill rakers on 1st arch; 193–242 scales along lateral line
Hucho taimen

Chum Salmon *Oncorhynchus keta*

Size 45–90cm; maximum 100cm; fishes with a mean length of 75cm weigh 4.9kg. **Distinctive features** 10 or more branched rays in anal fin; 150–160 scales along lateral line. **Distribution** native to the north Pacific and associated large rivers in North America and Asia. Occurs sporadically in northern European seas and some rivers as a result of regular introductions to the White Sea area. **Reproduction** August–December in areas of coarse gravel where a reasonable current is present. The eggs are laid in nests excavated by the female, and hatch in 90–130 days. The fry remain in the river for several months, but have normally migrated to the sea by the end of their first year. The adults mature after 3–4 years and migrate back to their parent rivers. 2,008–4,388 eggs per female. **Food** invertebrates when young, large invertebrates (mainly crustaceans) and fishes when adult. **Value** a major commercial and sporting species both in the sea and in fresh water.

Humpback Salmon *Oncorhynchus gorbuscha*

Size 40–50cm; maximum 64cm; fishes with a mean length of 50cm weigh about 1.7kg. **Distinctive features** 10 or more branched rays in anal fin; 177–240 scales along lateral line. **Distribution** native to the north Pacific and associated large rivers in North America and Asia. Occurs sporadically in northern European seas and some rivers as a result of introduction to the White Sea area. **Reproduction** September–October, in nests among gravel in running water. The eggs hatch after 100–120 days and the young migrate very quickly downstream to the sea, where they grow, maturing after 2 years. 1,090–1,629 eggs per female. **Food** mainly invertebrates (especially larger crustaceans) and fishes. **Value** a major commercial and sporting species in some north Pacific coastal areas, and fresh waters.

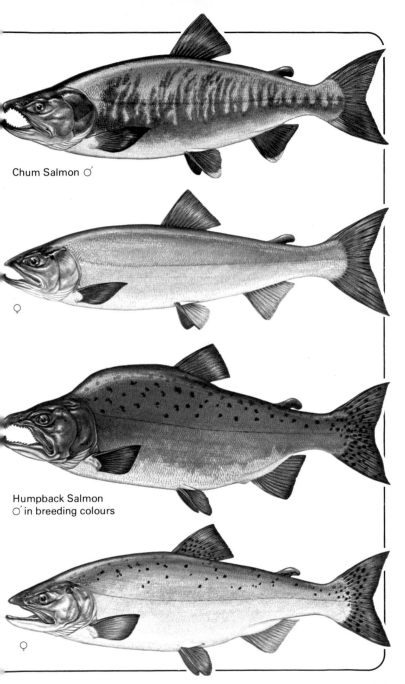

Chum Salmon ♂

♀

Humpback Salmon
♂ in breeding colours

♀

91

Atlantic Salmon *Salmo salar*

Size 40–100cm; maximum 120cm; British rod record 29.028kg. **Distinctive features** 10 or less branched rays in anal fin; vomer toothed posteriorly but not anteriorly. **Distribution** anadromous native species widely found in the Atlantic areas of northern Europe and eastern Canada in clear stony rivers, streams and accessible lakes. **Reproduction** October–January. Eggs, laid in redds among gravel in running water, hatch into alevins, which change to fry, then to parr. After 2–6 years these become silver coloured and migrate to the sea as smolts. Major growth occurs in the sea (fishes returning within 1 year are called *grilse*; later than 1 year *salmon*). A 10kg female carries about 22,000 eggs. **Food** invertebrates when small, invertebrates and fishes when larger. **Value** a major commercial species, netted off Atlantic coasts and estuaries and off Greenland. An important sport species angled for in rivers and lakes – fly fishing, spinning and trolling all successful in various waters.

Atlantic Salmon
fry

parr

smolt

♂

♀

93

Trout *Salmo trutta*

Size 50cm; maximum 70cm; British rod record 8.745kg. **Distinctive features** 10 or less branched rays in anal fin; vomer toothed anteriorly and posteriorly; less than 130 scales along lateral line. **Distribution** occurs all over Europe in all kinds of running and standing waters. Migratory populations occur in rivers all along the European coast from Spain northwards. **Reproduction** September—October in small rivers and streams, where the female lays her eggs in a nest (redd) which she cuts out in the gravel. The eggs hatch in approximately 150 days and the fry spend a year or more in the nursery stream before moving down into a larger river or lake (or the sea in the case of the migratory sea trout). Adults mature after 3—5 years and many live up to 20 years. The mean number of eggs is about 5,400 per female. **Food** invertebrates when young, invertebrates and some fishes (especially in the case of sea trout) when adult. **Value** an important commercial species in some areas, and possibly the most important single sport species over Europe as a whole.

Rainbow Trout *Salmo gairdneri*

Size 25—45cm; maximum 70cm; British rod record 5.953kg. **Distinctive features** 10 or less branched rays in anal fin; caudal and adipose fins heavily spotted; broad pink band along sides. **Distribution** native to the western coastal basins of North America where both migratory and purely freshwater populations occur. Has been introduced widely all over Europe, although it is only in some places that self-maintaining populations have developed. **Reproduction** October—March, the eggs being laid in nests dug out of gravel in running water. The eggs hatch after 100—150 days and the young gradually move into larger rivers and lakes. 1,000—5,000 eggs per female. **Food** invertebrates when young, invertebrates and fishes when adult. **Value** of major importance as a commercial species in many fish farms all over Europe and as a sporting species in rivers and lakes.

Trout: resident freshwater form (brown trout) ○

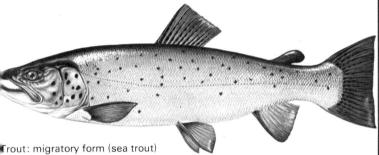

Trout: migratory form (sea trout)

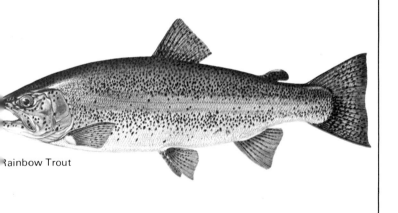

Rainbow Trout

Charr *Salvelinus alpinus*

Size 15–40cm; maximum 88cm; British rod record
0.8kg. **Distinctive features** 10 or less branched rays
in anal fin; vomer toothless posteriorly; body uni-
formly coloured with pale spots. **Distribution** much
of the Northern Hemisphere in clear cool lakes. In
Arctic seas migratory stocks are found, maturing in
the sea and entering rivers to spawn. These fishes
are larger than the freshwater forms, some of which
are dwarf races. **Reproduction** October–March,
among gravel in both lakes and rivers. After hatching the young move into lakes or the sea, maturing
in 3–6 years. 560–7,300 eggs per female. **Food**
mainly invertebrates, especially planktonic crustaceans. **Value** netted in Arctic areas during the
spawning migration. A sporting species in some
lakes.

Brook Charr *Salvelinus fontinalis*

Size 20–35cm; maximum 50cm; British rod record
1.162kg. **Distinctive features** 10 or less branched
rays in anal fin; vomer toothless; body strongly
patterned with dark and light areas. **Distribution**
native to western North America, but introduced to
many parts of Europe where it has become established. **Reproduction** October–March among gravel
in running waters. The eggs hatch in spring and the
young spend about 2 years in nursery areas before
moving into larger rivers or lakes. Adults mature at
2–3 years of age. 100–5,000 eggs per female.
Food mainly invertebrates, but fishes are eaten by
large adults. **Value** a major sport species in North
America, but not yet angled for in many places in
Europe.

American Lake Charr
Salvelinus namaycush

Size 30–50cm; maximum 126cm – this fish
weighed 46.3kg. **Distinctive features** 10 or less
branched rays in anal fin; vomer toothless; body
covered with light yellowish spots. **Distribution**
widespread in northern U.S.A. and central Canada.
It was introduced to Europe where established
populations are found in large deep lakes in
Sweden and Switzerland. **Reproduction** September–November, spawning over stones and gravel.
Eggs hatch in 100–150 days and the young move
offshore soon afterwards. Adults mature after 6–8
years, but may live up to 25 years. An 80cm fish
carries about 18,000 eggs. **Food** invertebrates
when young, but other fishes (especially *Coregonus*) as increase in size occurs. **Value** an important commercial and sport species in North
America, but as yet of little importance in Europe.

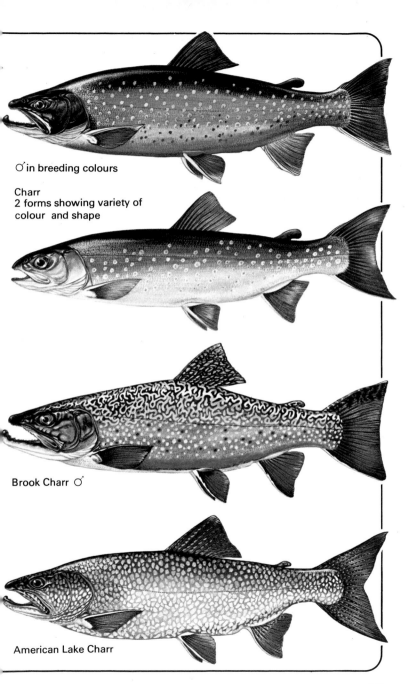

♂ in breeding colours

Charr
2 forms showing variety of
colour and shape

Brook Charr ♂

American Lake Charr

Huchen *Hucho hucho*

Size 50–100cm; maximum 120cm – this fish weighed 21kg. **Distinctive features** 10 or less branched rays in anal fin; vomer toothless; dark spots on body; 16 gill rakers on 1st arch. **Distribution** occurs only in the basin of the River Danube, particularly the middle and upper reaches. **Reproduction** March–May, spawning among gravel in flowing water. The eggs hatch in about 35 days and adults mature in 4–5 years. They may reach an age of 15 years or more. Females with a mean weight of 5kg carry about 5,000 eggs. **Food** invertebrates and fishes when young, but mainly fishes (especially *Chondrostoma*) when larger. **Value** a highly prized sport species whose numbers have diminished alarmingly in recent years.

Taimen *Hucho taimen*

Size 50–100cm; maximum 150cm; maximum weight 80kg. **Distinctive features** 10 or less branched rays in anal fin; vomer toothless; dark spots on body; 11–12 gill rakers on 1st arch. **Distribution** found in rivers throughout Siberia (e.g. Ob, Lena) and occasionally in lakes. **Reproduction** May, spawning over gravel in flowing water. Eggs hatch in about 30–35 days and adults mature after about 5 years. 10,000–34,000 eggs per female. **Food** some invertebrates when young, but mainly fishes thereafter. **Value** important both as a commercial and sporting species in several areas.

Adriatic Salmon
Salmothymus obtusirostris

Size 25–40cm; maximum 50cm; maximum weight about 5kg. **Distinctive features** 101–103 lateral scales; head short. **Distribution** found only in waters in Dalmatia this species is considered by many ichthyologists to be derived from isolated populations of Salmon. Several local races are recognized. **Reproduction** October–December among gravel in running water. **Food** invertebrates when young, invertebrates and fishes when older. **Value** of little commercial or sporting interest.

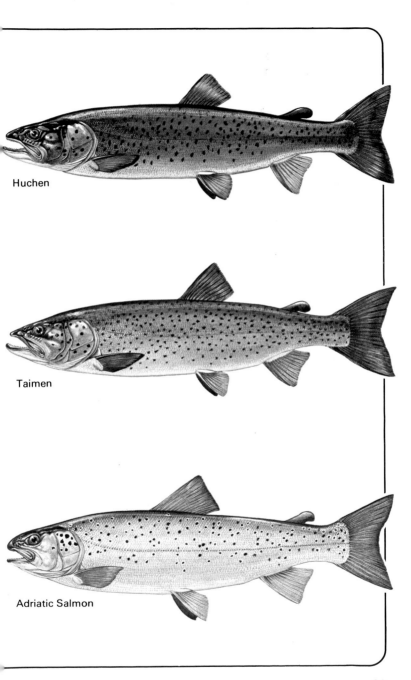

Huchen

Taimen

Adriatic Salmon

Family **COREGONIDAE**

The Coregonidae, commonly known as whitefishes or ciscoes, are closely related to the Salmonidae and, like them, possess a well-developed adipose fin. The elongate body is covered by relatively large scales, but unlike the Salmonidae, obvious spotting or colour patterning of any kind is absent. Most forms are silvery brown, grey or grey-blue. Teeth are usually either very small or absent.

Members of the family are restricted to the Northern Hemisphere and are found in cool, unpolluted waters in northern Europe, Asia and North America. Their identification presents enormous difficulties, and while it is accepted that there are probably only 3 genera present (*Stenodus*, *Prosopium* and *Coregonus*), the number of species within these (especially *Coregonus*) is a matter of considerable dispute. There are probably between 20 and 30 species altogether in the world today. The problem in assigning *Coregonus* to particular species lies in the apparent plasticity of form which these fishes are able to exhibit in different habitats. It appears that many of the characters which are normally used to diagnose species (shape, size, growth rate, and numbers of scales and gill rakers) are very variable and directly influenced by the environment. Much of the proof for this variability has been obtained from experimental work moving certain races from one environment to

Fig. 33 Complete gill arch and raker systems from *Coregonus lavaretus* (a) and *C. albula* (b)

another or rearing different species together in experimental ponds. There is therefore available within the group a large number of scientific names, some of which refer to single populations occurring in a lake or river system.

The Coregonidae are mainly a freshwater group, although some anadromous populations occur in northern seas. They are common in many lakes, especially large, cool unpolluted waters in highland or northern areas. Many forms are entirely pelagic, and some benthic in habit, while other populations are benthic in habit at one time of the year (usually winter) and pelagic at another (summer). They often move around in large shoals and feed on benthic invertebrates and zooplankton. Spawning takes place during the colder months of the year (often under ice), and huge numbers congregate in the spawning areas at this time. The eggs are laid in open water, usually over a stony or gravelly bottom, and hatch in the spring. The young are pelagic for at least the first year.

Although of no value as sport fishes, the Coregonidae form the basis of some of the most important commercial freshwater fisheries in the world, and are a major source of fish flesh in parts of Europe (Scandinavia and the alpine countries), northern Asia and North America (especially the Great Lakes and other large waters in Canada). Fishes are caught in trap nets, gill nets and by seining, and are sometimes dried or smoked. Adult fishes have a pleasant slightly oily flesh which has often a

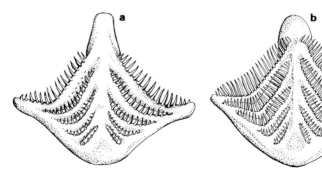

characteristic odour, likened to that of fresh cucumbers. In recent years the populations in many of the most important waters have collapsed under fishing pressure, pollution and other man-made impacts, and fisheries which yielded up to 40 million fishes annually now give nothing. In Russia, coregonid species have been introduced to large reservoirs created there, and form the basis of several important fisheries.

Seven main species may be recognized in Europe. Several of these are very similar to forms found in North America.

Key to European Coregonidae

1   Mouth large, oblique and terminal; lower jaw prominent and articulating with cranium behind posterior margin of eye; small teeth present on jaws; 19—26 gill rakers   *Stenodus leucichthys*

Mouth small, lower jaw not prominent and articulating before, or under, eye; jaws toothless or occasionally with minute teeth   **2**

2   Mouth terminal or superior; maxillary reaching behind anterior margin of eye   **3**

Mouth inferior; maxillary not reaching behind anterior margin of eye   **4**

3   Mouth superior, upper jaw shorter than lower; 36—52 gill rakers   *Coregonus albula*

Mouth terminal, upper jaw equal to lower; 49—68 gill rakers   *Coregonus peled*

4   Well-developed snout; distance between anterior of eye and tip of snout more than twice eye diameter; 35—44 gill rakers   *Corregonus oxyrinchus*

Snout not well developed; distance between anterior of eye and tip of snout less than twice eye diameter   **5**

5   Maxillary wide and short, width usually more than half length, length usually less than 22 per cent head length; snout humped before eyes; 20—29 gill rakers   *Coregonus nasus*

Maxillary narrow and long, width usually less than half length, length usually more than 22 per cent head length; snout not humped before eyes   **6**

6   Length of lower jaw exceeding minimum body depth; 17—48 gill rakers   *Coregonus lavaretus*

Length of lower jaw less than minimum body depth; 16—29 gill rakers   *Coregonus pidschian*

Inconnu *Stenodus leucichthys*

Size 50—80cm; maximum 130cm; maximum weight about 35kg. **Distinctive features** prominent lower jaw with small teeth; usually large. **Distribution** occurs in Europe and North America in many lakes and rivers whose basins are linked to the Arctic Ocean and northern Caspian Sea, where it is found in some coastal areas. **Reproduction** October—November, usually in the lower or middle reaches of large rivers. Adults mature at 8—10 years of age and may live up to 20 years. 130,000—420,000 eggs per female. **Food** invertebrates when young, but mainly fishes (e.g. *Coregonus*) when adult. **Value** of little sporting significance but an important commercial species in both Canada and Russia. Most fishes are caught in nets during spawning migration and many are stored after smoking or drying.

Cisco *Coregonus albula*

Size 15—25cm; maximum 33cm; fishes with a mean weight of 18cm weigh 60g. **Distinctive features** mouth superior; 36—52 gill rakers; usually small. **Distribution** found in many parts of northern and central Europe, usually in deep cold lakes. **Reproduction** October—December over gravel or stones at depths of 2—3m or more. Eggs hatch after 100—120 days and the young move into deeper water. Adults mature after 2—3 years and may live up to 10 years. 1,700—4,800 eggs per female. **Food** invertebrates, especially planktonic crustaceans. **Value** of no sporting importance, but important commercially in many areas, fishes being caught in nets and traps during their spawning migration. Sometimes smoked.

Peled *Coregonus peled*

Size 30—40cm; maximum 50cm; maximum weight about 5kg. **Distinctive features** mouth terminal and toothless; 49—68 gill rakers. **Distribution** found in much of northern Europe, particularly in lakes in arctic areas of Siberia, Finland and Sweden. **Reproduction** September—November, in shallow water in both lakes and rivers—often migrating considerable distances to the spawning grounds. 29,000—105,000 eggs per female. **Food** invertebrates, especially planktonic crustaceans. **Value** a very important commercial species, netted in large numbers in many Russian waters.

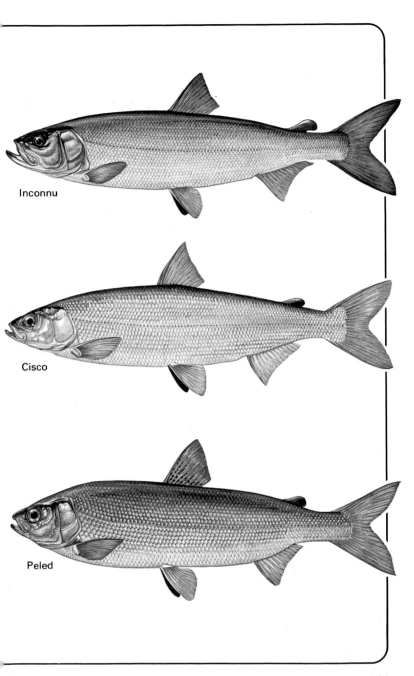

Inconnu

Cisco

Peled

Arctic Whitefish *Coregonus pidschian*

Size 20–30cm; maximum 50cm; a 48cm fish weighs about 1.25kg. **Distinctive features** mouth inferior; maxillary narrow and long; 16–29 gill rakers. **Distribution** arctic areas of Europe in rivers, lakes and some coastal areas of the Baltic. **Reproduction** October–December, eggs hatching in spring. Adults mature at 2–4 years and live up to 12 years. 8,000–50,000 eggs per female. **Food** invertebrates, especially crustaceans. **Value** of considerable commercial importance in many areas.

Broad Whitefish *Coregonus nasus*

Size 35–60cm; maximum 86cm – this fish weighed 10kg. **Distinctive features** mouth small, toothless and inferior; maxillary wide and short; snout humped. **Distribution** mainly in lakes and the lower reaches of rivers associated with the Arctic Ocean. **Reproduction** October–November in rivers, the young migrating back to lakes where they mature after 4–5 years; they live for up to 10 years. 14,000–29,000 eggs per female. **Food** invertebrates, especially insects and molluscs. **Value** caught in a few areas where it is gill netted and sometimes dried and smoked.

Common Whitefish
Coregonus lavaretus

Size 15–40cm; maximum 57cm; maximum weight about 2.8kg; British rod record 652gm. **Distinctive features** mouth small, toothless and inferior; 17–48 gill rakers. A variable species forming local races in different lakes. **Distribution** north-western and central Europe in large cold lakes and in the Baltic area, migrating into rivers to spawn. **Reproduction** October–January, over gravel. Eggs hatch in about 100 days. Young mature in 3–4 years and live up to 10 years. 1,000–28,000 eggs per female. **Food** invertebrates and planktonic crustaceans when young, but both bottom-dwelling and planktonic forms later. **Value** of commercial importance in various countries, and caught mainly by gill nets. Occasionally angled for.

Houting *Coregonus oxyrinchus*

Size 25–40cm; maximum 50cm; maximum weight about 2kg. **Distinctive features** mouth small, toothless and inferior; well-developed snout. **Distribution** northern Europe, especially the Baltic where large populations formerly occurred in brackish water, only running into fresh water to spawn. **Reproduction** October–December, in the lower reaches of rivers. After hatching, the young migrate to the sea, where they mature in 3–4 years. **Food** invertebrates, planktonic crustaceans when young, planktonic and benthic forms later. **Value** locally important in some areas and caught during the autumn spawning migration.

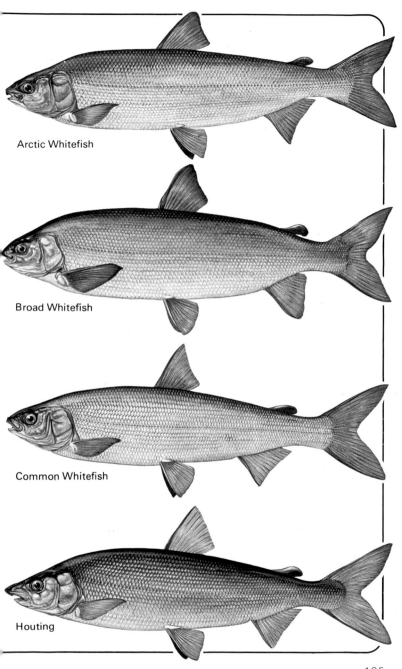

Arctic Whitefish

Broad Whitefish

Common Whitefish

Houting

Family THYMALLIDAE

The Thymallidae, or graylings, are found in the Northern Hemisphere (Europe, Asia and North America) where 6 species in 1 genus occur. All live in swift-flowing streams and cold lakes, occasionally in estuaries. The name refers to the flesh which is supposed to smell like the herb thyme. The high dorsal fin is characteristic of the family, only 1 species of which occurs in Europe.

Grayling *Thymallus thymallus*

Size 25—35cm; maximum 50cm; maximum weight 4.675kg. **Distinctive features** adipose and large dorsal fins. **Distribution** found in clean cool rivers (occasionally lakes) in parts of Europe, especially northern areas. Sometimes in estuaries. **Reproduction** March—May, eggs laid in nests in gravel hatch in 20—30 days and the young mature at 3—4 years. They live up to 15 years. Females about 45cm long carry about 10,000 eggs. **Food** mainly invertebrates, especially insects. Larger individuals may eat small fishes. **Value** of some commercial importance to fisheries especially in Russia. A sport fish in some countries, such as Britain, where it is caught on worms or artificial flies.

Family OSMERIDAE

The Osmeridae or smelts occur all round the Northern Hemisphere where various species are marine, anadromous or freshwater in habit. There are 6 genera with 10 species in the Atlantic, Arctic or Pacific Oceans and their basins. All have adipose fins and are small, silvery, slender fishes with elongate laterally compressed bodies and large mouths. Most smelts are popular food species and have a characteristic odour, similar to fresh cucumber. Only 1 species occurs in fresh water in Europe.

Smelt *Osmerus eperlanus*

Size 10—20cm; maximum 31cm; fishes 16cm long weigh about 32g. **Distinctive features** small silvery fish with an adipose fin; large mouth and teeth. **Distribution** round the coast of north-western Europe and in the estuaries and lower reaches of unpolluted rivers. Some populations in lakes are purely freshwater. **Reproduction** March—May, spawning among weeds in rivers above estuaries, or at the edges of lakes. Eggs hatch in 20—35 days and the young move down to the sea, maturing after 2 years. They live up to 8 years. 10,000—40,000 eggs per female. **Food** invertebrates (especially crustaceans) when young, invertebrates and fishes when older. **Value** of commercial value in some rivers where they are caught by nets and traps.

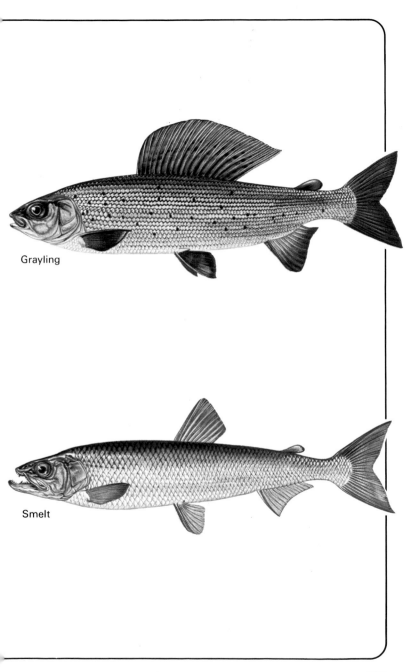

Grayling

Smelt

107

Family UMBRIDAE

The Umbridae, or mudminnows, occur in Europe, Asia and North America in weedy ponds and streams. Mudminnows are small pugnacious fishes with round fins and dull colours. There are 3 genera and 5 species. Only 2 occur in Europe.

Key to European Umbridae

1   More than 14 dorsal rays; 33—35 lateral scales; body blotched; lower jaw light *Umbra krameri*

    Less than 14 dorsal rays; 35—37 lateral scales; body striped; lower jaw dark *Umbra pygmaea*

Mudminnow *Umbra krameri*

Size 5—9cm; maximum 11.5cm; maximum weight 27gm. **Distinctive features** more than 14 dorsal rays. **Distribution** native to Europe, mainly the Danube basin, although introduced elsewhere. **Reproduction** February—April in nests which the female guards. Young mature in 2 years and live up to 7 years. 1,580—2,710 eggs per female. **Food** invertebrates, especially insect larvae and crustaceans. **Value** of no commercial or sporting importance, but kept in aquaria.

Eastern Mudminnow *Umbra pygmaea*

Size 4—8cm; maximum 10cm. **Distinctive features** less than 14 dorsal rays. **Distribution** native to eastern temperate North America, but introduced to Europe. **Reproduction** March—April, among weeds in shallow water. Eggs hatch in 5—10 days and fishes mature in 2 years. **Food** invertebrates, especially insect larvae and crustaceans. **Value** of no commercial or sporting value, but often kept in aquaria.

Family ESOCIDAE

The Esocidae, or pike, occur in lakes and slow-flowing rivers in temperate Europe, Asia and North America. All have an elongate head, a massive mouth and large teeth. Although widespread, only 1 genus exists, with 5 species. 1 species occurs in Europe.

Pike *Esox lucius*

Size 30—120cm; maximum 150cm; weight up to 34kg. **Distinctive features** head and snout large, with enormous mouth and teeth. **Distribution** common in standing and slow-flowing waters in temperate Europe, Asia and North America. **Reproduction** February—May among weed. The adhesive eggs hatch after 10—15 days and larvae attach to weed for a short time. They mature in 3—4 years and may live to 25 years. 16,600—79,700 eggs per female. **Food** invertebrates at first, but soon fishes and other vertebrates are eaten. **Value** of commercial importance and a popular table fish in central and other parts of Europe. A major sport species.

Mudminnow

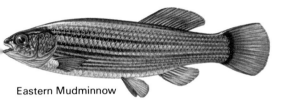

Eastern Mudminnow

Pike

Family CYPRINIDAE

The Cyprinidae, often known as carp or minnows, is a very large and variable family found in most parts of the world except South America and Australia. They are all freshwater species and only a few are able to venture occasionally into the brackish water of estuaries. This is the largest family of fishes in the world with some 275 genera and about 2,000 species. It is the dominant family in European fresh waters in terms of numbers of species.

Members of the family may be small to large fishes of quite variable shape. The mouth is variable in size and position but never possesses teeth. These are replaced functionally by pharyngeal bones with 1—3 rows of teeth which grind food against a pair of horny pads on the opposite side of the pharynx. These are important in identification, the number of rows, and teeth in each row, being indicated thus: 4.1.1. In this example, it means that the pharyngeal bone concerned has 3 rows of teeth, with 4 teeth on the inside row and 1 on each of the other rows (see fig. 3b). One or two sensory barbels are often present just beside the mouth. The fins are all moderately developed and usually soft rayed, except for the stiffened leading rays of the dorsal and anal fins in a few species. The body is usually well covered with cycloid scales and in most fishes a lateral line is present. The sexes often appear different during the spawning season, the males becoming brightly coloured with well-developed tubercles on the head, body and fins in some species; the shape, position, size and number of these tubercles are useful aids in identification.

As might be expected, from the large number of species, the Cyprinidae show considerable differences in habit and habitat, and occupy a variety of niches in fresh waters. Most species feed on invertebrates and only occasionally on fishes. A number are omnivorous, feeding both on invertebrates and plants. A few species are purely plant feeders and such fishes have proved to be important to man in two ways — as efficient producers of fish flesh, and as potential vegetation controllers.

There are 80 species in Europe.

Key to European Cyprinidae

1 More than 14 branched rays in dorsal fin; a serrated ray present in the dorsal, and usually the anal, fin **2**

Less than 14 branched rays in dorsal fin; a serrated ray never present in the anal fin **4**

2 Four barbels present; pharyngeal teeth triserial *Cyprinus carpio*

No barbels; pharyngeal teeth uniserial **3**

3 More than 31 scales along lateral line; less than 34 gill rakers on 1st gill arch; dorsal fin convex; 1st dorsal ray feeble, weakly serrated
Carassius carassius

Less than 31 scales along lateral line; more than 34 gill rakers on 1st gill arch; dorsal fin concave; 1st dorsal ray strong, coarsely serrated
Carassius auratus

4 Leading ray of dorsal fin distinct and much shorter than 2nd; lips thick
Pachychilon pictum

Leading ray of dorsal fins close to, and about the same size as, 2nd; lips normal **5**

5 Barbels present **6**

Barbels absent **22**

6 Undulating lateral line; scales absent *Aulopyge hugeli*

Straight or only moderately curved lateral line; scales present **7**

| **7** | Two pairs of barbels; pharyngeal teeth triserial | **8** |

Two pairs of barbels; pharyngeal teeth triserial **8**

One pair of barbels; pharyngeal teeth uni- or biserial **17**

8 Longest dorsal fin ray stiff, and with a serrated hind edge for most of its length **9**

Longest dorsal fin ray without serrations, or if these are present they occur only on the lower half **10**

9 Lateral line with 55–65 scales *Barbus barbus*

Lateral line with 49–51 scales *Barbus comiza*

10 Body with dark spots or marks **11**

Body without dark spots or marks **14**

11 Numerous distinct small dark spots on body and fins, but not on head; 12 rays in dorsal fin **12**

Many large dark marks often forming a mosaic on back and fins, and extending onto head; 11 rays in dorsal fin; 48–55 scales in lateral line
Barbus meridionalis

12 Barbels long, more than 3 times eye diameter, 60–71 scales in lateral line *Barbus ciscaucasicus*

Barbels short, less than 3 times eye diameter **13**

13 Lower part of longest dorsal ray slightly serrated; belly yellowish; 49–52 scales in lateral line *Barbus albanicus*

Longest dorsal ray without serrations; belly whitish *Barbus prespensis*

14 Barbels very short, equal to, or less than, eye diameter *Barbus cyclolepis*

Barbels longer, greater than eye diameter **15**

15 More than 60 scales in lateral line **16**

Less than 60 scales in lateral line *Barbus graecus*

16 Usually 7 branched dorsal rays; barbels long, anterior barbel reaching beyond anterior eye margin; 67–76 lateral scales *Barbus brachycephalus*

Usually 8 branched dorsal rays; barbels short, anterior barbel never reaching anterior eye margin; 58–65 lateral scales *Barbus capito*

17 Mouth terminal; scales very small, more than 80 in lateral line; pharyngeal teeth uniserial *Tinca tinca*

Mouth inferior; scales large, always less than 50 in lateral line; pharyngeal teeth biserial **18**

18 Caudal peduncle short, deep and laterally compressed at origin; its thickness at anal fin equal to, or less than, minimum body depth; its depth at caudal fin more than one-third caudal peduncle length; barbels usually not reaching posterior end of preopercular *Gobio gobio*

Caudal peduncle long, thick at origin, slender at end; its thickness at anal fin greater than minimum body depth; length of caudal peduncle less than one-third minimum body depth; barbels usually reaching beyond posterior edge of eye **19**

19 Dorsal fin with 8 branched rays; throat naked; colours bright; eye diameter equal to inter-orbital width *Gobio kessleri*

Dorsal fin with 7 branched rays **20**

20 Throat scaled; eye diameter equal to inter-orbital width
Gobio uranoscopus

Throat naked **21**

21   Eye diameter equal to, or slightly greater than, inter-orbital width
Gobio albipinnatus

      Eye diameter much less than inter-orbital width; colour variegated
Gobio ciscaucasicus

22   Undulating lateral line; abdomen with a scaleless dermal keel starting at throat   *Pelecus cultratus*

      Lateral line not undulating; keel, if present, starting behind ventral fins **23**

23   Mouth inferior, as a transverse cleft; lower jaw trenchant and covered with cartilage   **24**

      Mouth terminal, oblique or, if inferior, crescentic; never as an inferior transverse cleft covered with cartilage   **32**

24   Less than 56 or more than 66 scales in lateral line   **25**

      56–66 scales in lateral line   **26**

25   Lateral line with 52–54 scales   *Chondrostoma kneri*

      Lateral line with 88–90 scales   *Chondrostoma phoxinus*

26   Darkish line along side; pharyngeal teeth 5.5 (occasionally 5.6)
Chondrostoma genei

      No darkening along side, or if so, pharyngeal teeth 6.5   **27**

27   Body deep, greatest depth more than twice that of head
Chondrostoma soetta

      Body less deep, greatest depth less than twice that of head   **28**

28   Pharyngeal teeth 6.6 or 7.6   **29**

      Pharyngeal teeth 6.5 (occasionally 5.5)   **30**

29   11 rays in dorsal fin, 12 rays in anal fin; pharyngeal teeth usually 6.6
Chondrostoma toxostoma

      12 rays in dorsal fin, 13–14 rays in anal fin; pharyngeal teeth usually 7.6
Chondrostoma nasus

30   Snout small and rounded, its length usually less than half eye diameter
Chondrostoma polylepis

      Snout prominent, length usually more than half eye diameter   **31**

31   Mouth cleft straight; depth of body usually more than 0.22 times length; sometimes with dark lateral band   *Chondrostoma colchicum*

      Mouth cleft rounded; depth of body usually less than 0.22 times length; never with dark lateral band   *Chondrostoma oxyrhynchus*

32   Scaleless abdominal keel before vent   **33**

      No scaleless keel on abdomen behind ventral fins   **42**

33   Scaled dorsal keel behind dorsal fin; pharyngeal teeth uniserial
Vimba vimba

      No keel behind dorsal fin   **34**

34   Pharyngeal teeth uniserial; anal fin with 23–43 branched rays   **35**

      Pharyngeal teeth biserial   **37**

35   Less than 30 branched rays in anal fin; 51–60 scales along lateral line; mouth subterminal   *Abramis brama*

      More than 30 branched rays in anal fin   **36**

36   Lateral line with 49–52 scales; mouth subterminal   *Abramis sapa*

Lateral line with 65–75 scales; mouth terminal *Abramis ballerus*

37 Scaled keel immediately behind ventral fins **38**

Scaleless keel only in front of vent, not reaching ventral fins
Chalcalburnus chalcoides

38 Scaleless dorsal groove in adults before dorsal fin; scales thick, firmly embedded; 19–24 branched rays in anal fin *Blicca bjoerkna*

No scaleless dorsal groove before dorsal fin; scales thin, easily detached
39

39 Gill rakers long, crowded; pharyngeal teeth usually serrated **40**

Gill rakers short, well spaced; pharyngeal teeth not serrated
Alburnoides bipunctatus

40 Body slim, maximum depth about twice that of caudal peduncle **41**

Body stout, maximum depth about three times that of caudal peduncle
Alburnus charusini

41 More than 17 rays in anal fin *Alburnus alburnus*

Less than 18 rays in anal fin *Alburnus albidus*

42 Lateral line incomplete, short, ending well before dorsal fin **43**

Lateral line complete, or if incomplete, ending below or behind dorsal fin **48**

43 Lateral stripe dark, running full length of body; 4–14 scales along lateral line **44**

Lateral stripe pale silver-blue or green-blue **45**

44 Ventral fin with 8 rays; lateral line short, only 4–6 scales long
Phoxinellus minutus

Ventral fin with 9–10 rays; more than 6 scales on lateral line
Phoxinellus hispanicus

45 Mouth subterminal; body deep; 8–10 branched rays in anal fin
Rhodeus sericeus

Mouth terminal; body elongate; 10–13 branched rays in anal fin; lower jaw with a tubercle entering a notch in upper jaw **46**

46 Anal fin with less than 12 rays *Leucaspius stymphalicus*

Anal fin with more than 12 rays **47**

47 Anal fin with 14–20 rays; ventral fin with 10 rays; pharyngeal teeth 5.4
Leucaspius delineatus

Anal fin with 14 rays; ventral fin with 9 rays; pharyngeal teeth 5.5
Leucaspius marathonicus

48 Scales very thin, rudimentary or absent **49**

Scales normal **54**

49 Most of body without scales **50**

Most of body covered in thin or rudimentary scales **51**

50 No scales on body except along lateral line *Paraphoxinus alepidotus*

Some scales on body although not on back, or caudal peduncle
Paraphoxinus ghethaldii

51 Body covered by thin fragile scales *Paraphoxinus epiroticus*

Body covered with rudimentary scales **52**

52 No dark spots along sides *Paraphoxinus croaticus*

Dark spots along sides **53**

53 Relatively few brown spots, rarely below lateral line *Paraphoxinus pstrossi*

Relatively many dark brown spots, frequently below lateral line
Paraphoxinus adspersus

54 Branchiostegal membranes attached under eye; lower jaw with a tubercle entering notch in upper jaw; mouth terminal, very large
Aspius aspius

Branchiostegal membranes attached behind eye; upper jaw not notched to receive tubercle in lower jaw; mouth inferior or subterminal, if terminal then small **55**

55 Origin of dorsal fin slightly behind vertical from posterior end of ventral fin base; pharyngeal teeth biserial **56**

Origin of dorsal fin above ventral fins **60**

56 Scales large, less than 45 along lateral line **57**

Scales small, more than 45 along lateral line **58**

57 Body deep, greatest depth (which is at the dorsal fin) usually about twice depth of head or more; profile not, or hardly, concave just behind head *Scardinius erythrophthalmus*

Body less deep, greatest depth (which occurs well in front of dorsal fin) less than twice depth of head; profile clearly concave behind head
Scardinius graecus

58 Large vague dark spots on body, sometimes forming a longitudinal pattern or stripe; no distinct dark speckles on sides; horny tubercles present on heads of mature males *Phoxinus phoxinus*

Small distinct dark speckles on body, but no large vague dark spots; horny tubercles never present on heads of mature males **59**

59 Body deep, maximum depth exceeding length of caudal peduncle, and more than 24 per cent of body length *Phoxinus percnurus*

Body elongate, maximum depth less than length of caudal peduncle, and less than 24 per cent of body length *Phoxinus czekanowskii*

60 Pharyngeal teeth uniserial **61**

Pharyngeal teeth biserial **68**

61 Dorsal fin with 11 or more rays; normally with a coloured band along side of body **62**

Dorsal fin with 10 or less rays; rarely with a coloured band along side **65**

62 Lateral line with 55 or more scales *Rutilus frisii*

Lateral line with 50 or less scales **63**

63 Pectoral fins with 16 rays *Rutilus rutilus*

Pectoral fins with 17–18 rays **64**

64 Pharyngeal teeth 6.5; no marks along sides of body *Rutilus pigus*

Pharyngeal teeth 5.5; often with greyish stripes along sides of body
Rutilus rubilio

65 Pharyngeal teeth usually 4.4 *Rutilus macedonicus*

Pharyngeal teeth usually 5.5 **66**

66 Light grey band along side of body *Rutilus macrolepidotus*

114

	Marked dark band along side of body	**67**
67	Dorsal fin concave	*Rutilus lemmingii*
	Dorsal fin convex	*Rutilus alburnoides*
68	Dark band along side of body	**69**
	No dark band along side of body	**72**
69	Lateral band violet	*Leuciscus souffia*
	Lateral band dull grey or brown	**70**
70	Lateral band a think dark line from eye to base of tail	*Leuciscus polylepis*
	Lateral band broad	**71**
71	Lateral band rather faint; 62—64 scales on lateral line	*Leuciscus ukliva*
	Lateral band broad and dark; 70—72 scales on lateral line	*Leuciscus turskyi*
72	More than 54 scales on lateral line	**73**
	Less than 55 scales on lateral line	**74**
73	55—61 scales on lateral line; 12—14 rays in dorsal fin	*Leuciscus idus*
	73—75 scales on lateral line; 11 rays in dorsal fin	*Leuciscus microlepis*
74	More than 46 scales on lateral line	**75**
	Less than 47 scales on lateral line	**77**
75	Dorsal fin with 10—11 rays; 10—12 rays in anal fin	*Leuciscus leuciscus*
	Dorsal fin with 12—14 rays; 12—13 rays in anal fin	**76**
76	Lateral line with 48—49 scales; 12—14 rays in dorsal fin; scales with dark spots	*Leuciscus svallize*
	Lateral line with 49—54 scales; 12 rays in dorsal fin; scales with dark edges	*Leuciscus illyricus*
77	Anal fin truncated or only slightly emarginate; 43—45 scales on lateral line	*Leuciscus danilewskii*
	Anal fin rounded at tip; if, exceptionally, truncated, then 37—40 scales on lateral line	**78**
78	Less than 46 scales on lateral line; adults large, usually more than 15 cm long	*Leuciscus cephalus*
	More than 43 scales on lateral line; adults small, usually less than 15 cm long	**79**
79	Lateral line with 36—40 scales; length of head usually less than depth of body	*Leuciscus borysthenicus*
	Lateral line with 40—43 scales; length of head usually greater than depth of body	*Leuciscus aphipsi*

Roach *Rutilus rutilus*

Size 20—35 cm; maximum 44 cm — this fish weighed 2.1 kg; British rod record 1.757 kg. **Distinctive features** body with large silvery scales; pectoral fins with 16 rays. **Distribution** common in lakes, canals and slow-flowing rivers over most of northern Europe and Asia. Sometimes found in brackish water near the mouths of large rivers, e.g. in the Baltic and Black Seas. It is common also in parts of the Caspian Sea. **Reproduction** May—June, among weed in shallow water, usually in standing water but sometimes moving into fast-flowing water to spawn. The adhesive eggs hatch in 5—10 days and the larvae move round in large shoals, as do the adults which mature in about 2—3 years. 1,000— 14,600 eggs per female. **Food** an omnivorous species feeding on both aquatic plants (especially attached algae) and invertebrates of many kinds. **Value** commercially important in some parts of eastern Europe where it is caught in traps and nets. An important sport species in many countries where it is caught on set lines, using a variety of baits. Small roach are sometimes used as bait in pike fishing.

Danube Roach *Rutilus pigus*

Size 20—30 cm; maximum 40 cm; maximum weight about 1 kg. **Distinctive features** rather slender fish with large silvery scales (44—49 along lateral line). **Distribution** found in slow-flowing or still waters in parts of the Danube basin and northern Italy. **Reproduction** April—May, among weed, etc. The adults mature after 2—3 years. 35,000—60,000 eggs per female. **Food** invertebrates, especially worms, molluscs and crustaceans, and some aquatic plants. **Value** of little commercial value, it is sometimes sought after as a sport species.

Adriatic Roach *Rutilus rubilio*

Size 20—25 cm; maximum 30 cm. **Distinctive features** body with large silvery scales and greyish stripes along sides. **Distribution** found over most of Italy and basins draining into the Adriatic Sea. Occurring mainly in slow-flowing and standing waters. **Reproduction** April—May, spawning in shoals among weed in shallow water. **Food** mainly invertebrates, particularly insect larvae and worms. **Value** of some local importance to net fishermen; is also angled for in some places.

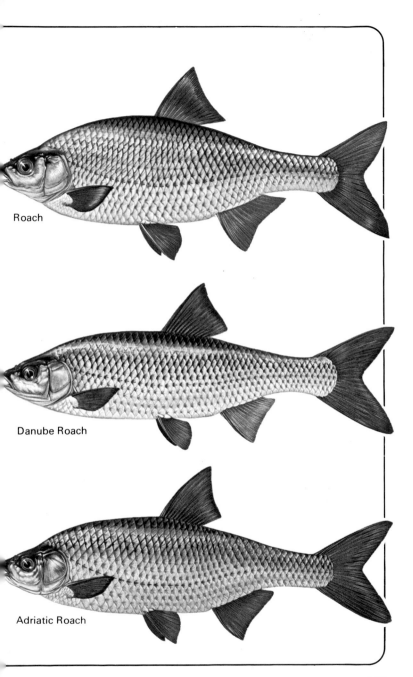

Roach

Danube Roach

Adriatic Roach

117

Portuguese Roach
Rutilus macrolepidotus

Size 12–15 cm; maximum 18 cm. **Distinctive features** large silvery scales on body and a light grey band along each side. **Distribution** found only in a few areas in Portugal, in lakes and lowland rivers. **Reproduction** April–May, mainly among weed in shallow water. **Food** invertebrates, especially worms, crustaceans and insect larvae. **Value** of little commercial or sporting significance.

Pardilla Roach *Rutilus lemmingii*

Size 15–20 cm. **Distinctive features** dark band along each side; mouth slightly inferior. **Distribution** in standing and slow-flowing waters in Portugal and south-east Spain. **Reproduction** April–May, spawning in large shoals among weed in shallow water. **Food** invertebrates, especially worms, crustaceans and insect larvae. **Value** of little commercial or sporting importance.

Macedonian Roach
Rutilus macedonicus

Size 12–15 cm; maximum 18 cm. **Distinctive features** large silvery scales on body and only rarely with a dark band along side; pharyngeal teeth usually 4.4 (see page 110). **Distribution** occurring only in rich slow-flowing or standing waters in a few small basins running into the north-west of the Aegean Sea. **Reproduction** April–May, shoaling among weed in shallow water. **Food** invertebrates, mainly worms, crustaceans and insect larvae. **Value** of no commercial or sporting significance.

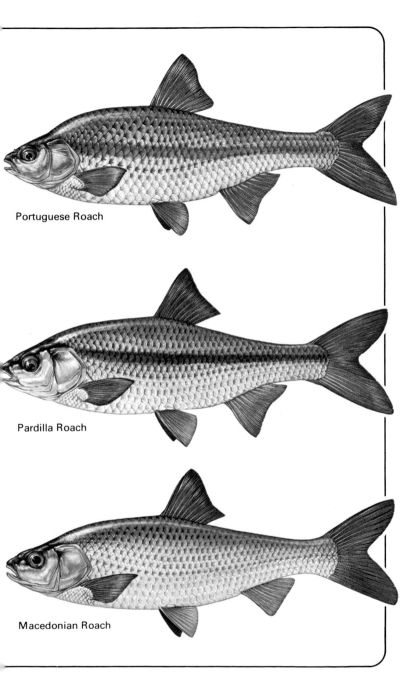

Portuguese Roach

Pardilla Roach

Macedonian Roach

119

Pearl Roach *Rutilus frisii*

Size 40–50 cm; maximum 71 cm; maximum weight about 7.1 kg. Distinctive features body with large silvery scales, 60 or more scales along lateral line. Distribution found in a few areas of Germany and Austria in the Upper Danube Basin, in basins entering the Black Sea, the Sea of Azov and the Caspian Sea. Occurring particularly in the lower reaches of rivers. Reproduction April–May, in shallow water among weed or over gravel and stones. The young hatch in about 10 days and mature after 3–5 years. Large migrations occur along rivers, and into and out of lakes at various times of the year. Average about 138,400 eggs per female. Food a wide variety of invertebrates, together with some plant material and small fishes. Value of considerable commercial value in many areas near the Black and Caspian Seas, and many thousands of large specimens are netted annually from some rivers. Also important as a sport species in some regions.

Calandino Roach *Rutilus alburnoides*

Size 12–15 cm; maximum 20 cm. Distinctive features marked dark band along each side; dorsal fin convex. Distribution found only in rich slow-flowing or standing waters in Portugal and southwest Spain. Reproduction April–May, among weed and stones in shallow water. Food invertebrates, notably worms and insect larvae. Value of little commercial or sporting significance.

Moranec *Pachychilon pictum*

Size 12–15 cm; maximum 16 cm. Distinctive features a small slender fish with scattered dark spots; lips very thick. Distribution found only in two areas of Albania (Ohrid and Skutari). Reproduction shoaling in shallow water during May–August. Food invertebrates, especially crustaceans and insect larvae. Value of no commercial or sporting value.

Greek Minnowcarp
Phoxinellus minutus

Size 4–5 cm; maximum 6 cm. Distinctive features lateral line very short (extending to only 4–6 scales); ventral fin with 8 rays; dark stripe along each side. Distribution found only in Lake Ohrid in Albania. Reproduction spawning habits, etc. unknown. Food mainly zooplankton, especially crustaceans. Value of no commercial or sporting significance.

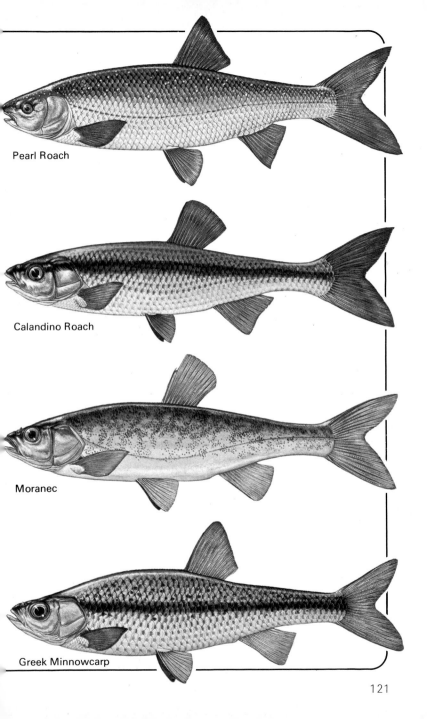

Pearl Roach

Calandino Roach

Moranec

Greek Minnowcarp

121

Spanish Minnowcarp
Phoxinellus hispanicus

Size 4—6cm. **Distinctive features** dark stripe along each side; more than 6 scales on lateral line; 9—10 rays in ventral fin. **Distribution** found only in streams in the River Guadiana basin in southern Spain. **Reproduction** shoaling in small streams during May—July. **Food** mainly invertebrates, especially insects. **Value** of no commercial or sporting value.

Adriatic Minnow
Paraphoxinus alepidotus

Size 8—9cm; maximum 10cm. **Distinctive features** body virtually without scales except for a few along the lateral line. **Distribution** found only in a few basins in Dalmatia draining into the eastern Adriatic Sea. **Reproduction** spawning habits, etc. unknown. **Food** invertebrates, especially small crustaceans and insect larvae. **Value** of no commercial or sporting significance.

Croatian Minnow
Paraphoxinus croaticus

Size 8—9cm; maximum 10cm. **Distinctive features** body with rudimentary scales, but no dark spots along sides. **Distribution** found only in south Croatia. **Reproduction** spawning behaviour, etc. unknown. **Food** invertebrates (mainly crustaceans and insect larvae) and some detritus. **Value** of no commercial or sporting value.

Dalmatian Minnow
Paraphoxinus ghethaldii

Size 9—12cm; maximum 13cm. **Distinctive features** most of body without scales, but some present on body, although not on back or caudal peduncle. **Distribution** found only in the Popovo basin in the Herzegowina area of Yugoslavia. **Reproduction** spawning habits unknown. **Food** invertebrates, mainly crustaceans. **Value** of no commercial or sporting value.

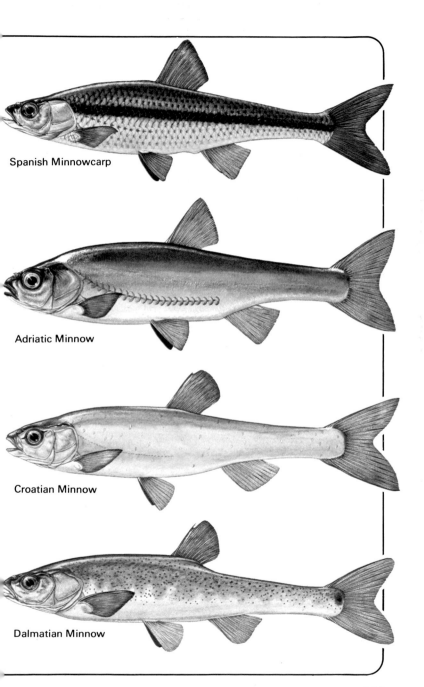

Spanish Minnowcarp

Adriatic Minnow

Croatian Minnow

Dalmatian Minnow

South Dalmatian Minnow
Paraphoxinus pstrossi

Size 8–9cm; maximum 10cm. **Distinctive features** a few dark spots along sides, but mostly above lateral line. **Distribution** found only in certain coastal areas of south-west Yugoslavia. **Reproduction** spawning behaviour unknown. **Food** invertebrates, including crustaceans and insect larvae. **Value** of no commercial or sporting value.

Greek Minnow
Paraphoxinus epiroticus

Size 9–10cm; maximum 12cm. **Distinctive features** body covered with thin fragile scales. **Distribution** found only in Dalmatia in Lake Janina and the River Luro. **Reproduction** spawning behaviour not recorded. **Food** invertebrates, including crustaceans and insect larvae. **Value** of no sporting or commercial value.

Spotted Minnow
Paraphoxinus adspersus

Size 8–9cm; maximum 10cm. **Distinctive features** dark spots along sides, many of them below lateral line. **Distribution** found only in some waters in Dalmatia. **Reproduction** spawning behaviour unknown. **Food** invertebrates, especially worms, crustaceans and insect larvae. **Value** of no commercial or sporting value.

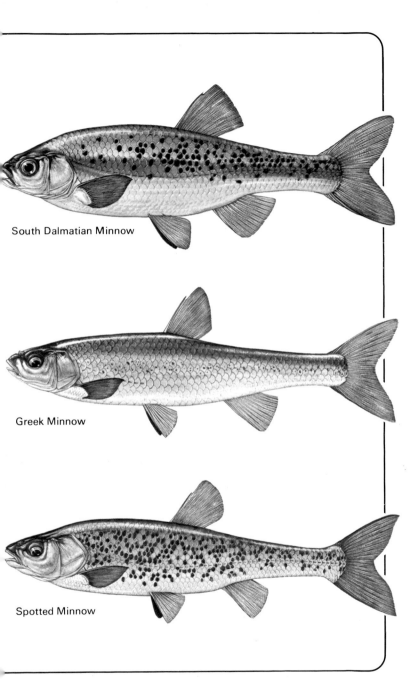

South Dalmatian Minnow

Greek Minnow

Spotted Minnow

Belica *Leucaspius delineatus*

Size 5–9cm; maximum 12cm. **Distinctive features** lateral line incomplete, extending over first 2–13 scales only; ventral fin with 10 rays. **Distribution** found in small ponds, and the lower reaches of some rivers in central and eastern Europe from the Rhine basin in the west to the Volga basin in the east. **Reproduction** June–July, spawning among weeds in shallow water. Matures after 2 years and lives only about 5 years. **Food** invertebrates (especially crustaceans and some insect larvae) and fine plant material. **Value** of local commercial importance in net fisheries in parts of Russia. Rarely angled for but occasionally kept in aquaria.

Tsima *Leucaspius marathonicus*

Size 8–10cm; maximum 12cm. **Distinctive features** lateral line incomplete, extending only over first 2–13 scales; ventral fin with 9 rays. **Distribution** found only in waters in the Marathon area of Greece. **Reproduction** reproductive habits unknown. **Food** invertebrates, mainly crustaceans, insect larvae and aerial insects. **Value** of little commercial or sporting value.

Marida *Leucaspius stymphalicus*

Size 8–10cm; maximum 12cm. **Distinctive features** lateral line incomplete, extending only to first 2–13 scales; anal fin with less than 12 rays. **Distribution** found only in Morea in southern Greece. **Reproduction** reproductive habits unknown. **Food** invertebrates, mainly crustaceans, insect larvae and aerial insects. **Value** of little commercial or sporting value.

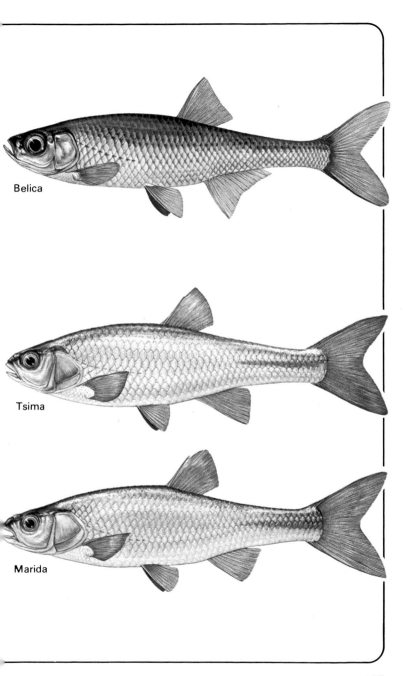

Belica

Tsima

Marida

127

Dace *Leuciscus leuciscus*

Size 15—25cm; maximum 30cm; British rod record 574g. **Distinctive features** body with large silvery scales, 49—52 along lateral line; anal fin concave; 10—11 rays in dorsal fin. **Distribution** found in rivers and streams throughout Europe except the extreme north-west and south-west. Occasionally in brackish water near river mouths. **Reproduction** March—May, among stones and plants in running water. The adults mature after 3—4 years. 2,500—27,500 eggs per female. **Food** mainly invertebrates, especially aquatic insects — both larvae and adults. **Value** of some commercial importance in parts of Russia. A sport species in some parts of western Europe.

Danilewskii's Dace
Leuciscus danilewskii

Size 15—20cm; maximum 25cm. **Distinctive features** body covered by large silvery scales, 43—45 along the lateral line. **Distribution** found only in running water in the basin of the River Don. **Reproduction** March—May, spawning among gravel, stones and weed in streams. Matures after 3—4 years. **Food** invertebrates, especially insects. **Value** of little commercial or sporting value.

Adriatic Dace *Leuciscus svallize*

Size 15—25cm. **Distinctive features** body with large silvery scales, 48—49 along lateral line; anal fin with 13 rays. **Distribution** found only in clear streams and rivers in south-west Yugoslavia (Dalmatia) and Albania. **Reproduction** little is known about the reproductive habits of this species. **Food** invertebrates, including worms, crustaceans and aquatic flying insects. **Value** of some local commercial importance in net fisheries; angled for in a few areas.

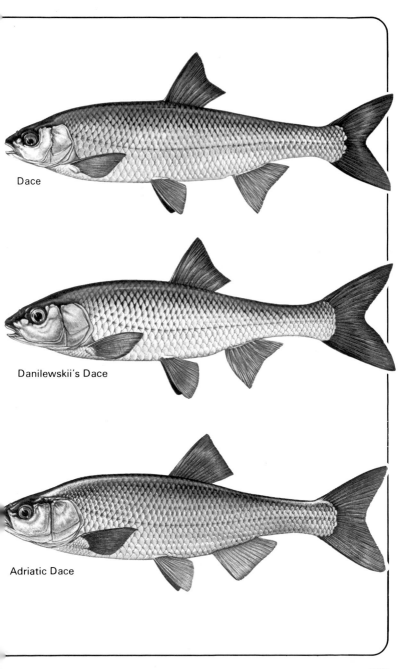

Dace

Danilewskii's Dace

Adriatic Dace

129

Yugoslavian Dace *Leuciscus illyricus*

Size 15—20cm; maximum 25cm. **Distinctive features** body with large silvery scales, 49—54 along lateral line; 12 rays in dorsal fin. **Distribution** found only in western Yugoslavia (Dalmatia) where it is found in a variety of waters. **Reproduction** reproductive habits unknown. **Food** invertebrates, especially worms, crustaceans and insect larvae. **Value** of minor local commercial (not fishery), and angling importance.

Chub *Leuciscus cephalus*

Size 30—50cm; maximum 80cm; British rod record 3.345kg. **Distinctive features** body with large silvery scales, less than 46 along lateral line; forehead wide and flat; anal fin rounded. **Distribution** found in running water (occasionally in lakes) throughout most of central and southern Europe. Occurs sometimes in brackish water (e.g. Baltic Sea). **Reproduction** April—June among stones and plants in slow-flowing water. The eggs hatch in 6—8 days and the adults are mature after 3—4 years. 50,000—200,000 eggs per female. **Food** mainly invertebrates and some plant material when young, large invertebrates and fishes when adult. **Value** only locally of importance as a commercial species, when it is caught by nets. It is of considerable sporting value in many parts of Europe.

Black Sea Chub
Leuciscus borysthenicus

Size 15—35cm; maximum 40cm. **Distinctive features** body with large silvery scales, 36—40 along lateral line; anal fin squarish. **Distribution** found in small lakes and in the lower reaches of rivers (e.g. Dniester, Dnieper) entering the Black Sea. **Reproduction** May—June, spawning among weed and stones in slow-moving water. Adults mature after 3—4 years. On average about 2,500 eggs per female (this number is for small fishes in the River Kuban). **Food** invertebrates when young, invertebrates and small fishes when older. **Value** of little commercial or sporting value.

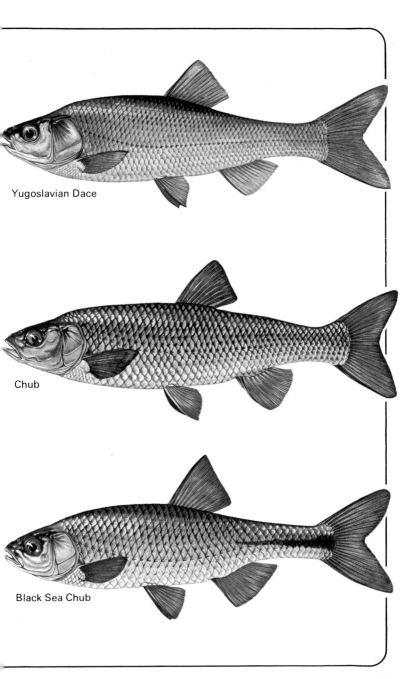

Yugoslavian Dace

Chub

Black Sea Chub

131

Caucasian Chub *Leuciscus aphipsi*

Size 12–15cm; maximum 18cm. **Distinctive features** body with large silvery scales, 40–43 along lateral line; anal fin slightly rounded. **Distribution** found only in the Rivers Afips and Psekups (mountainous tributaries of the River Kuban in western Caucasia). **Reproduction** May, spawning in running water. Males bear tubercles during spawning period. **Food** invertebrates, especially insect larvae. **Value** of no commercial or sporting value.

Blageon *Leuciscus souffia*

Size 12–18cm; maximum 25cm. **Distinctive features** body with large scales, those along the lateral line with a yellowish tinge; distinct violet band along sides. **Distribution** found in a few lakes and in the middle reaches of rivers (e.g. Rhône) in central Europe. **Reproduction** March–May over gravel and stones in flowing water. 5,500–8,000 eggs per female. **Food** invertebrates, especially crustaceans and insect larvae. **Value** of little value, although occasionally eaten locally or used as bait in sport fishing.

Croatian Dace *Leuciscus polylepis*

Size 15–20cm; maximum 25cm. **Distinctive features** body covered by large scales – a thin dark grey or brown stripe along sides from eye to base of tail. **Distribution** found only in northern Yugoslavia (Croatia). **Reproduction** reproductive habits unknown. **Food** invertebrates, especially worms, crustaceans and insect larvae. **Value** of little commercial or sporting value.

Ukliva Dace *Leuciscus ukliva*

Size 15–20cm; maximum 25cm. **Distinctive features** body with well-developed large scales, 62–64 scales along lateral line; a broad, although rather faint dark line along sides. **Distribution** found only in the Cetina basin in south-western Yugoslavia (Dalmatia). **Reproduction** breeding habits unknown. **Food** invertebrates, especially worms, crustaceans and insect larvae. **Value** of little commercial or sporting value.

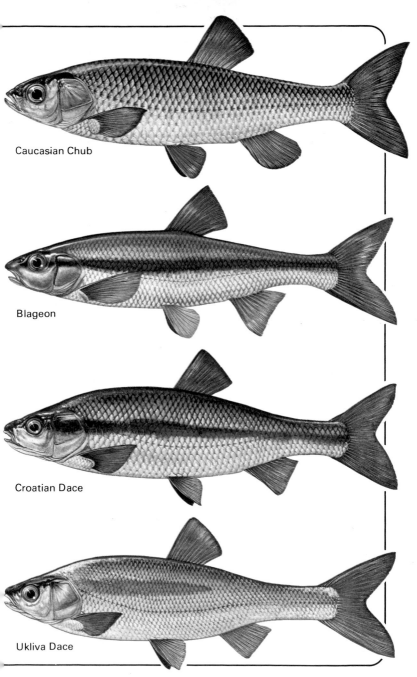

Caucasian Chub

Blageon

Croatian Dace

Ukliva Dace

133

Makal Dace *Leuciscus microlepis*

Size 20–25cm; maximum 30cm. **Distinctive features** body covered with well-developed scales, 73–75 along lateral line; sometimes with a faint longitudinal band along sides. **Distribution** found only in streams and lakes in south-western Yugoslavia (Dalmatia). **Reproduction** reproductive habits not known. **Food** invertebrates, especially insect larvae. **Value** of no commercial or sporting value.

Turskyi Dace *Leuciscus turskyi*

Size 15–20cm; maximum 25cm. **Distinctive features** body with well-developed scales, 70–72 along lateral line; a broad dark lateral band on each side. **Distribution** found only in streams and lakes in the Narenta basin in south-western Yugoslavia (Dalmatia). **Reproduction** reproductive habits not known. **Food** invertebrates, especially worms, crustaceans and insect larvae. **Value** of little commercial or sporting value.

Orfe *Leuciscus idus*

Size 35–50cm; maximum 100cm; British rod record 1.771kg. **Distinctive features** body with well-developed scales, 55–61 along lateral line; 12–14 rays in dorsal fin. **Distribution** native to most of Europe and parts of Asia east of the Rhine. Introduced successfully to several countries west of the Rhine. Found sometimes in brackish water, it occurs mainly in rivers and some lakes. **Reproduction** April–May, in shallow water among weed and stones. The eggs hatch in 15–20 days and the adults mature at 5–7 years. 39,000–114,000 eggs per female. **Food** invertebrates, especially molluscs, crustaceans and insect larvae, and some plant material, when young; invertebrates and some fishes when larger. **Value** of considerable commercial importance in Russia, where large numbers are taken in nets and traps. Angled for in some parts of Europe. The golden variety is very popular as an aquarium or pond fish.

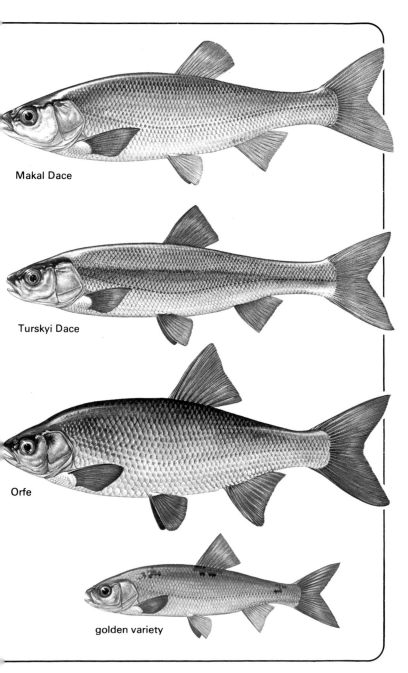

Makal Dace

Turskyi Dace

Orfe

golden variety

Swamp Minnow *Phoxinus percnurus*

Size 10—15 cm; maximum 19 cm; maximum weight about 100 g. **Distinctive features** scales small, 70—80 along lateral line; body deep and covered with small brown spots. **Distribution** found in ponds and lakes in parts of central Europe and in the basins of all rivers which flow into the Arctic Ocean. **Reproduction** June—July, spawning among water plants to which its adhesive eggs are attached. The eggs hatch in 5—8 days and the adults mature after 2—3 years. 1,600—18,700 eggs per female. **Food** invertebrates, especially worms, crustaceans and insect larvae. **Value** of considerable commercial importance in parts of Russia, and used as a bait species for sport fishing elsewhere.

Minnow *Phoxinus phoxinus*

Size 6—10 cm; maximum 14 cm. **Distinctive features** scales small, 80—100 along lateral line; numerous brown and black blotches along sides, sometimes uniting to form stripes; males brightly coloured during spawning. **Distribution** found in rivers and lakes over almost the whole of Europe and northern Asia. **Reproduction** June—July, spawning in shoals over stones and gravel (to which the eggs adhere) in running water. The eggs hatch in 5—10 days and the adults mature after 2—3 years. 200—1,000 eggs per female. **Food** invertebrates, especially crustaceans and insect larvae, and some plant material. **Value** of commercial importance in parts of Russia. A valuable bait species elsewhere. Commonly used also as an aquarium and laboratory fish.

Poznan Minnow
Phoxinus czekanowskii

Size 5—8 cm; maximum 12 cm. **Distinctive features** scales small, 90—94 along sides; body with numerous dark spots. **Distribution** found in rivers and lakes in many basins whose waters enter the Arctic Ocean. **Reproduction** June—July, among weed in both running and standing water. **Food** invertebrates, especially crustaceans and insect larvae. **Value** of some commercial value in certain areas of Russia.

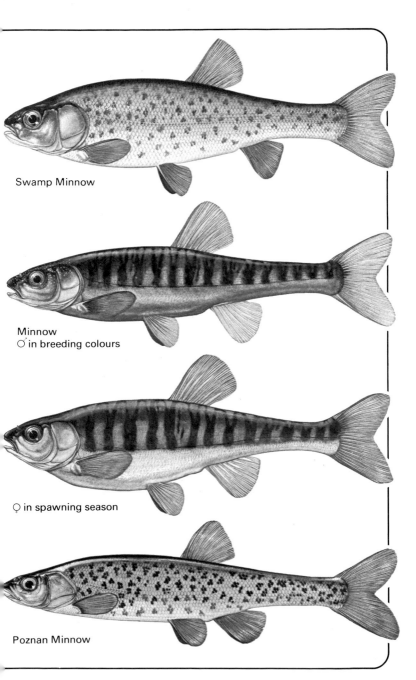

Swamp Minnow

Minnow
♂ in breeding colours

♀ in spawning season

Poznan Minnow

137

Rudd *Scardinius erythrophthalmus*

Size 15–30cm; maximum 45cm; British rod record 2.041 kg. **Distinctive features** body with large silvery scales, 40–43 along lateral line; lower fins bright red; origin of pelvic fins anterior to that of dorsal fin. **Distribution** found in lakes and slow-flowing rivers throughout much of Europe. **Reproduction** May–June, spawning in shoals among weed. The eggs hatch in 5–8 days and the adults mature after 2–3 years. 90,000–200,000 eggs per female. **Food** invertebrates (especially molluscs and insect larvae) and aquatic vegetation. **Value** of little commercial value, but of value as a sport and a bait species in some countries. The golden variety is commonly kept in aquaria and ponds.

Greek Rudd *Scardinius graecus*

Size 20–35cm; maximum 40cm. **Distinctive features** body with large silvery scales, greatest body depth anterior to dorsal fin. **Distribution** found only in lakes and slow-flowing waters in southern Greece. **Reproduction** April–June, spawning in shoals among weed in shallow water. **Food** invertebrates and various plant species. **Value** of some local importance as both a commercial and a sport species.

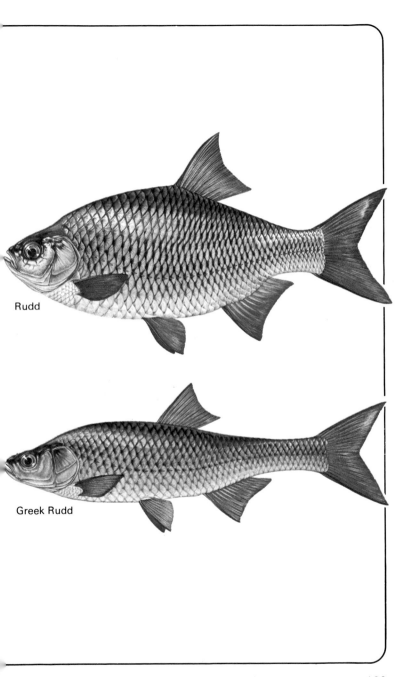

Rudd

Greek Rudd

139

Asp *Aspius aspius*

Size 50–75 cm; maximum 120 cm; maximum weight about 12 kg. **Distinctive features** body with well-developed scales, 64–76 along lateral line; mouth large, lower jaw with a tubercle entering notch in upper jaw. **Distribution** found in the middle reaches of rivers in central Europe from Holland to the west of the Caspian Sea. Occurs occasionally in lakes and in brackish water in estuarine areas. **Reproduction** April–June, spawning among stones and gravel in flowing water. The eggs hatch in 10–15 days and the adults mature at 4–5 years of age. 58,000–500,000 eggs per female. **Food** invertebrates (especially crustaceans) when young, mainly fishes when larger. **Value** of considerable commercial value in some areas where it is caught in nets and traps (e.g. Volga). It is also prized as a sport fish in some areas.

Tench *Tinca tinca*

Size 20–40 cm; maximum 65 cm; British rod record 4.110 kg. **Distinctive features** body deep, with small, deeply embedded scales, 95–120 along lateral line; one pair of small barbels at mouth; fins very rounded. **Distribution** found in rich, weedy lakes and slow-flowing rivers over most of Europe except northern areas. **Reproduction** May–July, spawning among weed in shallow water. The eggs hatch in 3–5 days, and adults mature after 3–4 years. They may live up to 10 years. 280,000–827,000 eggs per female. **Food** invertebrates, especially molluscs, crustaceans and insect larvae. **Value** of little commercial importance, but valued as a sport species in many countries where it is caught by baited hooks of various types. The golden variety is a popular aquarium and pond fish.

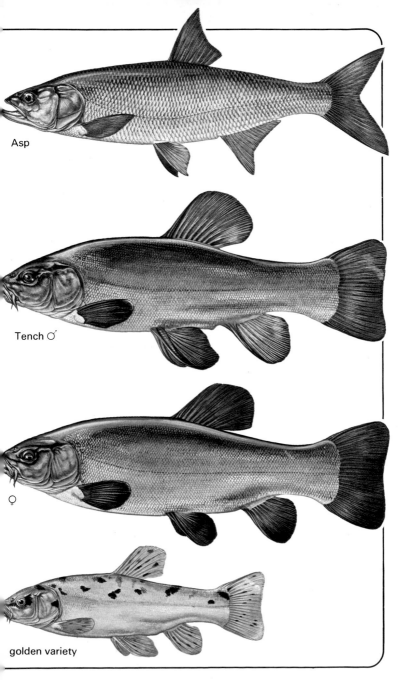

Asp

Tench ♂

♀

golden variety

Nase *Chondrostoma nasus*

Size 20–40cm; maximum 51cm; maximum weight 2.5kg. **Distinctive features** prominent snout and well-developed lips; 13–14 rays in anal fin. **Distribution** found in the middle reaches of large rivers in central and eastern Europe. **Reproduction** March–May, spawning, after migrating upstream, over gravel and stones in flowing water. The adults mature after 3–4 years and may live for at least 9 years. On average, about 10,000 eggs per female. **Food** mainly material grazed off the surface of stones (e.g. filamentous algae and various invertebrates). **Value** of considerable commercial importance in the Dnieper, Volga and other rivers where it is caught in nets and traps. It is of little sporting significance.

Italian Nase *Chondrostoma soetta*

Size 25–35cm; maximum 45cm. **Distinctive features** well-developed lips; body deep, greatest depth more than twice that of head. **Distribution** found only in the middle reaches of large alpine rivers in northern Italy (e.g. Po). **Reproduction** reproductive habits not known. **Food** mainly invertebrates (especially molluscs and insect larvae) and fine plant material (algae). **Value** of some local commercial importance in net and trap fisheries. Not angled for.

Caucasian Nase *Chondrostoma colchicum*

Size 20–25cm; maximum 29cm. **Distinctive features** snout well developed, mouth cleft straight and transverse. Often a longitudinal band of dark spots runs laterally from head to tail. **Distribution** found in the middle reaches of large rivers (e.g. Kuban) in Caucasian area of southern Russia. **Reproduction** Breeding habits little known. Males with well-developed tubercles. **Food** invertebrates (molluscs and insect larvae) and attached algae and other small plants. **Value** of little commercial, and no sporting value.

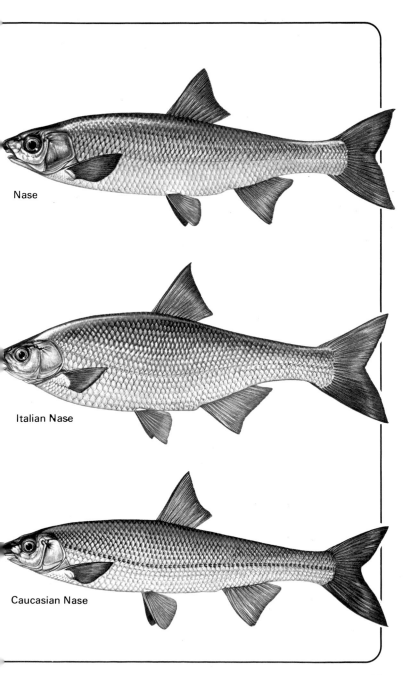

Nase

Italian Nase

Caucasian Nase

Iberian Nase *Chondrostoma polylepis*

Size 15–20cm; maximum 25cm. **Distinctive features** usually small, with a rounded snout; anal fin with 12 rays. **Distribution** found only in rivers in Portugal (e.g. Douro, Mondego), and western Spain. **Reproduction** reproductive habits unknown. **Food** benthic invertebrates (especially molluscs and insect larvae) and various plants (mainly attached algae). **Value** of little commercial, and no sporting value.

Terek Nase
Chondrostoma oxyrhynchum

Size 15–20cm; maximum 24cm. **Distinctive features** moderate snout, mouth cleft rounded; body elongate, its length about 5 times its depth; 11–12 rays in anal fin; never with a dark lateral band. **Distribution** found only in rivers entering the western Caspian Sea (e.g. Kuma and Sulak). **Reproduction** reproductive habits unknown. **Food** invertebrates and attached algae. **Value** of little commercial and no sporting value.

Laska Nase *Chondrostoma genei*

Size 15–20cm; maximum 30cm. **Distinctive features** snout and lips moderately developed; darkish band along either side. **Distribution** found mainly in the middle reaches of large rivers in central and northern Italy. **Reproduction** March–May, spawning in flowing water over stones and gravel. **Food** invertebrates and fine plant material. **Value** of little commercial or sporting value.

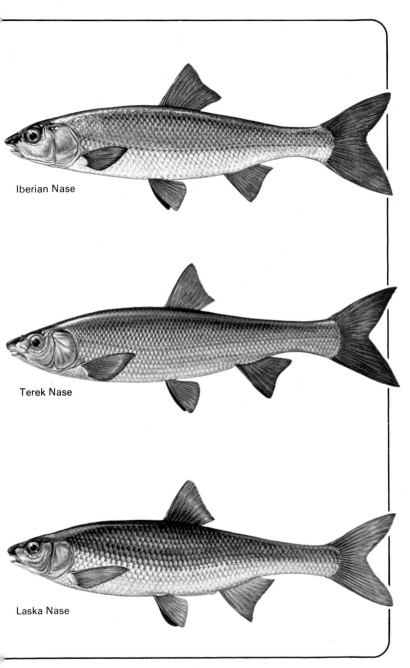

Iberian Nase

Terek Nase

Laska Nase

145

French Nase
Chondrostoma toxostoma

Size 20–25cm; maximum 30cm. **Distinctive features** snout small; mouth small and arched; 11 rays in dorsal fin and 12 rays in anal fin. **Distribution** found only in rivers in south-western France, Spain and Portugal. **Reproduction** March–May, spawning over gravel and stones in fast-flowing water, often in quite small tributaries. **Food** invertebrates and fine plant material (mainly attached algae). **Value** of no commercial or sporting value.

Dalmatian Nase *Chondrostoma kneri*

Size 15–18cm; maximum 20cm. **Distinctive features** mouth semicircular in shape; scales relatively large, 52–54 along lateral line. **Distribution** found only in the middle reaches of rivers in western Yugoslavia (Dalmatia). **Reproduction** March–May, spawning over gravel and stones in running water. **Food** invertebrates and attached algae. **Value** of no commercial or sporting value.

Minnow Nase *Chondrostoma phoxinus*

Size 10–12cm; maximum 15cm. **Distinctive features** very small and slim with small scales, 88–90 along lateral line. **Distribution** found only in fast-running water in certain rivers in western Yugoslavia (Dalmatia and Bosnia). **Reproduction** reproductive habits not known. **Food** invertebrates, attached algae and other fine plant material. **Value** of no commercial or sporting value.

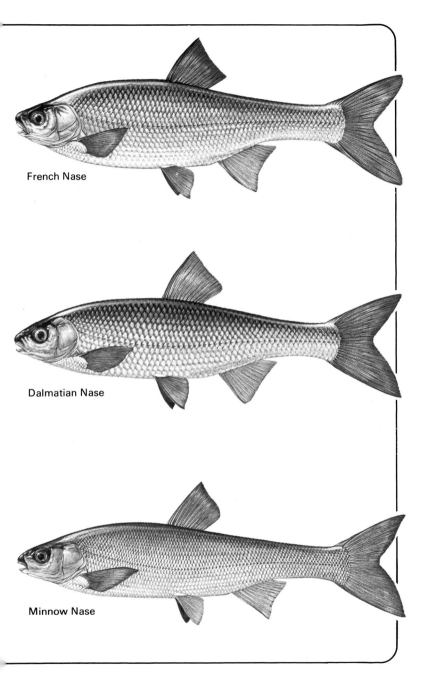

French Nase

Dalmatian Nase

Minnow Nase

147

Gudgeon *Gobio gobio*

Size 10–15cm; maximum 20cm; British rod record
113g. **Distinctive features** 2 well-developed
barbels; scales large, 40–45 along lateral line.
Distribution found in streams and rivers throughout
temperate Europe and Asia. **Reproduction** May–
June, among stones and weed in running water.
The young hatch after 15–20 days and adults
mature after 2–3 years, living up to a maximum of
8 years. 800–3,000 eggs per female. **Food** invertebrates, especially molluscs, crustaceans and insect
larvae. **Value** of little commercial significance, but
occasionally used as a bait species in sport fishing,
or angled for in its own right.

Kessler's Gudgeon *Gobio kessleri*

Size 10–12cm; maximum 15cm. **Distinctive features** 1 pair of long barbels reaching hind edge of
eye; dorsal fin with 8 branched rays. **Distribution**
found only in rivers in central Europe in the area of
the Danube basin. **Reproduction** reproductive
habits not well known. **Food** invertebrates, especially crustaceans and insect larvae. **Value** of no
commercial or sporting value.

Danube Gudgeon *Gobio uranoscopus*

Size 10–12cm; maximum 15cm. **Distinctive features** 1 pair of long barbels which can reach back
beyond the eyes; very few spots on body and fins,
but a blue band running along lateral line. **Distribution** living in fast-running water in the middle and
upper reaches of streams in the Danube basin.
Reproduction May–June, among weed and stones
in flowing water. **Food** invertebrates, especially
worms, crustaceans and insect larvae. **Value** of no
commercial or sporting value.

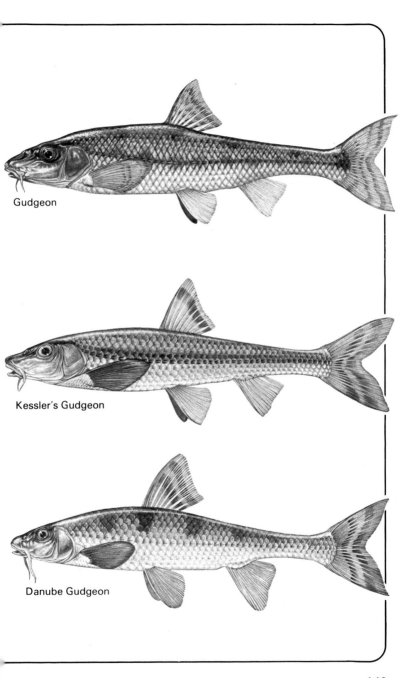

Gudgeon

Kessler's Gudgeon

Danube Gudgeon

149

Whitefin Gudgeon *Gobio albipinnatus*

Size 10–12cm; maximun 13cm. **Distinctive features** 1 pair of long barbels reaching posterior margin of eye; dorsal and caudal fins without dark spots; throat mostly without scales. **Distribution** found only in the middle and upper reaches of rivers in central and eastern Europe, notably the Volga, Dnieper, and Don. **Reproduction** reproductive habits little known. **Food** invertebrates, mainly worms, crustaceans and insect larvae. **Value** of no commercial or sporting value.

Caucasian Gudgeon *Gobio ciscaucasicus*

Size 11–14cm; maximum 15cm. **Distinctive features** barbels very long, reaching beyond posterior edge of eye; 42–46 scales along lateral line; throat usually scaleless. **Distribution** found only in streams and rivers in south-western Russia (Transcaucasia), notably the Kuban, Kuma, Terek, and Sulak. **Reproduction** May–June, but spawning habits little known. **Food** bottom-dwelling invertebrates, especially crustaceans and insect larvae. **Value** of no commercial or sporting significance.

Dalmatian Barbelgudgeon *Aulopyge hugeli*

Size 9–12cm; maximun 13cm. **Distinctive features** a well-developed snout with 4 barbels; body scaleless, but with an undulating lateral line running from head to caudal fin. **Distribution** found only in running water in parts of western Yugoslavia (Dalmatia and Bosnia). **Reproduction** reproductive habits little known. **Food** invertebrates, especially worms and insect larvae. **Value** of minor local commercial significance, but of no sporting value.

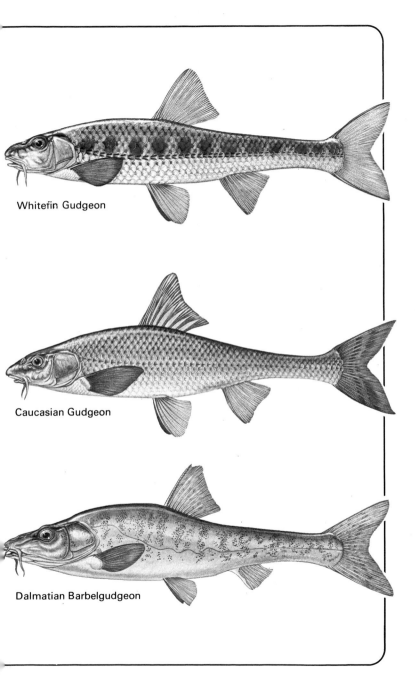

Whitefin Gudgeon

Caucasian Gudgeon

Dalmatian Barbelgudgeon

151

Barbel *Barbus barbus*

Size 25–75cm; maximum 90cm; British rod record 6.237kg. **Distinctive features** inferior mouth with 4 sensory barbels; 55–65 lateral scales; last unbranched ray in dorsal fin thickened and with numerous denticles posteriorly. **Distribution** found in the middle reaches of rivers in middle Europe from eastern England to the Black Sea. **Reproduction** May–July among gravel and stones in flowing water. The eggs (which are reputed to be poisonous) hatch in 10–15 days and the young mature after 4–5 years. 3,000–32,000 eggs per female. **Food** invertebrates (mainly worms, molluscs and insect larvae) and some plant material when young; invertebrates and small fishes when older. **Value** of some commercial importance locally, where it is caught by traps and nets. An important angling species in several countries.

Turkish Barbel *Barbus cyclolepis*

Size 20–30cm; maximum 35cm. **Distinctive features** inferior mouth with 4 short barbels – these are equal to, or less than, eye diameter. **Distribution** found only in running water in a few basins emptying into the Black and Aegean Seas (e.g. Rivers Maritza and Struma). **Reproduction** April–July, over gravel and stones in running water. **Food** mainly invertebrates, but some plant food when young, and fish and fish eggs when older. **Value** of no commercial or sporting value.

Macedonian Barbel *Barbus prespensis*

Size 20–25cm; maximum 30cm. **Distinctive features** 4 barbels round inferior mouth; longest dorsal ray without denticles posteriorly. **Distribution** found only in one small area of northern Greece. **Reproduction** reproductive habits unknown. **Food** mainly invertebrates, especially insect larvae. **Value** of little commercial or sporting value.

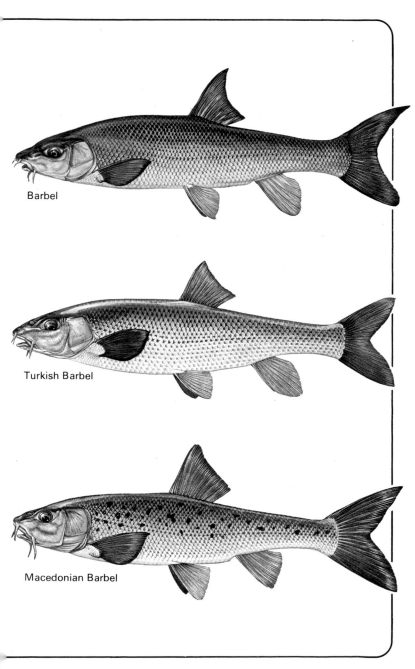

Barbel

Turkish Barbel

Macedonian Barbel

153

Caucasian Barbel
Barbus ciscaucasicus

Size 25–35cm; maximum 39cm. **Distinctive features** 4 long barbels around inferior mouth, these being more than 3 times the diameter of the eye in length; 60–71 scales along lateral line; body, especially above the lateral line, covered with numerous dark spots. **Distribution** found only in the middle and upper reaches of rivers entering the western Caspian Sea (e.g. Kuma and Terek). **Reproduction** May–July, spawning over stones and gravel, sometimes in quite small tributaries. **Food** mainly invertebrates, especially insect larvae. **Value** of minor commercial, and no angling importance.

Greek Barbel *Barbus graecus*

Size 30–40cm; maximum 45cm. **Distinctive features** body without dark spots or marks; 4 barbels around inferior mouth, each longer than eye diameter; less than 60 scales along lateral line. **Distribution** found only in western Greece in the River Aspropotamus. **Reproduction** habits not known. **Food** benthic invertebrates, especially insect larvae and molluscs. **Value** of little commercial or sporting value.

Albanian Barbel *Barbus albanicus*

Size 30–40cm; maximum 45cm. **Distinctive features** 4 short barbels around inferior mouth, each less than 3 times eye diameter; 49–52 scales along lateral line; lower part of longest dorsal ray slightly serrated posteriorly. **Distribution** found only in the Janina area of Albania. **Reproduction** habits unknown. **Food** mainly benthic invertebrates, especially insect larvae. **Value** of little commercial or sporting value.

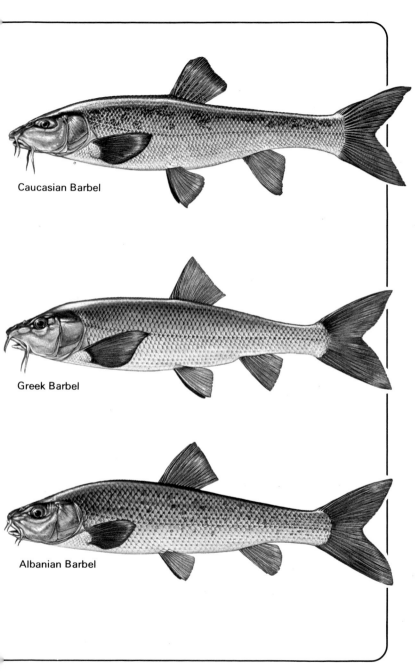

Caucasian Barbel

Greek Barbel

Albanian Barbel

Mediterranean Barbel
Barbus meridionalis

Size 20–30cm; maximum 40cm; a 20cm fish weighs about 150g. **Distinctive features** numerous large dark spots, often forming a mosaic on back and fins; 48–55 lateral scales; longest ray of dorsal fin without posterior serrations. **Distribution** middle reaches of rivers in south-western and central Europe. **Reproduction** May–July, in running water over gravel and stones – sometimes in areas of vegetation. **Food** mainly benthic invertebrates, but some plant food when young, and fishes when adult. **Value** of local commercial and sporting significance.

Bulatmai Barbel *Barbus capito*

Size 60–90cm; maximum 105cm. **Distinctive features** 4 barbels around inferior mouth, anterior barbel never reaching margin of eye; 58–65 lateral scales. **Distribution** lower and middle reaches of rivers entering Caspian and Aral Seas; also in salt water in these areas, migrating into fresh water at the spawning season. **Reproduction** in running water, young maturing in 6–7 years. **Food** benthic invertebrates, especially insect larvae. Plant material and fishes are also eaten. **Value** of local commercial value, taken in traps and nets in rivers during the spawning season.

Aral Barbel *Barbus brachycephalus*

Size 80–100cm; maximum 120cm; maximum weight about 22.5kg. **Distinctive features** 4 barbels around inferior mouth reaching back beyond margin of eye; 67–76 lateral scales. **Distribution** brackish waters of the Aral and Caspian Seas, and in fresh water only in the lower reaches of rivers there (e.g. Volga, Ural), often only for spawning. **Reproduction** April–July, in rivers easily accessible from the sea. Up to 1,259,000 eggs per female. **Food** invertebrates (mainly molluscs in the Aral Sea). **Value** of commercial importance in the Aral and Caspian areas, where fishes are caught in nets and traps during the spawning migration.

Iberian Barbel *Barbus comiza*

Size 20–30cm; maximum 35cm. **Distinctive features** 2 pairs of barbels around inferior mouth; largest dorsal ray stiff with a serrated hind edge; 49–51 lateral scales. **Distribution** in a few rivers in south-western Portugal and Spain (e.g. Gaudalquivir, Tagus). **Reproduction** reproductive habits not known. **Food** mainly benthic invertebrates, especially insect larvae. **Value** of no commercial or sporting value.

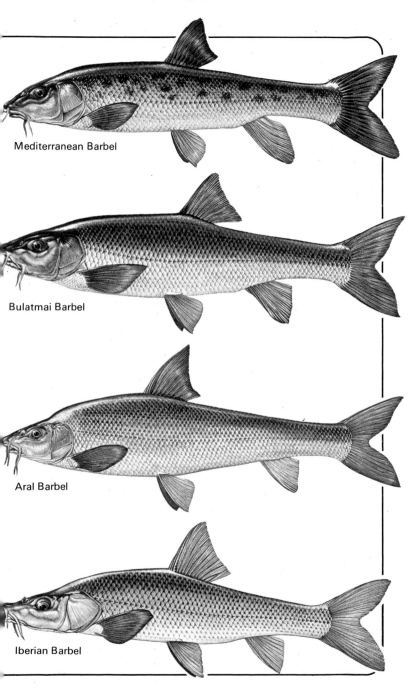

Mediterranean Barbel

Bulatmai Barbel

Aral Barbel

Iberian Barbel

Bleak *Alburnus alburnus*

Size 12–15 cm; maximum 25 cm; British rod record 111 g. **Distinctive features** body slim; base of anal fin longer than that of dorsal fin; more than 17 rays in anal fin. **Distribution** found in slow-flowing rivers and lakes throughout much of Europe from France east to the Caspian Sea. **Reproduction** May–July among stones and gravel in shallow water. The eggs hatch in 5–10 days and the young mature after 2–3 years. 5,000–6,500 eggs per female. **Food** invertebrates, especially crustaceans and insects (larvae and adults). **Value** important commercially only locally, and may be used for animal food or to produce a material used for covering artificial pearls. This is made from the fishes' scales. Of some sporting value.

White Bleak *Alburnus albidus*

Size 10–15 cm; maximum 20 cm. **Distinctive features** body slim, maximum depth about twice that of caudal peduncle; 13–18 rays in anal fin. **Distribution** found only in waters in western Yugoslavia and in north and south Italy. **Reproduction** reproductive habits not well known. **Food** invertebrates, especially worms, crustaceans, insect larvae and adults. **Value** of little commercial or sporting value.

Caucasian Bleak *Alburnus charusini*

Size 8–10 cm; maximum 12 cm. **Distinctive features** maximum depth of body about 3 times that of caudal peduncle. 41–47 scales along lateral line. **Distribution** found in lakes and slow-flowing rivers in several river basins (e.g. Kuma, Terek) in Transcaucasia between the Black and Caspian Seas. **Reproduction** little is known about the reproductive habits of this species. **Food** invertebrates, mainly crustaceans, insect larvae and adults. **Value** of no commercial or sporting significance.

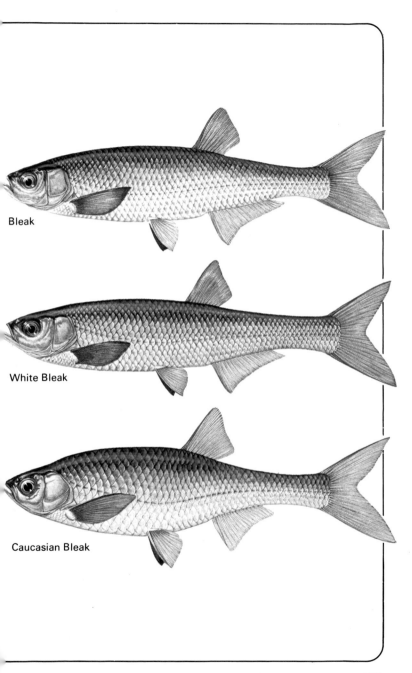

Bleak

White Bleak

Caucasian Bleak

Shemaya *Chalcalburnus chalcoides*

Size 15–30 cm; maximum 40 cm. **Distinctive features** slim, elongate body with 57–70 scales along lateral line; abdomen laterally compressed into a keel, which is free of scales posteriorly. **Distribution** found in most river basins entering the Black Sea and the western half of the Caspian Sea. It also occurs in salt water in these areas, but migrates into fresh water to breed. **Reproduction** May–July, spawning over gravel and stones in shallow fresh water. 15,500–23,500 eggs per female. **Food** invertebrates, especially worms, molluscs, crustaceans and insect larvae. **Value** of some commercial value in the Caspian area where large numbers are netted during the spawning migration.

Schneider *Alburnoides bipunctatus*

Size 10–12 cm; maximum 16 cm. **Distinctive features** pharyngeal teeth smooth; gill rakers short and set wide apart; 44–51 scales along lateral line. **Distribution** found in streams, rivers and occasionally lakes in parts of Europe from western France east to beyond the Caspian Sea. **Reproduction** May–July, spawning over gravel and small stones in running water. **Food** invertebrates, mainly insect larvae and adults. **Value** of no commercial value, but occasionally used as a bait species or kept in aquaria.

White Bream *Blicca bjoerkna*

Size 20–30 cm; maximum 35 cm; maximum weight 1.25 kg. **Distinctive features** body deep and strongly compressed; 40–45 scales along lateral line; anal fin with 19–24 branched rays. **Distribution** found in slow-flowing rivers and in lakes, in much of central and northern Europe from eastern England to the Caspian Sea. **Reproduction** May–July, spawning among plants in shallow water. The young mature after 3–5 years and may live up to 10 years 11,000–82,000 eggs per female. **Food** invertebrates, especially worms, molluscs and insect larvae. **Value** of some local importance both commercially (in net and trap fisheries) and as a sport species.

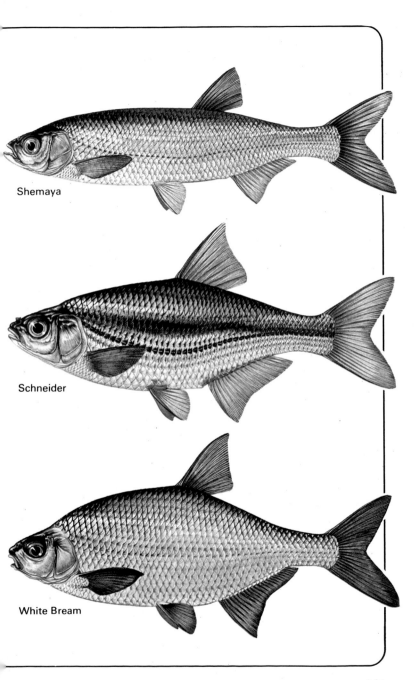

Shemaya

Schneider

White Bream

161

Bream *Abramis brama*

Size 30–50cm; maximum 80cm; British rod record
5.840kg. **Distinctive features** body very deep and
compressed laterally; 51–60 scales along lateral
line; less than 30 branched rays in anal fin. **Distribution** found in slow-flowing rivers and lakes throughout much of Europe from Ireland to the Aral Sea. It
also occurs in estuarine and brackish water in some
areas (e.g. Gulf of Finland). **Reproduction** May–
July, spawning among weeds in shallow water.
The eggs hatch in 5–10 days and the young mature
after 3–5 years. 104,000–587,000 eggs per female.
Food benthic invertebrates, especially worms, molluscs and insect larvae. **Value** of considerable commercial value in central Europe where large numbers
are caught in nets and traps. It is also important as a
sport species in many countries.

Whiteye Bream *Abramis sapa*

Size 15–25cm; maximum 39cm; maximum weight
800g **Distinctive features** deep, laterally compressed body with 49–52 scales along lateral line;
mouth subterminal; anal fin with 41–48 rays. **Distribution** found in slow-flowing rivers, some lakes,
and in brackish water in several river basins (e.g.
Danube and Volga) entering the northern Black
and Caspian Seas. Sea populations migrate to fresh
water to spawn. **Reproduction** April–May among
weed in running water. The young mature after 3–4
years and may reach over 8 years. 8,000–150,000
eggs per female. **Food** benthic invertebrates, mainly
molluscs, crustaceans and insect larvae. **Value** of
some local commercial importance in net fisheries
and sometimes sought as a sport fish.

Blue Bream *Abramis ballerus*

Size 20–30cm; maximum 45cm; specimens with an
average length of 18cm weigh about 92g. **Distinctive features** deep, laterally compressed body with
66–73 rather small scales along lateral line; anal fin
with 39–46 rays. **Distribution** found in slow-flowing rivers and lakes in lowland areas of central and
eastern Europe whose basins enter the Baltic,
Black and Caspian Seas, in the brackish waters of
which it also occurs. **Reproduction** April–June
among plants in shallow water. 4,200–25,400 eggs
per female. **Food** invertebrates, especially planktonic crustaceans. **Value** of little commercial or
sporting value.

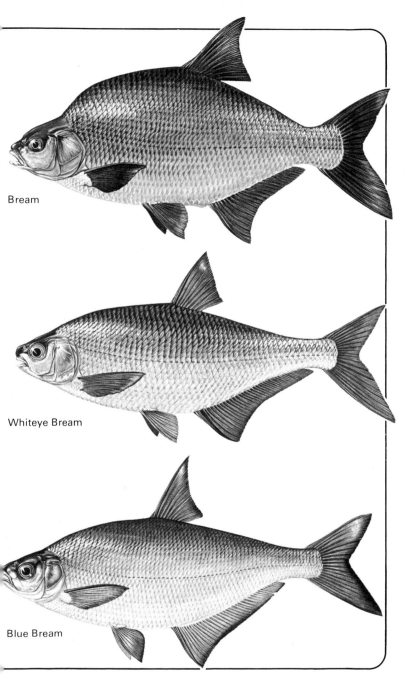

Bream

Whiteye Bream

Blue Bream

163

Vimba *Vimba vimba*

Size 20–30cm; maximum 50cm; specimens of average length 30cm weigh about 490g. **Distinctive features** sturdy, laterally compressed fish with 53–61 scales along lateral line; a scaleless abdominal keel before vent, and a scaled keel behind dorsal fin. **Distribution** found in the lower reaches of rivers, in some lakes and in basins linked to the Baltic, Black and Caspian Seas, in whose waters it also occurs. **Reproduction** May–July, spawning among weed and stones in shallow running water. The eggs hatch in 5–10 days and the young mature after 3–4 years. 27,000–115,500 eggs per female. **Food** benthic invertebrates, especially worms, molluscs and insect larvae. **Value** of considerable commercial value and caught in large numbers in nets and traps.

Chekhon *Pelecus cultratus*

Size 30–50cm; maximum 60cm; maximum weight 3.5kg. **Distinctive features** body elongate but strongly compressed laterally; lateral line undulating along sides; scales small, 90–115 along lateral line; well-developed keel along abdomen. **Distribution** found in central and eastern Europe in the basins of the Baltic and northern Black, Caspian and Aral Seas, occurring mainly in the lower reaches and estuaries of large rivers. **Reproduction** May–July, spawning in both fresh and brackish water. The eggs hatch in 3–4 days and the young mature in 3–4 years, living up to 9 years. 10,000–58,000 eggs per female. **Food** when young, invertebrates – especially crustaceans, insect larvae and adults. When adult, larger invertebrates and small fishes (e.g. herring and gobies). **Value** of considerable commercial importance in parts of south-eastern Europe; caught largely in nets and traps. As with the bleak, its scales are used in some places to coat artificial pearls.

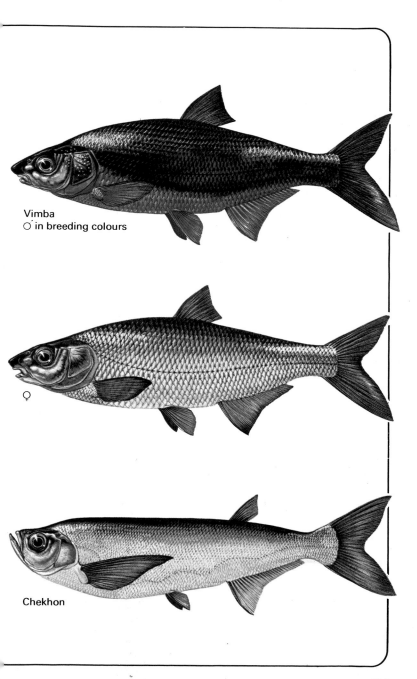

Vimba
♂ in breeding colours

♀

Chekhon

Bitterling *Rhodeus sericeus*

Size 5–8cm; maximum 10cm. **Distinctive features** body deep and compressed laterally; scales large, 32–40 laterally; lateral line incomplete; female bears long ovipositor. **Distribution** found in rich, slow-flowing rivers and lakes throughout much of the middle of Europe from France eastward to the Caspian Sea. Introduced successfully to a number of countries, such as England. **Reproduction** April–June, the fishes forming pairs and depositing eggs into the mantle cavity of large freshwater mussels, by means of an elongate ovipositor. The eggs hatch in 15–20 days and the young leave the mussel in a few days. The young mature after 2–3 years and may live up to 5 or more years. 40–100 eggs per female. **Food** both plants (mainly filamentous and other attached algae), and invertebrates (especially insect larvae and small crustaceans) are eaten. **Value** of little commercial value, but often used as a bait fish and very commonly kept in aquaria.

Crucian Carp *Carassius carassius*

Size 20–45cm; maximum 50cm; maximum weight 5kg; British rod record 2.253kg. **Distinctive features** body usually deep and laterally compressed; 31–36 scales along lateral line; dorsal fin convex, first ray feeble and weakly serrated. **Distribution** found in ponds, lakes and slow-flowing rivers throughout all of eastern and central Europe and many parts of the west. It is not native to many of these areas, but has been successfully introduced. **Reproduction** May–June, spawning in shallow water among thick weed growth. The eggs hatch after 5–8 days and the young mature after 3–4 years. 137,000–244,000 eggs per female. **Food** bottom-dwelling invertebrates and plants. **Value** of limited commercial importance (mainly in fish farms), but a useful sport species in some countries.

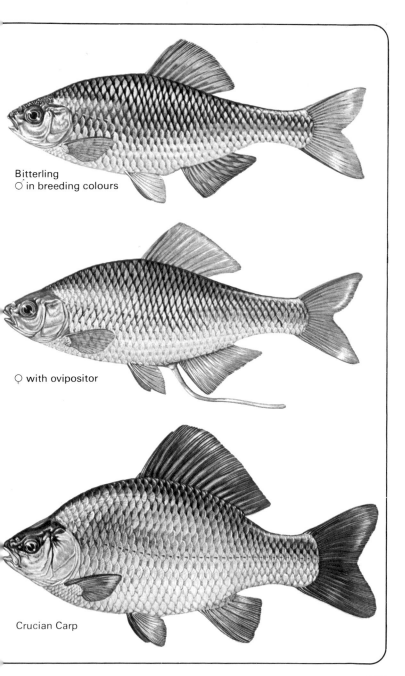

Bitterling
♂ in breeding colours

♀ with ovipositor

Crucian Carp

167

Goldfish *Carassius auratus*

Size 15—35cm; maximum 45cm; maximum weight about 3kg. **Distinctive features** body of moderate depth and laterally compressed; 27—31 scales along lateral line; dorsal fin concave, first ray strong and coarsely serrated. **Distribution** native to eastern Asia, this fish is now found in rich ponds, lake and slow-flowing rivers in many parts of Europe to which it has been introduced. **Reproduction** May—June, spawning among thick weed in shallow water. The eggs hatch in 5—8 days and the young mature at 2—4 years. They may live up to 20 years or more. 160,000—383,000 eggs per female. **Food** invertebrates and plant material. **Value** of some considerable commercial importance since the golden variety is one of the most popular aquarium fishes, and large numbers are reared on fish farms for this purpose. Of little sporting value although occasionally used as a bait species.

Carp *Cyprinus carpio*

Size 25—75cm; maximum 1.02m; British rod record 19.957kg. **Distinctive features** body covered with large scales; 33—40 scales along lateral line; upper lip with 2 long barbels and 2 short barbels. **Distribution** native to eastern Europe and Asia, this fish has been successfully introduced to many other countries where it is firmly established. It is found in rich ponds, lakes and slow-flowing rivers. **Reproduction** June—July, spawning among thick weed in shallow water. The eggs hatch in 3—6 days and the young mature after 3—5 years. 93,000—1,664,000 eggs per female. **Food** bottom-dwelling invertebrates and plant material. **Value** of considerable commercial value in many countries, particularly in central Europe, where many hundreds of fish farms are devoted to this species. Also of notable value as an elusive sport fish, when leather and mirror varieties are often encountered (see fig. 6). The golden and coloured varieties are popular pond fishes.

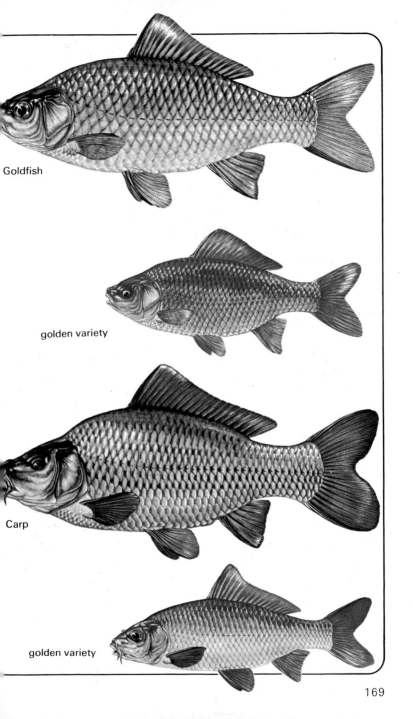

Goldfish

golden variety

Carp

golden variety

Family COBITIDAE

The Cobitidae, or loaches, are all freshwater, bottom-living fishes, found only in Europe and Asia. They occur in ponds, lakes and running waters of most kinds. There are many genera and species, particularly in southern Asia.

The body is characteristically very elongate, and usually cylindrical or only slightly compressed laterally. Scales may be absent, but where present they are normally very small and embedded within the skin. The eyes are small and usually rather dorsal in position, whilst the mouth is inferior with fleshy lips, and surrounded by 6 to 12 sensory barbels. The Cobitidae are related to the Cyprinidae, and possess pharyngeal teeth for crushing food. In some genera the head is unusual in that the anterior part articulates with the rest. There is a single dorsal fin, and all the fins are moderately developed.

Many members of the family are able to supplement inadequate oxygen supplies in stagnant water by swimming to the surface and swallowing air. Oxygen is absorbed from this in the gut, especially the hind portion, and the remainder is passed out through the anus. Some species which can breathe in this way (and presumably often have quantities of air inside them), are sensitive to changes in barometric pressure and become very active during rapidly decreasing atmospheric pressure preceding a storm.

Most of the species are nocturnal in habit, remaining hidden during daylight often under stones, among weed or buried in sand or gravel. The majority feed on benthic invertebrates, but a number are adapted for browsing on algae and various microscopic animals.

Altogether 12 species occur in European waters.

Key to European Cobitidae

1 Either 6 or 8 barbels **2**

10 barbels (4 on lower jaw) *Misgurnis fossilis*

2 No spine in cavity under eye; head not compressed laterally **3**

Spine in cavity under eye; head compressed laterally **5**

3 Caudal fin truncated *Noemacheilus barbatulus*

Caudal fin slightly emarginate **4**

4 Minimum body depth less than half caudal peduncle length; no dentiform process on the upper jaw *Noemacheilus merga*

Minimum body depth more than half caudal peduncle length; dentiform process usually present on upper jaw *Noemacheilus angorae*

5 Colour pattern on sides including one or more distinct rows of longitudinal spots **6**

Colour pattern on sides mottled with no distinct rows of spots **9**

6 No distinct dark line joining spots in lateral row **7**

Distinct dark line joining spots in lateral row **8**

7 Caudal fin with 14 branched rays; speckles above main lateral row also tending to form a distinct row *Cobitis taenia*

Caudal fin with less than 14 branched rays; speckles above main lateral row not forming a distinct row *Cobitis aurata*

8 Spotting relatively light; area above lateral row of spots forming a mainly clear band *Cobitis romanica*

Spotting relatively dark; many small spots in area above lateral row *Cobitis elongata*

9   Body coloration mainly in large patches   **10**

    Body coloration mainly as small dark speckles   **11**

10 Dark triangle formed by two halter-shaped stripes in front of eyes; no obvious elongate spots in front of dorsal fin   *Cobitis larvata*

    No dark triangle in front of eyes; two elongate spots in front of dorsal fin
                                                 Cobitis conspersa

11 Sides of body mainly with small speckles; suborbital spine strong, its branches similar in length   *Cobitis caucasica*

    Obvious dark streak running laterally on body; branches of suborbital spine greatly differing in length   *Cobitis caspia*

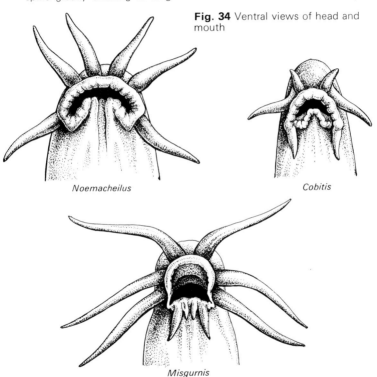

Fig. 34 Ventral views of head and mouth

Noemacheilus

Cobitis

Misgurnis

Stone Loach *Noemacheilus barbatulus*

Size 8–12 cm; maximum 18 cm. **Distinctive features** 6 barbels around mouth but no spine under eye; head rounded; caudal fin truncated. **Distribution** found in streams, rivers and some lakes throughout Europe except the extreme north and south. **Reproduction** April–May, among stones and weed in running water. The young mature after 2–3 years and may live up to 8 years. 500,000–800,000 eggs per female. **Food** benthic invertebrates, especially insect larvae of various kinds. **Value** occasionally eaten, but really of no commercial use. Sometimes used in sport fishing as a bait species.

Angora Loach *Noemacheilus angorae*

Size 6–8 cm; maximum 9 cm. **Distinctive features** 6 barbels around mouth; no spine under eye; head rounded; caudal fin slightly emarginate; body slim, minimum depth more than half length of caudal peduncle. **Distribution** found in rivers, streams and some lakes in certain basins entering the Black and Aegean Seas, e.g. Kamer and Coruh. **Reproduction** May–July, spawning among stones, gravel and plants in shallow running water. Specimens mature when they are longer than 5 cm. **Food** benthic invertebrates, especially worms and insect larvae. **Value** of no commercial or sporting value.

Terek Loach *Noemacheilus merga*

Size 6–8 cm; maximum 10 cm. **Distinctive features** 6 barbels around mouth; no spine under eye; head rounded; caudal fin emarginate; body rather deep, its minimum depth less than half the caudal peduncle length. **Distribution** found in running waters in basins of various rivers (e.g. Kuban, Kuma, Terek) in south-western Russia between the Black and Caspian Seas. **Reproduction** spawning habits little known. **Food** bottom-dwelling invertebrates, especially worms and insect larvae. **Value** of no commercial or sporting value.

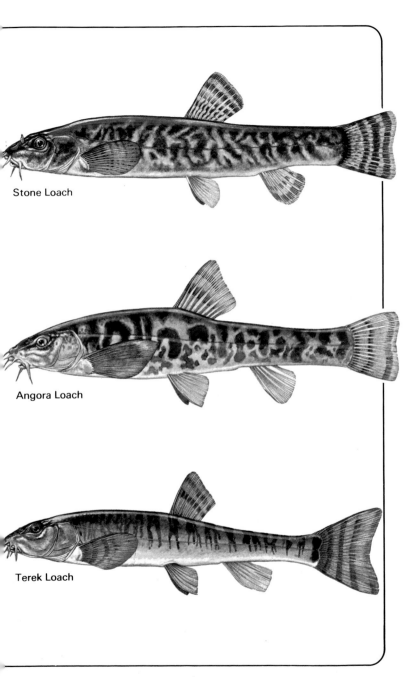

Stone Loach

Angora Loach

Terek Loach

Weather Loach *Misgurnis fossilis*

Size 15–30cm; maximum 50cm. Distinctive features 10 barbels around mouth; a large species with an elongate rounded body; several dark lateral stripes. Distribution found in rich ponds and small lakes in many parts of central and northern Europe. Reproduction April–June, among weeds in shallow water. The larvae possess fine external gills for a few days after hatching. 65,000–170,000 eggs per female. Food bottom-dwelling invertebrates, especially worms, molluscs and insect larvae. Value of little commercial or sporting value, although sometimes kept as an aquarium or pond fish.

Spined Loach *Cobitis taenia*

Size 8–10cm; maximum 14cm. Distinctive features 6 barbels around mouth, and a movable double spine below each eye; head compressed laterally; male pectoral fins with thickened second ray. Distribution found in slow-flowing streams and lakes over most of Europe except the extreme north. Reproduction April–July, among stones and weed in shallow running water. The larvae become bottom living almost immediately after hatching. Food bottom-dwelling invertebrates, especially worms, small molluscs and insect larvae. Value of no commercial or sporting value.

Golden Loach *Cobitis aurata*

Size 8–12cm; maximum 14cm. Distinctive features 6 barbels around mouth; a double spine beneath each eye; head compressed laterally; caudal fin with less than 14 branched rays. Distribution found only in the upper and middle reaches of streams in river basins emptying into the Black and Caspian Seas (e.g. Danube, Vordov and Kuban). Reproduction May–July, spawning among plants, gravel and stones in running water – especially in the upper reaches of streams and rivers. Food bottom-dwelling invertebrates, especially small worms and insect larvae. Value of no commercial or sporting value.

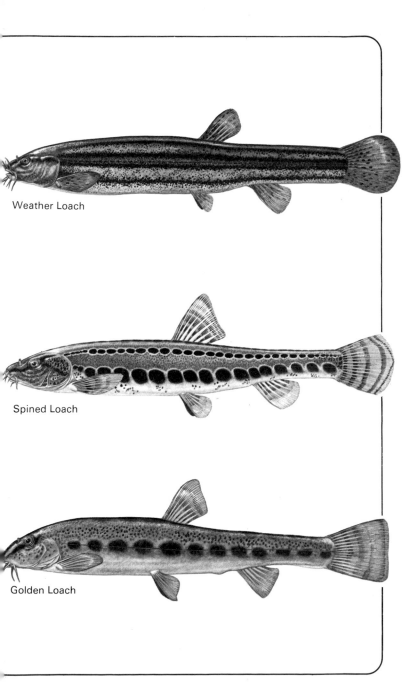

Weather Loach

Spined Loach

Golden Loach

Caspian Loach *Cobitis caspia*

Size 4–5cm; maximum 7cm. **Distinctive features** head compressed laterally; 6 barbels around the mouth; a double spine below each eye, the branches of this spine differing greatly in length. **Distribution** found in both fresh and brackish water in the lower reaches of rivers whose basins are linked to the west of the Caspian Sea (e.g. Kura and Ural). **Reproduction** April—May, among plants, gravel and sand in slow-flowing or even still water, usually in fresh, but sometimes in brackish habitats. **Food** bottom-living invertebrates, mainly worms, small molluscs and insect larvae. **Value** of no commercial or sporting value.

Caucasian Loach *Cobitis caucasicus*

Size 6–8cm; maximum 11cm. **Distinctive features** head compressed laterally; 6 barbels around mouth; a double spine below each eye – the branches of this spine of approximately equal length; sides of body marked with numerous small dark speckles. **Distribution** found only in the upper and middle reaches of certain rivers between the Black and Caspian Seas (e.g. Kuma and Terek). **Reproduction** May—July, among stones, gravel and plants in running water. **Food** bottom-dwelling invertebrates, especially worms and insect larvae. **Value** of no commercial or sporting value.

Venetian Loach *Cobitis conspersa*

Size 6–8cm; maximum 9cm. **Distinctive features** head compressed laterally; 6 barbels around mouth; a double spine under each eye; 2 elongate dark spots in front of dorsal fin. **Distribution** found only in a few rivers in northern Italy (e.g. Brenta and Gua). **Reproduction** April—June, among plants and gravel in shallow running water. **Food** bottom-dwelling invertebrates, mainly worms and insect larvae. **Value** of no commercial or sporting value.

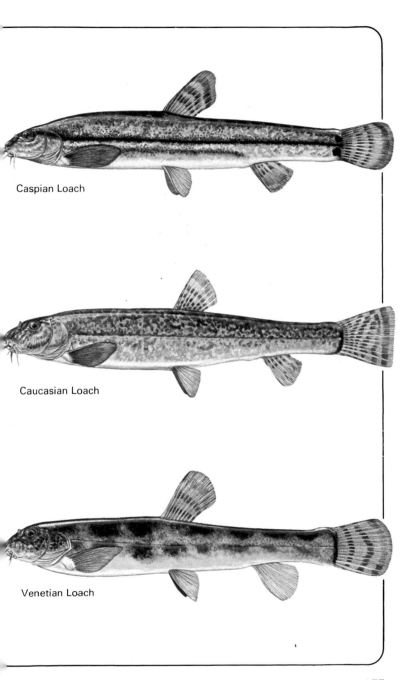

Caspian Loach

Caucasian Loach

Venetian Loach

Balkan Loach *Cobitis elongata*

Size 12–15cm; maximum 17cm. **Distinctive features** head compressed laterally; 6 barbels around
the mouth; a double spine below each eye; large
round dark spots along sides with a narrow dark
line running through them. **Distribution** found only
in streams in Yugoslavia and Rumania (e.g. Donau).
Reproduction April–June, in shallow running
water, spawning there on the bottom among stones
and gravel. **Food** bottom-living invertebrates,
mainly worms, small molluscs and insect larvae.
Value of no commercial or sporting value.

Italian Loach *Cobitis larvata*

Size 5–8cm; maximum 9cm. **Distinctive features**
head compressed laterally; 6 barbels around mouth;
a double spine below each eye; a dark triangle in
front of eyes; 2 dark spots on caudal peduncle.
Distribution found only in running water in the
region of northern Italy called Bergantino. **Reproduction** April–June, spawning among plants,
stones, gravel and sand in shallow running water.
Food mainly bottom-living worms and insect
larvae. **Value** of no commercial or sporting value.

Rumanian Loach *Cobitis romanica*

Size 8–10cm; maximum 12cm. **Distinctive features**
6 barbels around mouth; a double spine below each
eye; head compressed laterally; body relatively
lightly marked, a clear band running above the main
lateral row of spots. **Distribution** found only in the
upper reaches of certain tributaries of the Danube
in Rumania. **Reproduction** April–July, spawning on
the bottom in shallow running water among stones
and gravel. **Food** bottom-dwelling invertebrates,
especially worms, small molluscs and insect larvae.
Value of no commercial or sporting value.

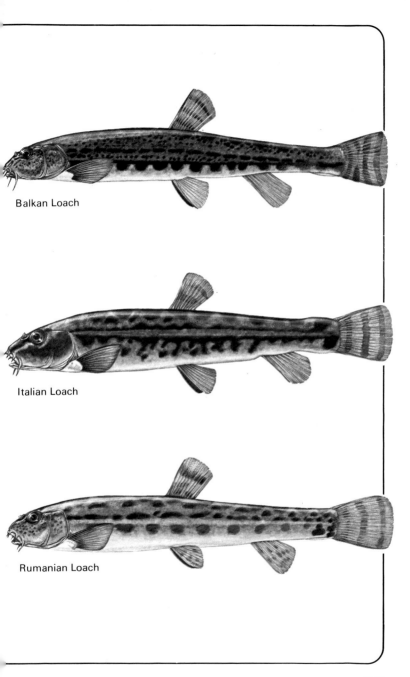

Balkan Loach

Italian Loach

Rumanian Loach

Family SILURIDAE

The Siluridae, a major family of catfishes in the Old World, are found in Europe and Asia — mainly the southern parts. There are 8 genera in the family, but only one of these occurs in Europe. All catfishes in this family are scaleless with an elongate body and a very large anal fin, terminating near the caudal fin. There is no adipose fin. Barbels are present on both upper and lower jaws. These fishes can grow to an enormous size and are among the largest freshwater fishes in the world. Only 2 species are found in Europe.

Key to European Siluridae

1   Lower jaw with 4 barbels   *Silurus glanis*

Lower jaw with 2 barbels   *Silurus aristotelis*

Wels *Silurus glanis*

Size 1–2 m; maximum 5 m – this fish weighed 306 kg; British rod record 19.730 kg. **Distinctive features** large flat head with 2 long barbels on upper jaw, and 4 short barbels on lower jaw; long anal fin. **Distribution** found in the lower reaches of large rivers and in rich muddy lakes in most of central and eastern Europe. Occurs also in brackish water in the Baltic and Black Seas. Introduced successfully to a number of other countries (e.g. England). **Reproduction** May–July, spawning in shallow water under thick vegetation where the male fish excavates a depression in which the eggs are laid. These are guarded by the male until they hatch in 2–3 days. The young mature after 4–5 years, and may live up to 15 years. 136,00–467,000 eggs per female. **Food** invertebrates when young, vertebrates (especially fishes but also frogs and waterfowl) when older. **Value** of considerable commercial importance in eastern Europe where it is caught in nets, in traps and on large baited hooks. It is also produced in a few fish farms. Prized as a large angling species in some areas, where it is caught on set lines baited with fishes or frogs.

Aristotle's Catfish *Silurus aristotelis*

Size 1–1.5 m; maximum about 2 m; maximum weight about 150 kg. **Distinctive features** large flat head with 2 long barbels on upper jaw and 2 short barbels on lower jaw; long anal fin. **Distribution** occurs only in southern Greece in the basin of the Akheloos river, where it is found in slow-flowing water or rich lakes. **Reproduction** June–August, spawning in a nest selected and guarded by the male until the eggs hatch. **Food** mainly zooplankton when very small, then changing to bottom-dwelling invertebrates and later to fishes when adult. **Value** of some minor local value commercially and for angling.

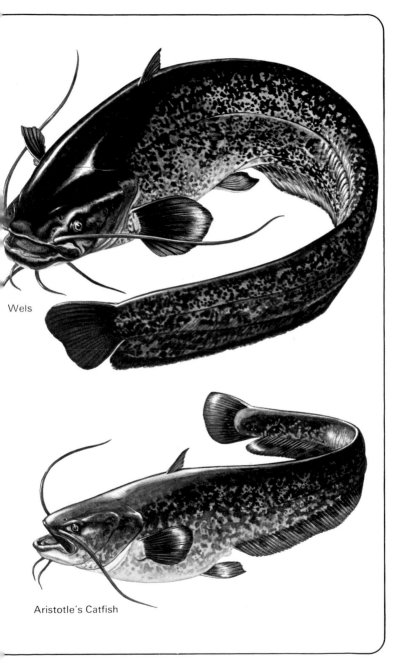

Wels

Aristotle's Catfish

Family ICTALURIDAE

The Ictaluridae, or North American catfishes, are native to rich lakes, ponds and slow-flowing rivers in North and Central America. There are 5 genera with some 25 species, all restricted to the New World, except a few species which have been introduced elsewhere. The body is elongate and scaleless, with a flattened head bearing barbels. An adipose fin is present, and dorsal and pectoral fins are armed with spines.

Several species have been introduced to Europe, but only 2 are established.

Key to European Ictaluridae

1   Barbs on posterior pectoral spines weak or absent; 17–21 anal rays; dorsal fin membranes darkened   *Ictalurus melas*

Barbs on posterior pectoral spines large; 21–24 anal rays; dorsal fin membranes not darkened   *Ictalurus nebulosus*

Black Bullhead *Ictalurus melas*

Size 20–30cm; maximum 45cm; maximum weight about 3kg. **Distinctive features** broad flat head with 8 barbels; barbs on posterior pectoral spines weak or absent; anal fin with 17–21 rays. **Distribution** native to eastern North America, but introduced to Europe (e.g. Italy) where it has established itself successfully. Occurs in rich slow-flowing rivers and lakes. **Reproduction** June–July, in a nest among logs, plants, etc. Eggs and young are guarded by both parents. **Food** both plants and invertebrates, especially crustaceans. Small fishes are also eaten. **Value** of little commercial or sporting value in Europe. Often kept in aquaria and ponds.

Brown Bullhead *Ictalurus nebulosus*

Size 20–30cm; maximum 45cm; maximum weight about 2.5kg. **Distinctive features** broad flat head with 8 barbels; barbs on posterior pectoral spines well developed; anal fin with 21–24 rays. **Distribution** native to eastern North America, but introduced to Europe (e.g. France), and successfully established in rich lakes and slow-flowing rivers. **Reproduction** June–July, in warm shallow water, spawning in a nest selected by both parents. Both parents guard the nest and the subsequent shoals of young fishes. 6,000–13,000 eggs per female. **Food** plants and invertebrates, especially large crustaceans. Fish and frogs are also eaten by large adults. **Value** of little commercial or sporting value in Europe, but kept in ponds and aquaria.

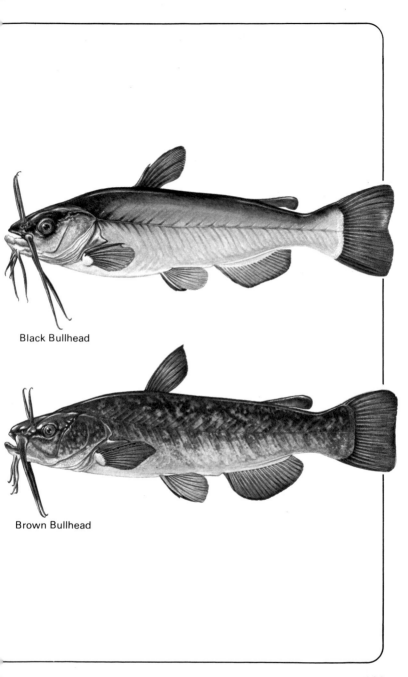

Black Bullhead

Brown Bullhead

Family ANGUILLIDAE

The Anguillidae, or eels, occur in Europe, Africa, Asia, North America and South America. The single genus contains 16 species. All are catadromous, moving early to fresh water and remaining there until maturity, then returning to the sea to breed. The body shape is characteristic, being elongate and round in cross-section. Pelvic fins are absent.

Only 1 species occurs in Europe.

Eel *Anguilla anguilla*

Size 40–90 cm; maximum about 2 m; British rod record 3.912 kg. **Distinctive features** elongate, cylindrical body with small gill openings; 1 pair of pectoral fins, but no pelvic fins. **Distribution** the European coast (including the Black Sea) and in a variety of fresh water habitats accessible from the sea. **Reproduction** adults spawn in the Sargasso Sea. Larvae (leptocephali) drift across the Atlantic for about 3 years before reaching Europe; they then migrate into fresh water as elvers, maturing at 8–15 years. These then migrate back to the Sargasso Sea. **Food** invertebrates (especially molluscs and crustaceans) and fishes. **Value** of commercial importance in many countries, where it is caught in traps, nets and by baited hooks. Often smoked. Of sporting value in a number of areas.

Family GADIDAE

The Gadidae, or cods, are mainly marine fishes, found in cool waters in the Northern and to a lesser extent the Southern Hemispheres. There are about 60 species, but few enter fresh water. Cods have wide heads with large jaws and numerous fine teeth. A slender barbel is found at the top of the chin. They are major commercial fishes, especially in the north Atlantic where many are also of sporting value.

Only 1 species occurs in fresh water in Europe.

Burbot *Lota lota*

Size 30–50 cm; maximum 120 cm; maximum weight about 32 kg. **Distinctive features** elongate body with 2 dorsal fins, the first shorter than the second; broad head with 1 long barbel on lower jaw, and 1 shorter barbel at each nostril. **Distribution** lakes and rivers throughout much of Europe, Asia and North America. **Reproduction** December–March, over stones and gravel in rivers and lakes. Eggs hatch in 40–50 days and the young mature after 3–4 years. 33,082–3,063,000 eggs per female. **Food** when young, invertebrates (especially crustaceans and insect larvae); when older, fishes. **Value** of commercial value, being caught by means of nets, traps and baited hooks, but of little sporting value.

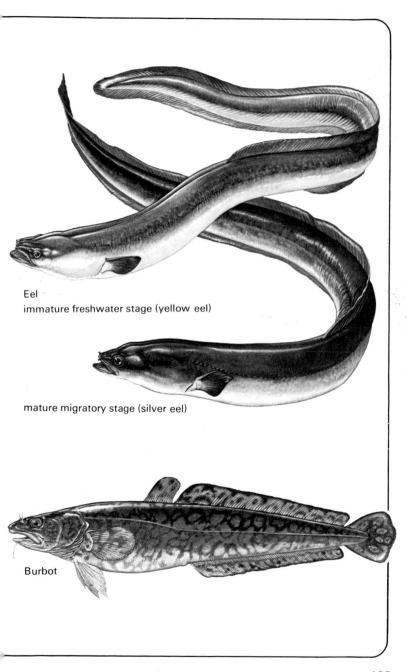

Eel
immature freshwater stage (yellow eel)

mature migratory stage (silver eel)

Burbot

Family GASTEROST-EIDAE

The Gasterosteidae, popularly known as sticklebacks, occur in a great variety of aquatic habitats in the Northern Hemisphere in Europe, Asia and North America. They are found in the sea, in estuaries and brackish waters, and in all kinds of fresh waters except where the flow is extremely fast. Although widespread, there are relatively few species, distributed in 5 genera.

Sticklebacks are all small laterally compressed fishes with well-developed dorsal and pelvic fin spines—these being characteristic of the family. There are really two dorsal fins, the first being represented by a series of spines. The pelvic fins have virtually been replaced by the spines. The mouth and teeth are small, but the latter are important for crushing and chewing. The body has no proper scales and is either naked or covered to a variable extent by bony plates.

Although small, sticklebacks are particularly aggressive fishes and feed on a great variety of invertebrates and fish fry. The European species have a very characteristic behaviour at spawning time, when the males establish territories in which each builds a nest. After spawning, the females are chased away and the eggs and subsequent fry are guarded carefully by the males. Further details of the spawning behaviour of the three-spined stickleback are described on pages 19 and 20.

Three species are found in fresh waters in Europe. A fourth species, *Spinachia spinachia* (L.), the sea stickleback, is found almost always in marine (occasionally estuarine) conditions.

Key to European Gasterosteidae occurring in fresh water

1   2—3 spines anterior to dorsal fin   *Gasterosteus aculeatus*

7—12 spines anterior to dorsal fin   **2**

2   Caudal peduncle usually with a well-developed lateral keel; body naked
Pungitius pungitius

Caudal peduncle smooth, with no lateral keel; body with lateral scutes
Pungitius platygaster

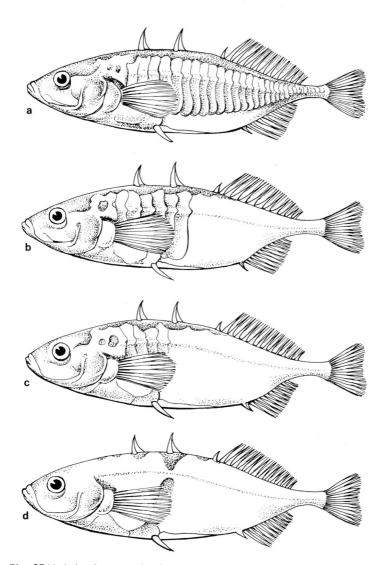

Fig. 35 Variation in armouring in different races of *Gasterosteus aculeatus*: a = trachurus type (mainly brackish); b and c = intermediate types; d = leiurus type (mainly freshwater)

Three-spined Stickleback
Gasterosteus aculeatus

Size 4–8 cm; maximum 11 cm. **Distinctive features** 3 strong spines anterior to dorsal fin; no scales on body but this may be protected by bony plates. **Distribution** found in many parts of Europe, especially areas which are not too far from the sea. Occurs in a wide variety of waters from the sea to rivers and lakes of all kinds. **Reproduction** March–June, when the male builds a nest of fibrous material and induces one or more females to lay in it. The eggs hatch in 5–20 days and they, and the young, are guarded by the male. The young mature after 1–2 years and rarely live beyond 4 years. 90–450 eggs per female. **Food** invertebrates (mainly worms, crustaceans and insect larvae) and sometimes small fishes. **Value** formerly used in parts of Europe for the production of fish meal, it is now of little commercial or sporting significance. It is commonly kept in aquaria, however, and is often used for teaching purposes.

Ten-spined Stickleback
Pungitius pungitius

Size 5–7 cm; maximum 9 cm. **Distinctive features** 7–12 – although usually 9 – stiff spines anterior to dorsal fin; body without scales. **Distribution** found in most parts of northern Europe, Asia and North America which are not too far from the sea. Found in both brackish and fresh waters. **Reproduction** April–July, the male builds a nest of fine plant material among vegetation, and induces one or more females to lay in it. The eggs hatch after 10–20 days; both they and the fry are guarded by the male. The young mature after 1 year. **Food** invertebrates, especially crustaceans and insect larvae. **Value** of no commercial or sporting value. Sometimes kept in aquaria.

Ukrainian Stickleback
Pungitius platygaster

Size 4–6 cm; maximum 7 cm. **Distinctive features** 8 or 9 strong spines anterior to dorsal fin; no scales present, but sides of body covered with inconspicuous bony scutes; ventral spine distinctly serrated. **Distribution** found in a variety of waters (both fresh and brackish) within basins linked to the north of the Black, Caspian and Aral Seas. **Reproduction** April–May, spawning in nests built by the males in shallow water, in well-vegetated areas. The male protects the eggs and young for some time. **Food** invertebrates, especially crustaceans and insect larvae. **Value** of no commercial or sporting value.

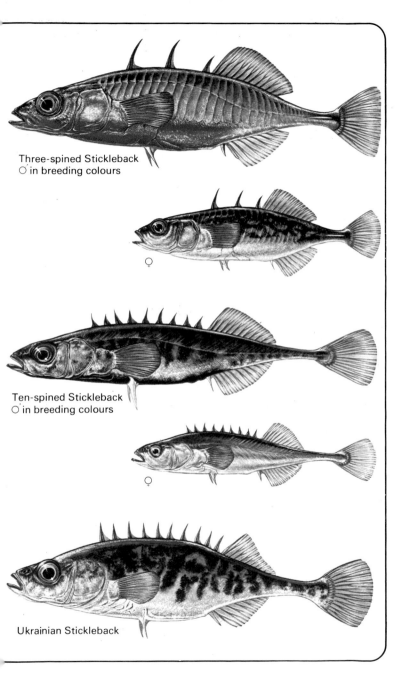

Three-spined Stickleback
○ in breeding colours

♀

Ten-spined Stickleback
○ in breeding colours

♀

Ukrainian Stickleback

Family SYNGNATHIDAE

The Syngnathidae, or pipefishes, are common in most seas and oceans, particularly among seaweed in shallow coastal areas. There are many genera and species, but only a few of these enter fresh water and even these are common only in estuaries, coastal lagoons and the lower reaches of some rivers.

The pipefishes have a very elongate body with or without pectoral and caudal fins. The dorsal fin is usually moderately well developed, but ventral fins are absent. There are no scales, but the body is covered with, and protected by, a series of bony rings which form a strong outer skeleton. The snout is very elongate, with a very small terminal mouth and two nasal openings on each side. There are no teeth. The gill opening is very small, situated behind the upper edge of the gill cover.

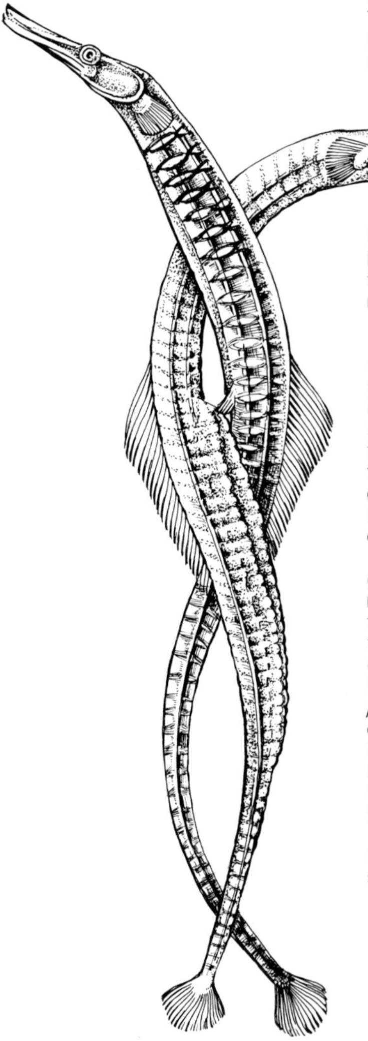

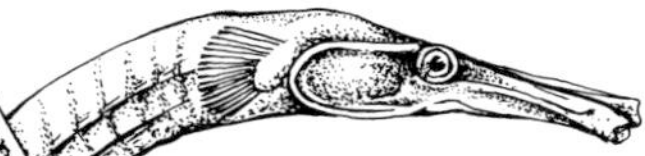

Fig. 36a Syngnathidae courtship behaviour: eggs being transferred from the female to the pouch of the male

Most members of the family are rather poor swimmers and live in protected places among weed and rocks. In such areas their elongate shape and mottled colouring give them considerable camouflage protection. Because of the minute size of the mouth, only small animals can be eaten—these are usually crustacean zooplankton and fish fry.

A very characteristic feature of the group is the fact that the male has a marsupial pouch on the underside of the tail and abdomen. It is formed by two folds of skin which are developed on either side and meet in the midline. In a few members (e.g. *Nerophis*) the pouch is absent and the eggs are attached directly to the abdomen. The inside of the pouch is lined with soft skin. During spawning the eggs are fertilized and placed in the brood pouch of the male, where

Fig. 36b Male pouch opened to show eggs

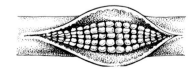

they remain for the full period of incubation. Soon after hatching, the young, which apart from size are very similar to the adults, are released and immediately start to fend for themselves.

Four species are found in fresh waters in some areas of Europe.

Key to European Syngnathidae occurring in fresh water

1 Pectoral fins absent in adults *Nerophis ophidion*

Pectoral fins present in adults **2**

2 Both halves of the pectoral ring mobile below and not fused; usually no median ventral bony plate under pectoral ring; proboscis strongly compressed laterally *Syphonostoma typhle*

Both halves of the pectoral ring fused below and immobile; median ventral bony plate present; proboscis subcylindrical and elongate **3**

3 Dorsal fins occupying 7—9 rings, and with 29—42 rays *Syngnathus nigrolineatus*

Dorsal fins occupying 11—13 rings, and with 41—62 rays *Syngnathus acus*

Black Sea Pipefish
Syngnathus nigrolineatus

Size 15—18cm; maximum 22cm. **Distinctive features** dorsal fins occupying 7—9 rings and with 29—42 rays; proboscis elongate and cylindrical. **Distribution** found among vegetation throughout the Black and Caspian Seas. Ascends the lower reaches of rivers entering these seas (e.g. Dniester, Volga) and occurs also in lakes on their plains. **Reproduction** May—August; after spawning eggs and fry are retained in pouches on males. Eggs hatch in 20—25 days and young mature after 1 year. **Food** invertebrates (mainly crustaceans) and fish larvae. **Value** of no commercial or sporting significance.

Mediterranean Pipefish
Syngnathus acus

Size 20—35cm; maximum 46cm. **Distinctive features** dorsal fin occupying 11—13 rings and with 41—62 rays; proboscis elongate and cylindrical. **Distribution** along Atlantic coasts from western Norway to northern Spain. Occurs in estuaries. **Reproduction** June—July, eggs are transferred from the female to the male's brood pouch where they are fertilized, and hatch in 30—35 days. 200—400 eggs per female. **Food** invertebrates (mainly crustaceans and fish larvae). **Value** of no commercial or sporting significance.

Broadnose Pipefish
Syphonostoma typhle

Size 20—30cm; maximum 37cm. **Distinctive features** proboscis compressed laterally. **Distribution** European coasts from Norway to the Mediterranean and Black Seas. Enters estuaries and lower reaches of rivers. **Reproduction** March—August, eggs being transferred from the female to the male brood pouch by an elongate tube. After fertilization, eggs remain in the pouch until they hatch after 25—30 days. Young mature in 1 year and live 3—4 years. 150—200 eggs per female. **Food** invertebrates (mainly crustaceans) and fish larvae. **Value** of no commercial or sporting significance.

Straightnose Pipefish
Nerophis ophidion

Size 15—25cm; maximum 30cm. **Distinctive features** no pectoral fins in fish longer than 10cm. **Distribution** European coast from northern Norway to the Mediterranean and Black Seas. Enters the lower reaches of rivers (e.g. Dniester, Dnieper). **Reproduction** May—August, eggs being fertilized by the male after transfer to his pouch. Young mature after 1 year and live for 3—4 years. 200—300 eggs per female. **Food** invertebrates (mainly crustaceans) and fish larvae. **Value** of no commercial or sporting significance.

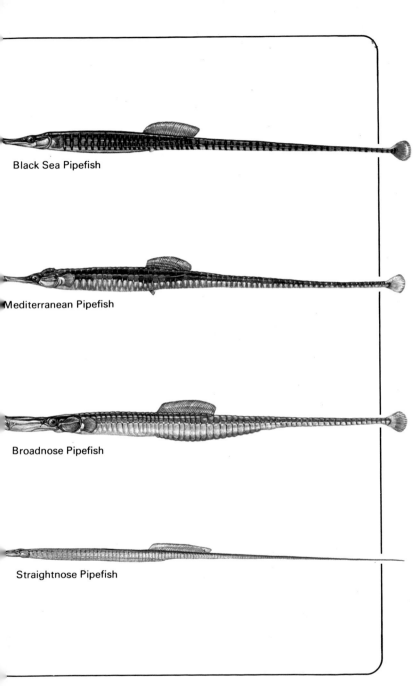

Black Sea Pipefish

Mediterranean Pipefish

Broadnose Pipefish

Straightnose Pipefish

Family CYPRINODONTIDAE

The Cyprinodontidae, or toothcarps, are found mainly in fresh water, but sometimes in brackish and occasionally marine situations. They occur only in warm water and are found in southern Europe, Africa, south-east Asia, South America and south-eastern U.S.A. They are all small fishes, often with a characteristically upturned mouth and well-developed, but small, teeth. Many species are very popular as aquarium fishes.

There are altogether some 45 genera with about 300 species, but only 3 of these occur in Europe.

Key to European Cyprinodontidae

1 Teeth unicuspid and conical; 12—14 rays in anal fin; 29—32 scales on lateral line
Valencia hispanica

Teeth tricuspid; 9—12 rays in anal fin; 25—30 scales on lateral line   **2**

2 9—10 rays in dorsal fin; male caudal fin bears several vertical bands; female sides mottled green-brown   *Aphanius iberus*

10—13 rays in dorsal fin; male caudal fin bears 1 vertical band; female sides grey with faint darker vertical bands   *Aphanius fasciatus*

Mediterranean Toothcarp
Aphanius fasciatus

Size 4—5cm; maximum 6cm. **Distinctive features** small fish with superior mouth; dorsal fin, with 10—13 rays, positioned well back and almost immediately above anal fin. **Distribution** found along the coastal regions of much of the northern Mediterranean area, occurring in a variety of fresh and brackish waters including small weedy ponds and ditches. **Reproduction** April—August, among vegetation. The eggs hatch in 10—15 days and the young mature within one year. **Food** invertebrates, especially crustaceans and insect larvae. **Value** of no commercial or sporting significance, although sometimes kept in aquaria.

Iberian Toothcarp *Aphanius iberus*

Size 3—4cm; maximum 5cm. **Distinctive features** small fish with superior mouth; dorsal fin, with 9—10 rays, placed well back and almost immediately above anal fin. **Distribution** found only in the coastal areas of south-eastern Spain in a variety of both fresh and brackish waters including small ditches and pools. **Reproduction** April—August, spawning among vegetation in shallow water. The eggs hatch in 10—15 days and the young mature within one year. About 200 eggs per female. **Food** invertebrates, mainly crustaceans and insect larvae. **Value** of no commercial or sporting value, although sometimes kept in aquaria.

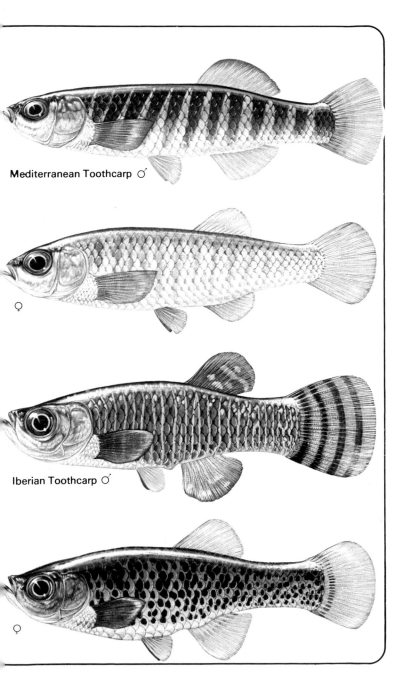

Mediterranean Toothcarp ♂

♀

Iberian Toothcarp ♂

♀

Valencia Toothcarp *Valencia hispanica*

Size 5—7cm; maximum 8cm. **Distinctive features** mouth terminal; dorsal fin anterior to anal fin, the latter with 12—14 rays. **Distribution** found only in coastal areas of south-east Spain, occurring in a great variety of waters (including small pools and ditches). Inhabits both fresh and brackish waters. **Reproduction** April—July, spawning among weed in shallow water. The eggs hatch in 12—15 days and the young mature after less than one year. About 200—250 eggs per female. **Food** invertebrates, especially crustaceans and insect larvae. **Value** of no real commercial or sporting value, although sometimes kept in aquaria.

Family POECILIIDAE

The Poeciliidae is a family of livebearing fishes found mainly in the warm temperate and tropical areas of North, Central and South America where more than 25 genera are known to occur. All are viviparous and in the males the anal fin is produced, its 3rd, 4th and 5th rays modified to form a copulatory organ.

Although very commonly kept in tropical aquaria in Europe, none are native here and only 1 species has been successfully introduced to the wild.

Mosquito Fish *Gambusia affinis*

Size 3—5cm; maximum 6cm. **Distinctive features** mouth superior; dorsal fin placed well back, above or posterior to anal fin; male with anal fin modified to form penis. **Distribution** native to south-eastern areas of North America, this species has been introduced to several parts of Europe in an attempt to control mosquitoes. It is now widely established in southern Europe and is found in a variety of fresh and brackish waters including small weedy ditches and pools. **Reproduction** mainly April—August. This is a livebearing species in which the females are fertilized internally by the males and give birth to some 50 young about 30 days afterwards. Several broods may be produced each year and the young mature within one year. **Food** invertebrates, especially crustaceans and insect larvae. **Value** of importance in mosquito control, especially in malarial areas. Commonly kept as an aquarium fish.

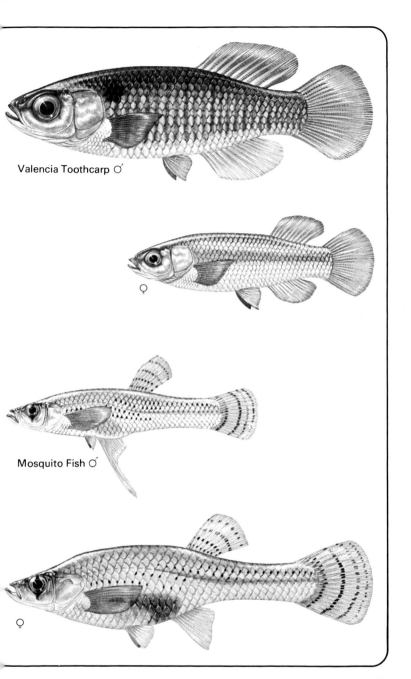

Valencia Toothcarp ♂

♀

Mosquito Fish ♂

♀

197

Family MUGILIDAE

The Mugilidae, or mullets, are common fishes in most oceans of the world, particularly in shallow inshore waters. Many species enter brackish and fresh water, but usually only estuaries, lagoons and the lower reaches of rivers, and for short periods. There are several genera with a total of about 100 species found in tropical and temperate waters. Only 1 genus occurs in Europe.

The mullets are elongate but sturdy fishes, whose bodies are only slightly compressed laterally. The mouth is terminal and large, but teeth are either very small or absent. In some species adipose eyelids are well developed. The function of these is believed to be that of protection and streamlining (see fig 37). The body is covered by large, usually cycloid scales which extend on to the head. There is no lateral line. The gill rakers are long and slender. There are two, well-separated dorsal fins, the anterior fin being short and supported by 1–5 strong spines. The second dorsal fin is longer, and supported by softer branched rays. The pectoral fins are set rather high and immediately behind the gill covers.

Mullets are fast-swimming shoaling fishes which often come into shallow waters in large numbers to feed. Much of their food consists of filamentous algae, but invertebrates are also eaten in some numbers. The gut is remarkably elongate, with a powerful muscular gizzard situated anteriorly, which crushes and breaks up food which is subsequently digested posteriorly in the intestine.

Spawning takes place in the sea, usually during spring in inshore waters. Relatively little is known about their breeding biology, however. Mullet fry commonly abound along some shores and enter streams in these areas. The adults run into larger rivers from time to time.

Although a widespread family, the importance of mullets to man can vary greatly from place to place. They are angled for along some coasts, usually by casting lines from the shore, but sometimes from boats. Commercial fishermen mostly use traps and seine nets, and catches in some areas are large — up to 20 million kg (19,683 tons) per annum in the Mediterranean area. In southern Russia the roe as well as the flesh of the fish is important commercially.

Six species occur around European shores and enter fresh waters from time to time.

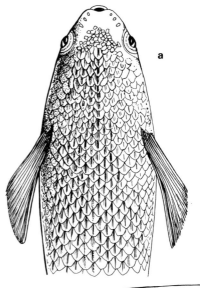

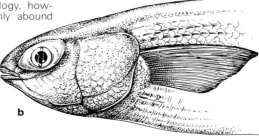

Fig. 37 Characteristic features of Mugilidae: a = dorsal view of sharp nose mullet showing sensory canals; b = side view of striped mullet showing adipose eyelid

Key to European Mugilidae

1 Preorbital bone posteriorly not reaching the level of the corner of the mouth; maxillary entirely concealed beneath preorbital bone; adipose eyelid well developed, covering eye to the pupil *Mugil cephalus*

Preorbital bone posteriorly reaching beyond level of the corner of the mouth; maxillary projecting from under preorbital bone at corner of mouth; adipose eyelid weakly developed, never reaching the pupil **2**

2 Upper lip very thick: its depth not less than $\frac{1}{10}$th of head length and more than $\frac{1}{2}$ of eye diameter; branches of the lower jaw not covered with scales **3**

Upper lip less thick: its depth less than $\frac{1}{10}$th of head length and not more than $\frac{1}{2}$ of eye diameter. Branches of the lower jaw scaled **4**

3 Upper lip smooth, its thickness about equal to the diameter of the eye
Mugil labeo

Upper lip with two rows of small warts, its thickness less than the diameter of eye *Mugil labrosus*

4 Some dorsal scales with several (2–5) canals; upper side of head scaled to the anterior nostrils; scales on the snout terminating in numerous rows of small scales; no elongate lobule above the base of the pectoral fin; several golden spots on gill covers *Mugil saliens*

Dorsal scales with single canals **5**

5 Upper side of head scaled to the nostrils or even anteriorly; posterior end of preorbital rounded or truncated vertically (but not obliquely); elongate lobule above base of pectoral fin *Mugil capito*

Scales on upper side of head not reaching anterior of nostrils, and terminating in a single series of small scales; posterior end of preorbital obliquely truncated; no elongate lobule above base of pectoral fin; 1 golden spot behind each gill cover, and 1 behind each eye *Mugil auratus*

Striped Mullet *Mugil cephalus*

Size 30–60 cm; maximum 70 cm; maximum weight about 6 kg. **Distinctive features** body covered with large cycloid scales extending on to head; 2 dorsal fins, the first with only 4 spiny rays; adipose eyelid well developed, covering eye to pupil. **Distribution** found widely all round Atlantic coastal areas of southern Europe (including the Mediterranean and Black Seas) and North America. It has been introduced to the Caspian Sea. Enters fresh waters via large estuaries and coastal lakes. **Reproduction** June–August, spawning in the sea. The young mature after 6–8 years. 5,000,000–7,200,000 eggs per female. **Food** mainly filamentous algae and other plant material, but also various invertebrates. **Value** of considerable commercial value; large catches are made by nets and traps in several countries. Angled for in estuarine waters in some places.

Golden Mullet *Mugil auratus*

Size 20–35 cm; maximum 50 cm. **Distinctive features** body covered with large cycloid scales which extend on to head; 2 dorsal fins, the first with only 4 spiny rays; no elongate lobule above base of pectoral fin; golden spot on gill cover and behind each eye. **Distribution** found all round the Atlantic coastal areas of southern Europe, including the Mediterranean and Black Seas. It has been successfully introduced to the Caspian Sea. Enters the lower reaches of a number of rivers (e.g. Dnieper). **Reproduction** August–September, spawning in the sea. The young mature after 3–5 years. 1,200,000–2,100,000 eggs per female. **Food** mainly filamentous algae and other bottom plant material, but also invertebrates (e.g. molluscs) at times. **Value** of considerable commercial value in net and trap fisheries, especially in the Mediterranean and Black Seas. Of little sporting significance.

Thinlipped Mullet *Mugil capito*

Size 25–40 cm; maximum 50 cm; British rod record 2.469 kg. **Distinctive features** body covered with large cycloid scales which extend on to head; 2 dorsal fins, the first with only 4 spiny rays; no golden spots on gill covers. **Distribution** found round all parts of the European coast (including the Mediterranean and Black Seas) except the extreme north. Enters the lower reaches of large rivers and some coastal lakes and lagoons. **Reproduction** August–September, spawning in the sea. The young mature after 3–5 years. **Food** mostly filamentous algae and associated invertebrates (e.g. molluscs). **Value** of considerable commercial and some sporting value in various parts of its range.

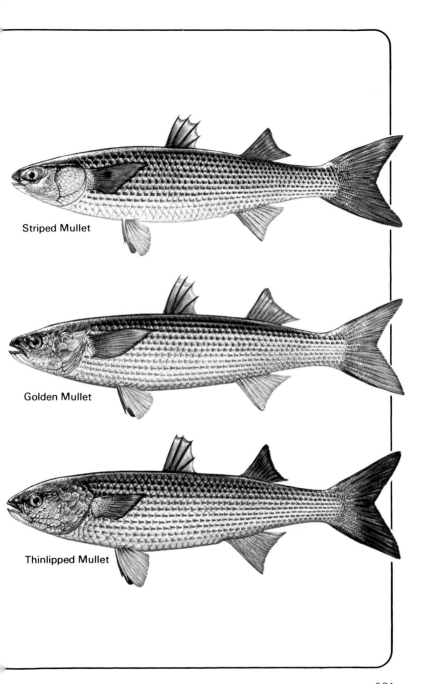

Striped Mullet

Golden Mullet

Thinlipped Mullet

201

Grey Mullet *Mugil labeo*

Size 15–20cm; maximum 25cm. **Distinctive features** body with large cycloid scales which extend on to head; 2 dorsal fins, the first with only 4 spiny rays; upper lip smooth and equal in thickness to the eye diameter. **Distribution** found in coastal areas of Europe from France round to the northern Mediterranean. Occurs in fresh water in the lower reaches of large rivers. **Reproduction** July–September, spawning in the sea. **Food** fine plant material and benthic invertebrates, especially molluscs and crustaceans. **Value** of considerable commercial value in coastal fisheries in France. Of little sporting significance.

Thicklipped Mullet *Mugil labrosus*

Size 30–50cm; maximum 90cm; British rod record 4.564kg. **Distinctive features** body covered with large cycloid scales which extend on to head; 2 dorsal fins, the first with only 4 spiny rays; upper lip very thick and with 2 rows of small warts. **Distribution** found in Atlantic coastal areas south of Norway and in the Mediterranean and Black Seas, occurring in fresh water in the lower reaches of some rivers. **Reproduction** June–August, in the sea. The young mature after 2–4 years. **Food** filamentous algae and other bottom plants, together with associated invertebrates. **Value** of considerable commercial value (along with other mullets) in net and trap fisheries. Considered to be a sport species in some areas.

Sharpnose Mullet *Mugil saliens*

Size 20–30cm; maximum 40cm. **Distinctive features** body covered with large cycloid scales which extend on to head; 2 dorsal fins, the first with only 4 spiny rays; several golden spots on gill covers. **Distribution** Atlantic coast of southern Europe and North Africa, Mediterranean and Black Seas. Has been introduced to the Caspian Sea. Found in fresh water in the lower reaches of a number of rivers (e.g. Guadalquivir) and coastal lagoons. **Reproduction** May–June, in shallow seas. **Food** mainly benthic algae and other plant material including associated invertebrates (e.g. molluscs). **Value** of some commercial significance in net and trap fisheries in the Mediterranean and Black Seas.

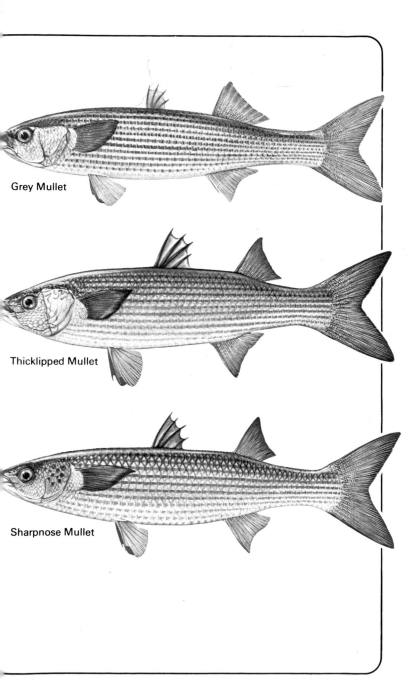

Grey Mullet

Thicklipped Mullet

Sharpnose Mullet

Family ATHERINIDAE

The Atherinidae, or sandsmelts, are found around the world except in high latitudes. They occur in the sea, brackish waters and various fresh waters. There are 50 genera and about 170 species. Most are small (less than 15 cm) although the largest species grow to more than 50 cm. All are silvery translucent fishes, usually with a lateral stripe. The lateral line is absent or small.

Only 3 species occur in Europe – they are mainly marine but may enter fresh water.

Key to European Atherinidae

1   Less than 55 lateral scales   *Atherina mochon*

     More than 55 lateral scales   **2**

2   Less than 12 branched rays in 2nd dorsal fin
              Atherina hepsetus

     More than 12 branched rays in 2nd dorsal fin
              Atherina presbyter

Sandsmelt *Atherina hepsetus*

Size 10–12 cm; maximum 15 cm. **Distinctive features** more than 55 lateral scales; less than 12 branched rays in dorsal fin. **Distribution** along the coasts of the Mediterranean, Black, and Caspian Seas, and in some estuaries. **Reproduction** June–August, spawning among vegetation to which the eggs adhere by filaments. **Food** invertebrates, mainly crustaceans. **Value** of no sporting value, and only minor commercial significance to local fisheries.

Mediterranean Sandsmelt
Atherina mochon

Size 8–12 cm; maximum 14 cm. **Distinctive features** less than 55 lateral scales. **Distribution** along the coasts of the Mediterranean, Black and Caspian Seas. Occurs in the lower reaches of some rivers (Dniester, Bug), and in lakes. **Reproduction** July–August, spawning among vegetation, to which the eggs attach by fine filaments. **Food** benthic invertebrates, especially crustaceans and (in fresh water) insect larvae. **Value** of no sporting, and only minor commercial, significance to fisheries in the Black and Caspian Seas.

Atlantic Sandsmelt *Atherina presbyter*

Size 10–13 cm; maximum 15 cm. **Distinctive features** more than 55 lateral scales; more than 15 branched rays in dorsal fin. **Distribution** along the coasts of Europe from Denmark to Spain and the western Mediterranean. Enters some estuaries. **Reproduction** April–July, in shallow water among seaweed to which the filamentous eggs attach. **Food** invertebrates, especially crustaceans. **Value** of no sporting, but minor commercial, importance in fisheries along the Mediterranean coast.

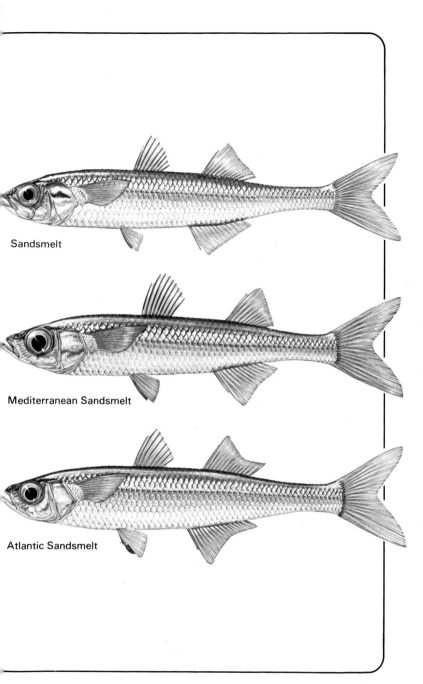

Sandsmelt

Mediterranean Sandsmelt

Atlantic Sandsmelt

Family SERRANIDAE

The Serranidae, or sea bass, as many of them are known, occur in most seas of the world – both temperate and tropical. Although many species are marine, a few occur in brackish or in fresh waters. They are characteristically well-built, deep-bodied fishes with spiny anterior dorsal fins and ctenoid scales.

Only 2 species enter fresh water in Europe.

Key to European Serranidae entering fresh water

1   Scales on interorbital space cycloid; teeth on head of vomer only; no spots on adults
Dicentrarchus labrax

Scales on interorbital space ctenoid; teeth over whole of vomer; spots present on adults, usually forming longitudinal series
Dicentrarchus punctatus

Sea Bass *Dicentrarchus labrax*

Size 40–70cm; maximum 100cm; maximum weight about 12kg; British rod record 8.220kg. **Distinctive features** 2 equal dorsal fins, which just meet each other; scales between eyes cycloid; large dark mark on gill cover, but none on body. **Distribution** found all round European coasts (including the Mediterranean and Black Seas) except in the extreme north. Enters the lower reaches of larger rivers. **Reproduction** March–June, in the sea. **Food** when young, invertebrates (especially molluscs and crustaceans) and some fishes; when adult mainly fishes (e.g. herring). **Value** of minor commercial importance in some countries. An important sporting species, offering exciting angling in some estuaries and coastal waters.

Spotted Bass *Dicentrarchus punctatus*

Size 25–40cm; maximum 100cm. **Distinctive features** 2 equal dorsal fins which just meet each other; scales between the eyes ctenoid; body with numerous dark spots, usually forming several longitudinal rows. **Distribution** found round the European coast from northern France to southern Italy. Absent from the eastern Mediterranean. Enters the lower reaches of rivers and their lagoons. **Reproduction** May–August, spawning in estuaries and along coasts. Where the water is fresh or brackish the eggs sink, whereas in sea water they float. **Food** invertebrates (especially molluscs and crustaceans) and fishes of various kinds. **Value** of some commercial and sporting significance in the western Mediterranean.

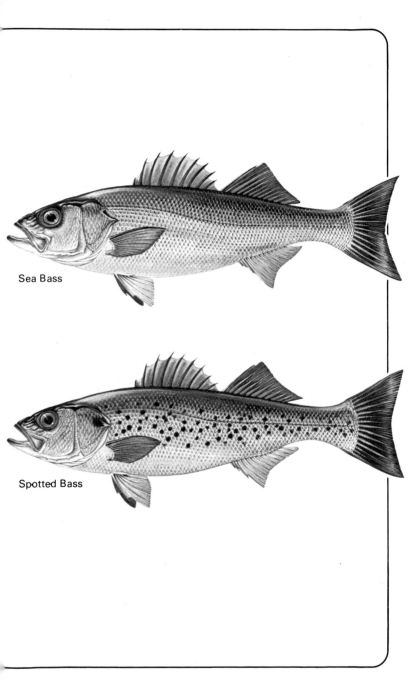

Sea Bass

Spotted Bass

Family PERCIDAE

The Percidae, or perches, as some members are commonly called, are restricted to the Northern Hemisphere and occur in various waters in Europe, northern Asia and North America. Successful introductions of at least one species (the perch) have been made in the Southern Hemisphere (Australia). There are 6 genera and about 16 species within the family — most of these being found in Europe. All but one are found in fresh water, but a few can live in estuaries and penetrate into brackish water. One species is largely marine.

Typical members of the family are elongate and rather compressed laterally. The mouth is usually large and carries several rows of teeth, many of them sharp, and some elongated to form canines. There are two dorsal fins, usually distinctly separated, with the anterior fin supported by 6–15 strong spines. The rays of the posterior dorsal fin are soft and branched. The body is covered by well-developed ctenoid scales which make the skin rough to the touch. In many species the scales extend on to the head which is also protected by spiny outgrowths from the opercular and other bones.

Several of the larger Percidae are of importance to sport fishermen, particularly the perch, the pikeperch

and other species of *Stizostedion*. In both Europe and North America large numbers of these fishes are angled for, using a variety of techniques including spinning and live baiting. These same larger species are important commercially in many countries, for the flesh is white, flaky and delicious when cooked properly. They are caught in traps, (perch in particular flock into these in enormous numbers in early summer) and nets. In 1934 the catch of perch alone from the Canadian side of the Great Lakes was over 25 million kg (24,603 tons). Lesser, but still valuable, catches are obtained from European waters.

All Percidae are carnivorous, and the larger species live mainly on other fishes. For this reason they are sometimes used to control numbers of prolific herbivorous fishes in fish farm ponds and elsewhere. In most species spawning takes place in pairs, trios or sometimes even larger numbers, when there are usually several males to one female. The eggs are laid over vegetation, or stones and gravel. In some species (for instance perch), eggs are laid in long strings; in others they are separate, and at spawning time are broadcast loose and fall down among the gravel and stones.

There are 12 species found in Europe. All of these are native.

Key to European Percidae

1 Eyes positioned dorsally on head *Romanichthys valsanicola*

Eyes positioned laterally or dorso-laterally on head **2**

2 Sensory organ cavities weakly developed on sides and top of head **3**

Large sensory organ cavities laterally and dorsally on head **9**

3 Maxillary bone free posteriorly, not covered by preorbital; body compressed laterally **4**

Maxillary bone covered posteriorly by preorbital; body fusiform **7**

4 Base of 1st dorsal fin longer than base of 2nd; ventral fins set close together, their interspace not exceeding $\frac{2}{3}$ of ventral fin width at base; teeth small, none of them canines *Perca fluviatilis*

Base of 1st dorsal fin equal to, or less than, base of 2nd; space between ventral fins at least $\frac{2}{3}$ as wide as ventral fin width at base **5**

5 Never more than 18 branched rays in dorsal fins; interorbital width much greater than eye diameter; canines present *Stizostedion marina*

More than 18 branched rays in dorsal fins; interorbital width shorter than, or equal to, eye diameter   **6**

6   Canines well developed; cheeks naked or only partly scaled; 80—97 scales along lateral line   *Stizostedion lucioperca*

     No canines in adults; cheeks completely scaled; 70—83 scales along lateral line   *Stizostedion volgensis*

7   1st dorsal fin with 13—15 spines; 2nd dorsal fin with 18—20 rays
                                           Aspro zingel

     1st dorsal fin with 8—9 spines; 2nd dorsal fin with 12—13 rays   **8**

8   Caudal peduncle as long as, or longer than, base of 2nd dorsal fin; 4—5 distinct dark bars across body   *Aspro streber*

     Caudal peduncle shorter than base of 2nd dorsal fin; 3 irregular dark bars across body   *Aspro asper*

9   Marked space between dorsal fins; maxillary free posteriorly
                                      Percarina demidoffi

     Dorsal fins united; maxillary covered by preorbital   **10**

10   Snout short, the same length as, or shorter than, eye diameter; dorsal fin with 11—16 spines; 35—40 scales along lateral line
                                      Gymnocephalus cernua

     Snout elongate, at least half as long again as eye diameter; dorsal fin with 17—19 spines; 50—62 scales along lateral line   **11**

11   Body length less than 5 times greatest depth; round black spots present on sides of body   *Gymnocephalus acerina*

     Body length more than 5 times greatest depth; 3 or 4 black transverse bands on sides of body   *Gymnocephalus schraetzer*

Fig. 38 Ctenoid scale from a perch, showing annual rings

Perch *Perca fluviatilis*

Size 20—35 cm; maximum 51 cm; maximum weight about 4.75 kg; British rod record 2.154 kg. **Distinctive features** separate dorsal fins, the first very spiny. **Distribution** in slow rivers and lakes over most of northern Europe, Asia and eastern North America. **Reproduction** April—June, in shallow water among vegetation. Eggs laid in ribbons about 1 m long hatch in 15—20 days. Young mature in 2—3 years and live to 10 years. 12,000—199,000 eggs per female. **Food** invertebrates (especially crustaceans and insect larvae) when young, invertebrates and fishes when older. **Value** caught commercially in some countries by traps, nets and baited lines. Also important as a sport species.

Pikeperch *Stizostedion lucioperca*

Size 30—70 cm; maximum 130 cm; maximum weight about 18 kg; British rod record 6.945 kg. **Distinctive features** dorsal fins almost touching; large canine teeth. **Distribution** slow rivers and rich lakes in Europe from the Netherlands to the Caspian Sea. Introduced to other areas (e.g. England). **Reproduction** April—June, among gravel and stones. The eggs are guarded by both parents and hatch in 5—10 days. Young mature in 3—5 years. 180,000—1,185,000 eggs per female. **Food** invertebrates at first, but almost entirely fishes thereafter. **Value** taken commercially in traps and nets. A prized sport species.

Sea Pikeperch *Stizostedion marina*

Size 30—50 cm; maximum 62 cm; specimens 54 cm long weigh about 1.7 kg. **Distinctive features** dorsal fins almost touching; large canine teeth; 78—84 lateral scales. **Distribution** Black and Caspian Seas and the lower reaches of rivers there (e.g. Bug and Dnieper). **Reproduction** April—May, over stones in fresh and salt water. Young mature after 3—5 years and live to 10 years. 13,000—126,000 eggs per female. **Food** invertebrates initially, but almost entirely fishes afterwards. **Value** of commercial significance in trap and net fisheries. Rarely angled for.

Volga Pikeperch *Stizostedion volgensis*

Size 25—40 cm; maximum 45 cm; mean weight about 1.3 kg. **Distinctive features** dorsal fins almost touching; no canine teeth in adults; 70—83 lateral scales. **Distribution** in the basins of rivers entering the Black and Caspian Seas (e.g. Volga and Danube). Occurs in slow rivers and lakes. **Reproduction** April—May, among stones and vegetation. Young mature after 3—4 years. **Food** large invertebrates, especially crustaceans, and fishes of various kinds. **Value** caught commercially in nets and traps. Of little angling importance.

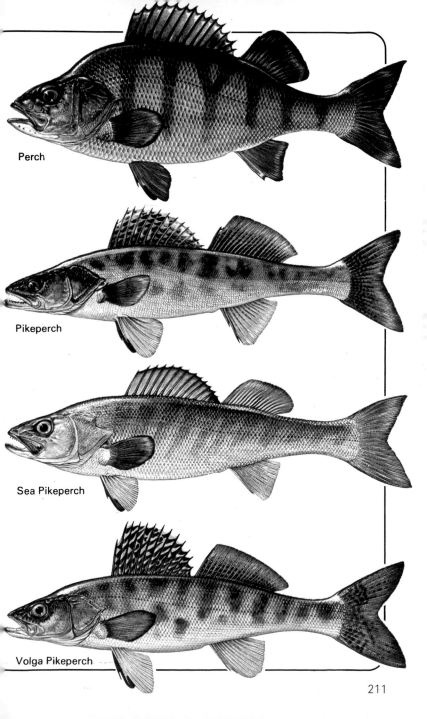

Perch

Pikeperch

Sea Pikeperch

Volga Pikeperch

211

Don Ruffe *Gymnocephalus acerina*

Size 12–18 cm; maximum 21 cm. **Distinctive features** two dorsal fins partially joined to one another, the anterior with 17–19 spines; 50–55 lateral scales. **Distribution** found only in slow-flowing waters and lakes in river basins entering the north of the Black Sea (e.g. Dniester, Dnieper, Don). **Reproduction** April–May, spawning among stones and vegetation in shallow water. **Food** invertebrates, especially crustaceans and insects; sometimes small fishes. **Value** of little commercial or sporting value.

Ruffe *Gymnocephalus cernua*

Size 10–15 cm; maximum 50 cm; British rod record 113 g. **Distinctive features** two dorsal fins partially joined to one another, the anterior with 11–16 spines; 35–40 lateral scales. **Distribution** found in slow-flowing rivers and lakes throughout much of Europe, except certain areas in the north and south. **Reproduction** April–May, spawning among stones and vegetation in shallow water. The eggs hatch in 8–12 days and the young mature after 2–3 years. 4,000–104,000 eggs per female. **Food** bottom-dwelling invertebrates (especially molluscs, crustaceans and insect larvae) and sometimes small fishes. **Value** of minor commercial and sporting value, although it is caught in a few areas.

Striped Ruffe
Gymnocephalus schraetzer

Size 15–20 cm; maximum 24 cm. **Distinctive features** two dorsal fins partially joined to one another, the anterior with 17–19 spines; 55–62 lateral scales. **Distribution** found only in the Danube basin, and occasionally in its estuary to the Black Sea. **Reproduction** April–May, spawning in shallow water among stones and vegetation. **Food** invertebrates (mainly molluscs, crustaceans and insects) but some fishes when larger. **Value** of little commercial or sporting value.

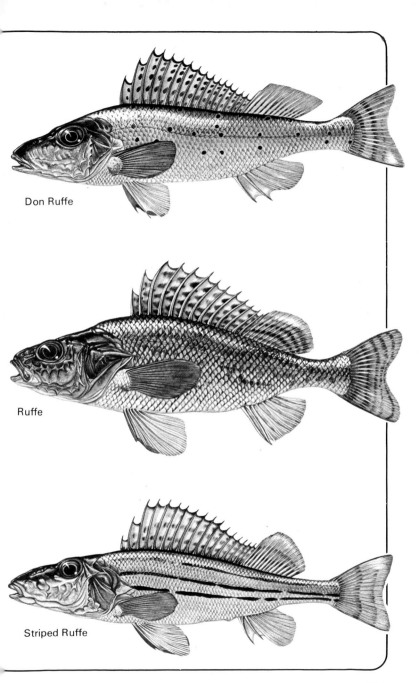

Don Ruffe

Ruffe

Striped Ruffe

Asper *Aspro asper*

Size 15–20cm; maximum 22cm. **Distinctive features** 2 well-separated dorsal fins, the anterior with 8–9 spines, the posterior with 12–13 rays; caudal peduncle shorter than base of posterior dorsal fin. **Distribution** found only in the River Rhône and its tributaries. **Reproduction** March–April, spawning among stones and vegetation in shallow water. **Food** mainly bottom-dwelling invertebrates (crustaceans and insects especially), but also fish eggs and fry. **Value** of no commercial or sporting value.

Streber *Aspro streber*

Size 12–15cm; maximum 22cm. **Distinctive features** 2 well-separated dorsal fins, the anterior with 8–9 spines, the posterior with 12–13 rays; caudal peduncle as long as, or longer than, base of posterior dorsal fin. **Distribution** found only in running water in the River Danube and its tributaries, and in the Vardar River which flows into the Aegean Sea. **Reproduction** March–April, among stones in fast-flowing water. **Food** invertebrates (mainly crustaceans and insect larvae) and some small fishes. **Value** of little commercial or sporting value.

Zingel *Aspro zingel*

Size 15–30cm; maximum 48cm. **Distinctive features** 2 well-separated dorsal fins, the anterior with 13–15 spines, the posterior with 18–20 rays; caudal peduncle shorter than base of posterior dorsal fin. **Distribution** only in running water in the basin of the River Danube. **Reproduction** March–May, in fast-flowing water among stones. About 5,000 eggs per female. **Food** benthic invertebrates (especially crustaceans and insect larvae) and small fishes. **Value** of no commercial or sporting value.

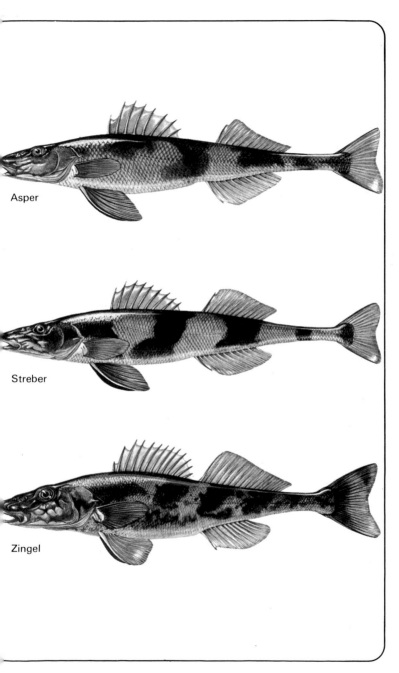

Asper

Streber

Zingel

Percarina *Percarina demidoffi*

Size 6—9cm; maximum 10cm. **Distinctive features** 2 well-separated dorsal fins, the anterior with 9—11 spines; a row of black spots along lateral line. **Distribution** found only in the northern area of the Black Sea and in the Sea of Azov, and in the lower reaches entering these areas. **Reproduction** June—July, spawning in shallow water in both fresh and sea water over sand and silt. The eggs hatch in 2 days and the young mature after 1 year. The adults rarely live longer than 3—4 years. A maximum of about 3,000 eggs per female. **Food** invertebrates, especially crustaceans and small fishes. **Value** of some commercial importance in local net fisheries.

Asprete *Romanichthys valsanicola*

Size 8—12cm; maximum 13cm. **Distinctive features** 2 well-separated dorsal fins, the posterior larger than the anterior; eyes positioned dorsally on head. **Distribution** found only in fast-flowing water in the upper reaches of certain rivers (Arges, Vilsan and Riul) in the Danube basin in Rumania. **Reproduction** reproductive behaviour unknown. **Food** invertebrates (mainly insect larvae) and small fishes. **Value** of no commercial or sporting value.

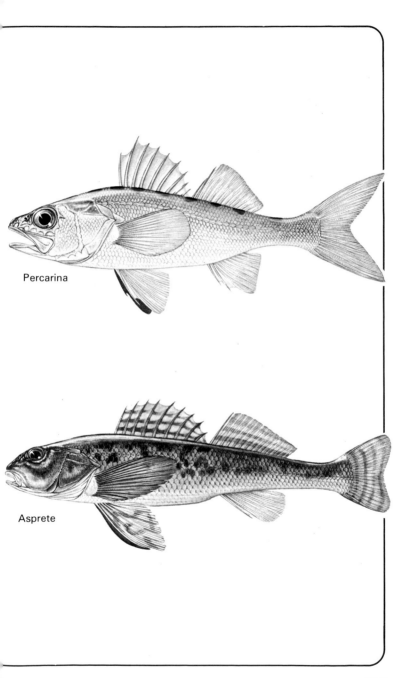

Percarina

Asprete

Family CENTRARCHIDAE

The Centrarchidae, commonly known as sunfishes, are native originally to a variety of waters, particularly rich well-weeded lakes and slow-flowing rivers in eastern North America. The present distribution of the family, however, is much wider than this, as various species have been successfully introduced to other parts of the world, including western North America and Europe. The family is a small but important one, including 30 species in 10 genera.

Most sunfishes are small to medium-sized, laterally flattened fishes with a well-developed dorsal fin, the anterior half of which has very spiny rays. The spiny portion and the soft-rayed portion of the dorsal fin are separated to a varying extent, but are always closer together than in most of the perch family. The other fins are also well-developed, particularly the anal fin, which is usually very similar in size to the posterior part of the dorsal fin. The mouth and eyes are large, and bands of small teeth are found on various parts of the mouth including the tongue.

The members of this family include several highly coloured and very attractive species which exhibit a number of interesting features of behaviour. The smaller species are popular with aquarists and pond keepers, and the larger species with anglers. The smallmouth bass and largemouth bass in particular are major sporting species, and are an important element in the gigantic sport fishery and associated tourist industries in eastern Canada. The originally important commercial fishery for these fishes is now of very little value.

The breeding biology of most species of Centrarchidae is now well documented and many common features are found throughout the family. Ripe fishes usually spawn in late spring or early summer, when the males select territories and dig out nests. These are simply circular depressions which can vary in size from 10—200cm in diameter, usually on a sandy or gravelly bottom, but often near the protection of logs, rocks or patches of vegetation. Males may return to the same nest in subsequent years and usually at least to the same general area of previous nests. On completion of the nest each pair of fishes indulge in considerable courtship display which ends in the spawning act. Eggs are laid regularly over a period of hours until the female is spent. The eggs are adhesive, and usually attach themselves to clean stones and gravel near the centre of the nest. During incubation the male guards the nest, fanning the eggs continually during this time. After hatching, the larvae still have considerable yolk sacs, and lie on the bottom of the nest for several days, still protected and cleaned by the male. Eventually they start to leave the nest but are still guarded by the male for several days. After this the family breaks up and the young fend for themselves.

Six species are known to have become established in various waters in Europe.

Key to European Centrarchidae

1   6 anal spines arising in a scaled groove; body with 7—9 horizontal rows of black spots below lateral line; base of anal fin about $1\frac{2}{3}$ times base of dorsal fin   *Ambloplites rupestris*

     3 anal spines, not arising in a groove; no horizontal rows of spots below lateral line; base of anal fin about $\frac{1}{3}-\frac{1}{2}$ times base of dorsal fin   **2**

2   More than 55 scales along lateral line; body length more than 3 times greatest depth   **3**

     Less than 50 scales along lateral line; body length less than 3 times greatest depth   **4**

3   Upper jaw extending back beyond eye; 60—68 scales along lateral line; pelvic fins not joined by membrane   *Micropterus salmoides*

Upper jaw extending back only to middle of eye; 68—78 scales along lateral line; pelvic fins joined by membrane   *Micropterus dolomieu*

4   Opercular flap all black, with no colour round edge   *Lepomis auritus*

Opercular flap with black centre, and yellow, orange or red spots or bands round margin   **5**

5   Pectoral fins about ⅓ of body length, pointed at leading edge; gill rakers knobbed; opercular flap short with a prominent red spot posteriorly
Lepomis gibbosus

Pectoral fins only about ¼ of body length, rounded at leading edge; gill rakers not knobbed; opercular flap with no prominent red spot posteriorly   *Lepomis cyanellus*

Fig. 39 Typical centrarchid behaviour; a male fish guards the nest and eggs

Largemouth Bass
Micropterus salmoides

Size 20—40 cm; maximum weight 83 cm; maximum weight 6.4 kg. **Distinctive features** upper jaw extending behind eye; 60—68 lateral scales. **Distribution** native to southern Canada and U.S.A., it has been introduced to Europe and is established in a number of countries. **Reproduction** March—July, spawning in pits dug out in sand and gravel. Eggs are guarded by the male and take 2—5 days to hatch. Young mature after 3—4 years and live up to 15 years. 751—11,457 eggs per female. **Food** invertebrates (especially crustaceans and insect larvae) when young, large invertebrates and fishes when adult. **Value** of little value in Europe, but a prized sport fish in North America where it is also caught commercially.

Smallmouth Bass
Micropterus dolomieu

Size 20—40 cm; maximum 58 cm; maximum weight 4.41 kg. **Distinctive features** upper jaw extending back to middle of eye; 68—78 lateral scales. **Distribution** native to eastern central North America, it has been introduced to Europe where it is now established (e.g. in France). **Reproduction** May—July, spawning in a nest excavated by the male among sand or gravel. The male guards eggs and fry which hatch after 4—10 days. The young mature in 3—4 years and may live to 15 years. 5,000—14,000 eggs per female. **Food** invertebrates (mainly crustaceans and insect larvae) when young, large invertebrates and fishes when older. **Value** of little significance in Europe, but formerly important commercially in North America and still a prized sport species there.

Rock Bass *Ambloplites rupestris*

Size 15—20 cm; maximum 34 cm; maximum weight 1.7 kg. **Distinctive features** anal fin with 6 spines arising in a scaled groove; 7—9 horizontal rows of black spots below lateral line. **Distribution** native to eastern central North America, it has been introduced to Europe and has become established in at least one country (England). **Reproduction** May—July, spawning in a nest excavated by the male among sand and gravel. The male guards the eggs (which hatch in 3—4 days) and early fry. Young fishes mature in 2—3 years and live to 10 years. 3,000—11,000 eggs per female. **Food** invertebrates (especially crustaceans and insect larvae) and small fishes. **Value** of no significance in Europe but a valuable commercial and sporting fish in North America.

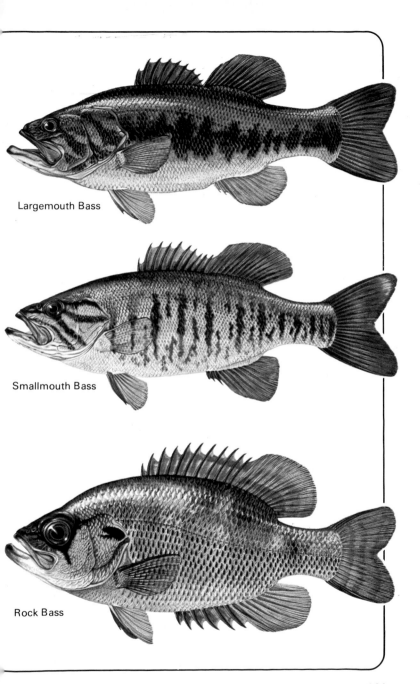

Largemouth Bass

Smallmouth Bass

Rock Bass

221

Pumpkinseed *Lepomis gibbosus*

Size 10—15 cm; maximum 22 cm; maximum weight about 300 g. **Distinctive features** single dorsal fin divided into two parts; gill rakers knobbed; opercular flap short with a prominent red spot posteriorly. **Distribution** native to fresh waters in eastern North America, this species has been introduced and become established in many parts of Europe. **Reproduction** May—July, spawning in shallow depressions among sand in weed beds. The eggs (which hatch in 3—5 days) and the fry are guarded by the male. The young mature after 2—3 years and may live for 9 years. 600—5,000 eggs per female. **Food** mainly invertebrates (especially crustaceans and insect larvae) but small fishes are eaten by adults. **Value** of little significance in Europe, but caught in some numbers in North America both commercially and as a sport fish.

Redbreast Sunfish *Lepomis auritus*

Size 12—15 cm; maximum 24 cm. **Distinctive features** single dorsal fin divided into two parts; opercular flap all black with no colour round edge. **Distribution** native to fresh waters in eastern North America, this species has been introduced and is established in Europe. **Reproduction** June—July, spawning in nest excavated by the male which also guards the eggs and fry. **Food** mainly invertebrates (especially insect larvae), but sometimes small fishes. **Value** of no importance in Europe and of only minor local sporting significance in North America.

Green Sunfish *Lepomis cyanellus*

Size 10—12 cm; maximum 30 cm — this fish weighed about 1 kg. **Distinctive features** single dorsal fin divided into two parts; gill rakers not knobbed; colour brown to olive with an emerald sheen; no red spot on opercular flap. **Distribution** native to fresh waters in eastern central North America, this species has been introduced to European waters and is established in West Germany. **Reproduction** May—August, spawning in a shallow nest excavated by the male in shallow water in areas sheltered by rocks and vegetation. The male guards and fans the eggs and protects the young for a short time. The eggs hatch in 3—5 days and the young mature after 2 years. They may live up to 9 years. **Food** mainly invertebrates (molluscs and insect larvae) but occasionally small fishes. **Value** of no commercial or sporting significance in Europe, but an important game species in some parts of the U.S.A.

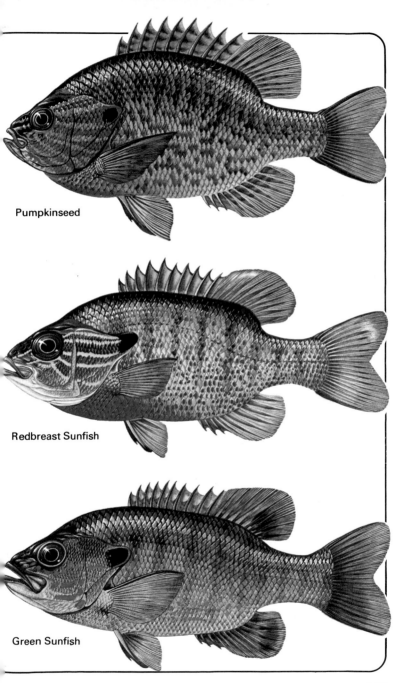

Pumpkinseed

Redbreast Sunfish

Green Sunfish

223

Family CICHLIDAE

The Cichlidae is a large family of fishes, many of them extremely colourful, and native mainly to tropical Africa, South America and Central America. They occur in a variety of habitats from large over-grown rivers to enormous deep lakes. They have only 1 pair of nostrils and the lateral line is usually in two parts. Breeding normally involves elaborate sexual display, nest building and parental care. Although common in tropical aquaria, only 1 species has been introduced successfully to natural waters in Europe.

Chanchito *Cichlasoma facetum*

Size 10–15cm; maximum 30cm. **Distinctive features** 1 pair of nostrils; large dorsal fin with erect spiny anterior rays; colour variable – brassy-yellow to greenish or even black, usually several dark transverse bands. **Distribution** native to South America, and known to tolerate much lower temperatures than most of the family, it has apparently been successfully introduced to southern Portugal. **Reproduction** June–August, spawning in a nest previously prepared by both male and female. Eggs hatch in 2–4 days and are protected by the parents for some time. **Food** invertebrates, especially molluscs and insect larvae. **Value** of no sporting or real commercial value other than its significance as an aquarium fish.

Family BLENNIIDAE

The Blenniidae, or blennies, are mainly small marine fishes, bottom living in habit. They are usually elongate with long dorsal fins stretching from head to tail. The bodies are characteristically marked with coloured blotches or stripes. Some have elaborate tentacles projecting from above the eye. A number of species occur round European coasts, but only 1 is found in fresh water.

Freshwater Blenny *Blennius fluviatilis*

Size 8–12cm; maximum 15cm. **Distinctive features** an enormous dorsal fin running from head to tail; small growth just above each eye; pelvic fins anterior to pectoral fins. **Distribution** found in fresh water in streams and lakes of basins associated with the western and north-eastern Mediterranean. **Reproduction** April–June, spawning in nests under stones. Eggs are guarded by the male. **Food** invertebrates (especially crustaceans and insects) and small fishes. **Value** of no commercial and little angling importance, except as bait.

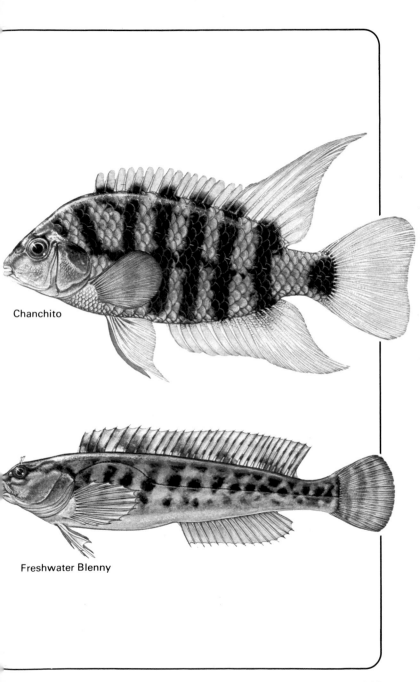

Chanchito

Freshwater Blenny

Family GOBIIDAE

The Gobiidae, commonly called gobies, is a very successful family of small fishes found in many parts of the world, both tropical and temperate. Most species are marine but many occur in brackish water and there is a considerable number of freshwater species. These occur in a variety of habitats, in both running and standing waters. Because of close relationships within genera, and the small size of many species, identification may often be difficult; it is further complicated by the fact that there are often considerable differences between the sexes.

The main characteristic of this family is the fact that the pelvic fins are united to form a single sucker-like fin. The body is normally rather elongate, although often broad and squat anteriorly. The head is large and the lips and cheeks well developed.

Sensory papillae and other protuberances are common on the head and often arranged in characteristic patterns. The lateral line is either incomplete or absent. There are two well-developed dorsal fins, but neither has strong spiny rays. The anal fin is usually similar in size to the second dorsal fin.

Gobies are often very abundant fishes, usually benthic in habit and common in shallow coastal areas. A number of species are pelagic. At spawning time, the males normally become much darker (some turn pure black), their fins elongate and the shape of the head alters. They build simple nests — usually in the shelter of shells, stones or weed, and guard the adhesive eggs laid in patches until the larvae emerge and swim away.

Altogether in Europe 22 species occur in fresh water or enter it from time to time during their life history.

Key to European Gobiidae found in fresh water

1 Body generally without scales; although there may be platelets or spikes; no sensory canals or pores on head   **2**

Body covered with scales; sensory canals and pores present on head   **6**

2 Body entirely naked; anterior nostrils not produced into tubules
Caspiosoma caspium

Body normally covered with platelets or spikes; anterior nostrils produced into tubules   **3**

3 6 rays in 1st dorsal fin, 12—13 rays in 2nd dorsal fin, 9—11 rays in anal fin; sparse spiny scales on side of body   *Benthophilus brauneri*

1—4 rays in 1st dorsal fin, 6—11 rays in 2nd dorsal fin, 6—10 rays in anal fin; no scales on side of body   **4**

4 Body covered in uniform bony granules, but without rows of larger granules   *Benthophilus granulosus*

3 rows of large spines on each side of body, usually with small bony granules between; abdomen and pectoral regions naked   **5**

5 Body densely covered with bony granules; 22—27 tubercles in the dorsal series; colour ash-grey, with no dark bands across back
Benthophilus macrocephalus

Body covered mainly with tubercles; very few bony granules present; 3 brownish bands across back   *Benthophilus stellatus*

6 2nd dorsal fin with less than 12 branched rays   **7**

2nd dorsal fin with more than 12 branched rays   **15**

7 Anterior nostrils produced into barbel-shaped tubercles overhanging mouth; 36—48 lateral scales   *Proterorhinus marmoratus*

Anterior nostrils not produced into barbel-shaped tubules; 45—79 lateral scales **8**

8 Swim-bladder present *Gobius ophiocephalus*

No swim-bladder present in adults **9**

9 Parietal and occipital areas not scaled **10**

Parietal and, usually, occipital areas scaled **14**

10 Anal fin with 10—13 branched rays; 42—58 lateral scales
Gobius melanostomus

Anal fin with 11—17 branched rays; more than 55 lateral scales **11**

11 2nd dorsal fin becoming lower posteriorly *Gobius fluviatilis*

2nd dorsal fin never becoming lower posteriorly, being either higher at the ends or of equal height throughout **12**

12 Caudal peduncle about 1½ times as long as deep; lateral lobules on collar of ventral sucker obtuse *Gobius syrman*

Caudal peduncle as long as deep, or only slightly longer; lateral lobules on collar of ventral sucker pointed **13**

13 Minimum body depth more than 8 per cent of body length; thickness of caudal peduncle less than 66 per cent of its depth *Gobius cephalarges*

Minimum body depth less than 8 per cent of body length; thickness of caudal peduncle more than 66 per cent of its depth *Gobius kessleri*

14 65—84 lateral scales; 8 or more pits in suborbital series
Gobius batracocephalus

47—69 lateral scales; 6 or more pits in suborbital series
Gobius gymnotrachelus

15 More than 60 lateral scales *Relictogobius kryzanovskii*

Less than 60 lateral scales **16**

16 Anal fin with 7 branched rays; 35—40 scales along lateral line **17**

Anal fin with 8—11 branched rays **18**

17 35 lateral scales; 8 branched rays in 2nd dorsal fin *Padogobius panizzai*

40 lateral scales; 9 branched rays in 2nd dorsal fin *Padogobius nigricans*

18 30 lateral scales; 8—9 branched rays in anal fin *Hyrcanogobius bergi*

More than 30 lateral scales; 8—11 branched rays in anal fin **19**

19 Space between dorsal fins about equal to length of 1st dorsal fin
Pomatoschistus longicaudatus

Space between dorsal fins much less than length of 1st dorsal fin **20**

20 More than 40 lateral scales *Pomatoschistus microps*

Less than 40 lateral scales **21**

21 Longitudinal stripes on both dorsal fins *Pomatoschistus canestrini*

No longitudinal stripes on dorsal fins *Pomatoschistus caucasicus*

227

Bighead Goby *Gobius kessleri*

Size 15–20cm; maximum 22cm. **Distinctive features** 2 dorsal fins and united pelvic fins; More than 55 lateral scales; pointed lateral lobules on collar of ventral sucker. **Distribution** found in the Black and Caspian Seas and in the basins of their northern rivers. Occurs commonly in the sea, in brackish water, in fast-flowing water and in lakes. **Reproduction** April–May, spawning in a nest which is subsequently guarded by the male. **Food** invertebrates, especially crustaceans. **Value** of some commercial importance to net fishermen in the Black and Caspian Seas. Of no angling importance.

Ginger Goby *Gobius cephalarges*

Size 18–22cm; maximum 24cm. **Distinctive features** 2 dorsal fins and united pelvic fins; more than 55 lateral scales; pointed lateral lobules on collar of ventral sucker. **Distribution** found in shallow stony areas in the Black and Caspian Seas and in many rivers associated with them. Many of the freshwater populations are non-migratory and spend all their lives in clear stony mountain streams. **Reproduction** March–May in the sea. Little is known about its reproductive habits. **Food** invertebrates (mainly molluscs and crustaceans) and small fishes. **Value** of some commercial value to local sea fishing. Not angled for.

Syrman Goby *Gobius syrman*

Size 18–22cm; maximum 25cm. **Distinctive features** 2 dorsal fins and united pelvic fins; more than 55 lateral scales; lateral lobules on collar of ventral sucker obtuse. **Distribution** found in the northern areas of the Black Sea (including the Sea of Azov) and the Caspian Sea. Enters estuaries and the lower reaches of rivers in these areas (e.g. Bug, Don). **Reproduction** April–May, spawning in a nest which is subsequently guarded by the male. **Food** invertebrates, especially crustaceans. **Value** of some commercial importance to net fishermen in the Black and Caspian Seas. Of no angling value.

Racer Goby *Gobius gymnotrachelus*

Size 12–15cm; maximum 17cm. **Distinctive features** 2 dorsal fins and united pelvic fins; 47–69 lateral scales; 6 or more pits in suborbital series. **Distribution** found in several streams and a few lakes in river basins north of the Black Sea (e.g. Danube, Dniester, Bug). It also occurs in brackish water here and throughout the Caspian Sea. **Reproduction** April–May, spawning in a nest prepared and subsequently guarded by the male. **Food** various invertebrates, especially crustaceans. **Value** of minor value to commercial net fishermen in the Black Sea. Of no angling importance.

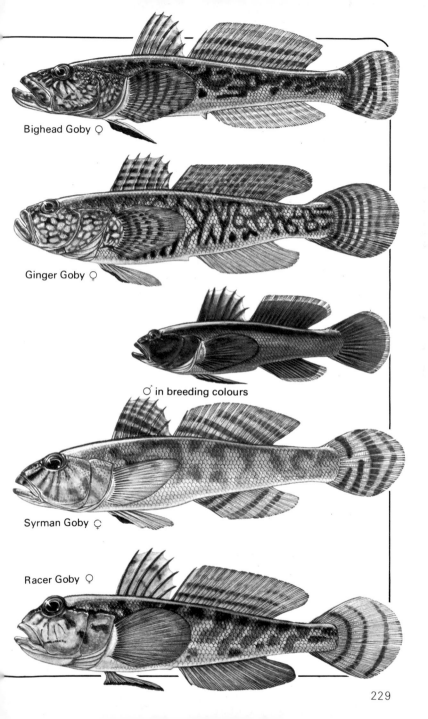

Bighead Goby ♀

Ginger Goby ♀

♂ in breeding colours

Syrman Goby ♀

Racer Goby ♀

229

Toad Goby *Gobius batracocephalus*

Size 25–30cm; maximum 35cm. **Distinctive features** 2 dorsal fins and united pelvic fins; 65–84 lateral scales; 8 or more pits in suborbital series. **Distribution** found along the northern coasts of the Black Sea, including the Sea of Azov. Occurs in brackish lagoons in estuarine areas but only occasionally enters rivers (e.g. Bug, Dnieper). **Reproduction** March–April, in coastal waters. The eggs are laid in a nest prepared and guarded by the male. **Food** invertebrates, particularly crustaceans, and some small fishes. **Value** a significant commercial species in net fisheries in the Black Sea.

Sand Goby *Gobius fluviatilis*

Size 15–18cm; maximum 20cm. **Distinctive features** 2 dorsal fins (the second fin becoming lower posteriorly), and united pelvic fins; 58–65 lateral scales. **Distribution** found in some brackish areas of the Black Sea (including the Sea of Azov) and the Caspian Sea, but most common in larger rivers in these areas (e.g. Danube, Dniester, Bug). **Reproduction** May–July, spawning in a nest prepared and guarded by the male. The young mature after 2 years. **Food** invertebrates, especially crustaceans. **Value** of considerable commercial value in both the Black and the Caspian Sea areas.

Round Goby *Gobius melanostomus*

Size 18–22cm; maximum 25cm. **Distinctive features** 2 dorsal fins and united pelvic fins; anal fin with 10–13 branched rays; 42–58 lateral scales. **Distribution** found in the Black and Caspian Seas, and in the lower reaches of large river systems associated with these (e.g. Dniester, Volga). **Reproduction** mainly May–July, but may extend well outside this in different areas. Spawns in both fresh and salt water. The young mature after 1 year. **Food** invertebrates, especially molluscs and crustaceans. **Value** an abundant species and of considerable commercial value in the Black Sea and the Caspian Sea where the catch may be marketed either fresh or canned.

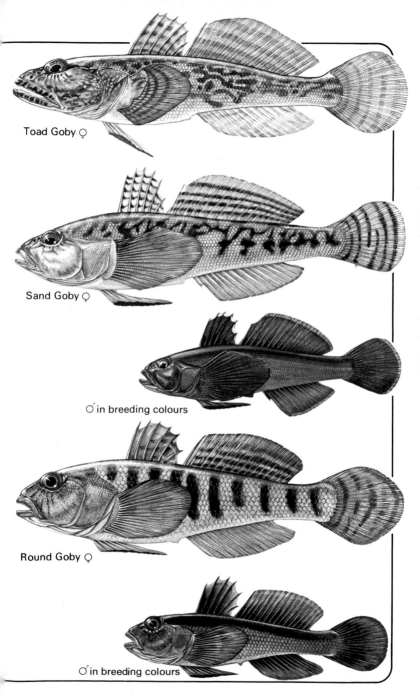

Toad Goby ♀

Sand Goby ♀

♂ in breeding colours

Round Goby ♀

♂ in breeding colours

231

Grass Goby *Gobius ophiocephalus*

Size 18—22 cm; maximum 25 cm. **Distinctive features** 2 dorsal fins and united pelvic fins; 45—79 lateral scales; swim-bladder present. **Distribution** found in coastal waters of the northern Mediterranean and the western and eastern Black Sea (including the Sea of Azov). Only occasionally occurs in fresh and brackish water. **Reproduction** March—April, spawning in nests built by the male from plant detritus, among thick vegetation. **Food** invertebrates, especially crustaceans. Sometimes small fishes. **Value** of some commercial value to net fisheries in the seas concerned.

Canestrini's Goby *Pomatoschistus canestrini*

Size 4—5 cm; maximum 6 cm. **Distinctive features** 2 dorsal fins and united pelvic fins; 34—38 lateral scales; longitudinal stripes on both dorsal fins. **Distribution** found only in fresh waters in Yugoslavia (River Jodro) and Italy. **Reproduction** little seems to be known about the reproductive habits of this species. **Food** invertebrates, especially crustaceans and insect larvae. **Value** of no commercial or sporting value.

Caucasian Goby *Pomatoschistus caucasicus*

Size 2—3 cm; maximum 4 cm. **Distinctive features** 2 dorsal fins and united pelvic fins; 30—36 lateral scales; no longitudinal stripes on dorsal fins. **Distribution** found all round the coasts of the Black Sea (including the Sea of Azov) and the Caspian Sea, and in estuaries and easily accessible fresh waters. **Reproduction** the spawning habits of this species are not known. **Food** invertebrates, especially crustaceans, and (in fresh water) insect larvae. **Value** of no commercial or sporting value.

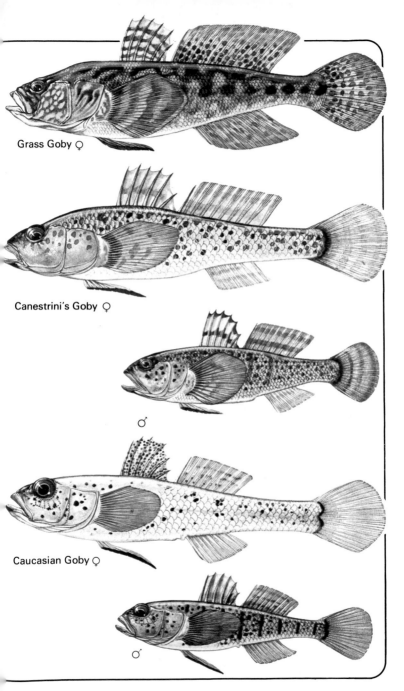

Grass Goby ♀

Canestrini's Goby ♀

♂

Caucasian Goby ♀

♂

233

Longtail Goby
Pomatoschistus longicaudatus

Size 3—4 cm; maximum 5 cm. **Distinctive features** 2 dorsal fins and united pelvic fins; 36—43 lateral scales; space between dorsal fins about equal to length of 1st dorsal fin. **Distribution** found in brackish waters in the Black Sea (including the Sea of Azov) and the Caspian Sea, and in lower reaches of several large rivers (e.g. Dnieper, Don). **Reproduction** nothing appears to be known about the reproductive habits of this species. **Food** invertebrates, especially crustaceans. **Value** of no commercial or sporting value.

Common Goby
Pomatoschistus microps

Size 3—6 cm; maximum 7 cm. **Distinctive features** 2 dorsal fins and united pelvic fins; 42—52 lateral scales; space between dorsal fins much less than length of 1st dorsal fin. **Distribution** found in shallow, often brackish water round the coasts of Europe from southern Norway to the Mediterranean and Black Seas. Common in estuaries. **Reproduction** April—September, spawning in a nest cleared by the male under a shell or stone. The male guards the eggs and fans water over them until they hatch. Fishes may spawn up to 8 times in a breeding season. The young mature after 1 year, and few fishes live beyond 2 years. **Food** mainly benthic invertebrates, especially crustaceans. **Value** of no commercial or sporting value.

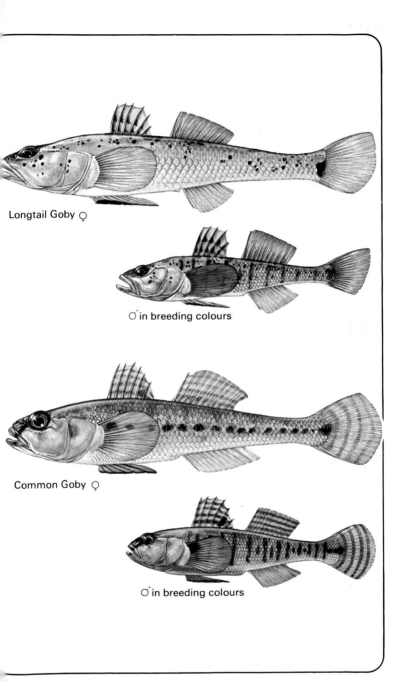

Longtail Goby ♀

♂ in breeding colours

Common Goby ♀

♂ in breeding colours

Berg's Goby *Hyrcanogobius bergi*

Size 2—3cm; maximum 3.5cm; this is one of the smallest European fishes. **Distinctive features** 2 dorsal fins and united pelvic fins; more than 30 lateral scales; 8—9 branched rays in anal fin. **Distribution** found only in the northern Caspian Sea, especially in or near the estuaries of the Volga, Emba and Ural Rivers. **Reproduction** July—September. Its reproductive habits are not well known. **Food** invertebrates, especially crustaceans. **Value** of no commercial or sporting value.

Relict Goby
Relictogobius kryzanovskii

Size 4—6cm; maximum 7cm. **Distinctive features** 2 dorsal fins (the second with more than 12 branched rays), and united pelvic fins; 63—72 lateral scales. **Distribution** found only in a salt lake on the coast of the Black Sea in the region of Novorossiisk. **Reproduction** little is known of the reproductive habits of this species. **Food** invertebrates, mainly crustaceans. **Value** of no commercial or sporting value.

Tubenose Goby
Proterhorinus marmoratus

Size 5—10cm; maximum 11cm. **Distinctive features** 2 dorsal fins (the second with less than 12 branched rays), and united pelvic fins; 36—48 lateral scales. **Distribution** found in shallow water round most of the coasts of the Black and Caspian Seas. Common in lagoons, some lakes and the lower reaches of many rivers flowing into these (e.g. Danube, Bug, Araks). **Reproduction** reproductive habits unknown. **Food** invertebrates, mainly crustaceans, and (in fresh water) insect larvae. **Value** of no commercial or sporting value.

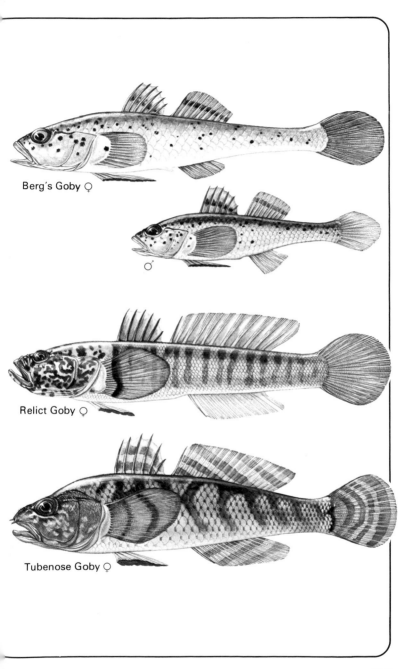

Berg's Goby ♀

♂

Relict Goby ♀

Tubenose Goby ♀

Panizza's Goby *Padogobius panizzai*

Size 3–5 cm; maximum 6 cm. **Distinctive features** 2 dorsal fins (the second with 8 branched rays), and united pelvic fins; about 35 lateral scales. **Distribution** found only in northern Italy in rivers near Venice (e.g. Po) and in Lake Garda and Lake Maggiore. **Reproduction** little is known of the reproductive biology of this species. **Food** invertebrates, particularly crustaceans and insect larvae. **Value** of no commercial or sporting value.

Italian Goby *Padogobius nigricans*

Size 4–5 cm; maximum 6 cm. **Distinctive features** 2 dorsal fins (the second with 9 branched rays), and united pelvic fins; about 40 lateral scales. **Distribution** found only in western Italy in clear running waters in the basins of the rivers Tiber and Arno. **Reproduction** April–July, spawning under stones in shallow running water. **Food** invertebrates, especially insect larvae. **Value** of no commercial or sporting value.

Caspian Goby *Caspiosoma caspium*

Size 3–4 cm; maximum 5 cm. **Distinctive features** 2 dorsal fins and united pelvic fins; body entirely naked; anterior nostrils produced into tubules. **Distribution** found in the northerly areas of the Black Sea (including the Sea of Azov) and the Caspian Sea. Common in the lower reaches of large rivers (e.g. Volga, Don, Dnieper) in these areas. **Reproduction** nothing is known of the reproductive habits of this species. **Food** invertebrates, mainly crustaceans, and (in fresh water) insect larvae. **Value** of no commercial or sporting value.

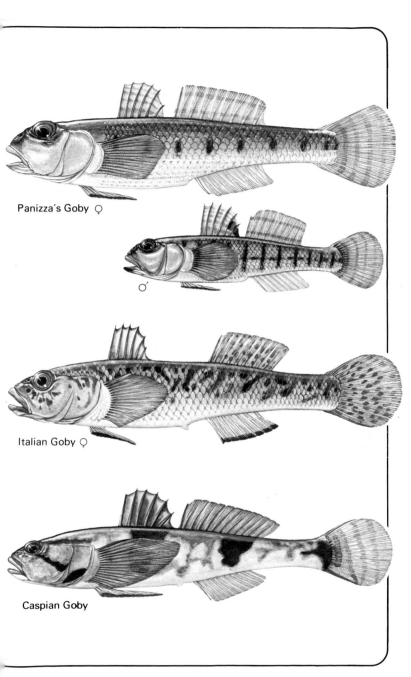

Panizza's Goby ♀

♂

Italian Goby ♀

Caspian Goby

239

Caspian Tadpole Goby
Benthophilus macrocephalus

Size 5—10cm. **Distinctive features** 2 dorsal fins and united pelvic fins; body densely covered in bony granules; 22—27 tubercles in the dorsal series. **Distribution** found throughout the Caspian Sea and in the Sea of Azov. Common in lagoons and the estuaries of the Volga and the Kuban. **Reproduction** little is known of the reproductive habits of this species. **Food** invertebrates, mainly worms, molluscs, crustaceans and insect larvae. **Value** of no commercial or sporting significance.

Stellate Tadpole Goby
Benthophilus stellatus

Size 8—12cm; maximum 14cm. **Distinctive features** 2 dorsal fins and united pelvic fins; large numbers of tubercles in characteristic patterns on head and body; 3 dark spots on back. **Distribution** found in brackish water areas of the Black Sea, the Sea of Azov and the Caspian Sea. Commonly found upstream in rivers in the Black Sea area (Danube, Dnieper, Don), but does not enter pure water in the Caspian basin. **Reproduction** May—June, after which all the adult males and females die; thus the whole life span is exactly 1 year. 700—2,500 eggs per female. **Food** invertebrates, mainly worms and molluscs. **Value** of no commercial or sporting significance.

Banded Tadpole Goby
Benthophilus brauneri

Size 4—5cm; maximum 6cm. **Distinctive features** 2 dorsal fins and united pelvic fins; 2 dark brownish bands around body; 2 oblique streaks on cheeks. **Distribution** found in the Caspian Sea and the lower reaches of the Dnieper and Bug. **Reproduction** spawning takes place in shallow brackish water, but little is known of its reproductive habits. **Food** invertebrates, especially crustaceans. **Value** of no commercial or sporting importance.

Rough Tadpole Goby
Benthophilus granulosus

Size 3—4cm; maximum 6cm. **Distinctive features** 2 dorsal fins and united pelvic fins; body covered in uniform bony granules, but without rows of larger granules. **Distribution** common throughout the Caspian Sea and in the estuary of the Volga. **Reproduction** nothing is known of the reproductive habits of this species. **Food** invertebrates, especially crustaceans, and some small fish larvae. **Value** of no commercial or sporting value.

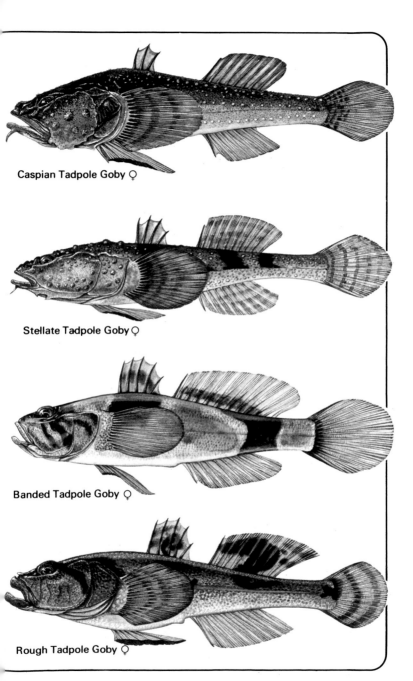

Caspian Tadpole Goby ♀

Stellate Tadpole Goby ♀

Banded Tadpole Goby ♀

Rough Tadpole Goby ♀

Family COTTIDAE

The Cottidae, or bullheads, are mainly small bottom-living fishes which occur in Europe, Asia and North America. They are mostly marine and over 300 species have been described.

Only 3 occur in fresh water in Europe.

Key to European Cottidae occurring in freshwater

1 Branchiostegal membrane free of isthmus, forming a fold; 4 yellow growths on head
Myoxocephalus quadricornis

Branchiostegal membrane attached to isthmus and not forming a free fold; no growths on head **2**

2 Lateral line extending to caudal fin; inner unpigmented pelvic ray more than $\frac{1}{2}$ length of longest ray *Cottus gobio*

Lateral line ending below 2nd dorsal fin; inner pigmented pelvic ray less than $\frac{1}{2}$ length of longest ray *Cottus poecilopus*

Bullhead *Cottus gobio*

Size 10–15cm; maximum 18cm. **Distinctive features** lateral line ending at caudal fin. **Distribution** in stony streams and some lakes in most of Europe except the extreme north and south. **Reproduction** March–May, spawning in nests under stones guarded by the male. Eggs hatch in 20–25 days and young mature in 2 years; rarely living longer than 6 years. About 100 eggs per female. **Food** mainly invertebrates, especially insect larvae, but also fish eggs and fry. **Value** of no commercial or sporting value.

Siberian Bullhead *Cottus poecilopus*

Size 8–10cm; maximum 13cm. **Distinctive features** lateral line ending below 2nd dorsal fin. **Distribution** in stony streams, rivers and some lakes in north and central Europe and northern Asia. **Reproduction** February–April, spawning in nests under stones. **Food** invertebrates, especially crustaceans and insect larvae. **Value** of no commercial or sporting significance.

Fourhorn Bullhead *Myoxocephalus quadricornis*

Size 10–25cm; maximum 60cm. **Distinctive features** 2 pairs of spongy growths on head. **Distribution** in the sea, and in brackish water along Arctic coasts of Europe, Asia and North America. Occurs as isolated populations in large lakes (e.g. Malarsee). **Reproduction** December–January, spawning among stones in areas guarded by the males. **Food** benthic invertebrates, especially crustaceans. **Value** of some value to local fisheries. Of no sporting significance.

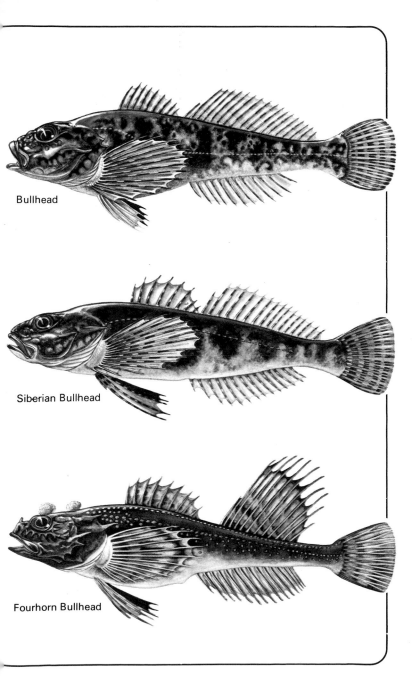

Bullhead

Siberian Bullhead

Fourhorn Bullhead

243

Family PLEURONECTIDAE

The Pleuronectidae, or flatfishes, is a large family of mainly marine fishes found in all seas of the world. There are many genera, but only 2 of these regularly enter fresh water in Europe. As their common name implies, these fishes are characteristically flattened and asymmetrical, with both eyes on the same side (usually the right, but reversed specimens occasionally occur).

Only 2 species (both catadromous) occur in fresh water in Europe.

Key to European Pleuronectidae entering fresh water

1 Bony tubercles present at bases of dorsal and anal fin rays; bony tubercles or platelets on body; 15–22 gill rakers on 1st arch
Platichthys flesus

No bony tubercles at bases of dorsal and anal fin rays, nor bony tubercles or platelets on body; 10–14 gill rakers on 1st arch
Liopsetta glacialis

Flounder *Platichthys flesus*

Size 20–30cm; maximum 50cm. **Distinctive features** flattened asymmetrically with both eyes on the same side; bony tubercles and platelets on body; 15–22 gill rakers on 1st arch. **Distribution** found all round the European coast from the Arctic Ocean to the northern Mediterranean and Black Seas. Common also in estuaries and lowland rivers and some lakes which are easily accessible from the sea. **Reproduction** February–May, spawning in the sea in deep water. The eggs hatch in 4–8 days and the larvae are pelagic for about 50 days before sinking to the bottom and developing their flattened form. The young mature after 3–4 years. 500,000–2,000,000 eggs per female. **Food** zooplankton when young, benthic invertebrates, especially worms, molluscs and crustaceans when older. **Value** of considerable commercial value in many sandy coastal areas where it is caught in traps and nets of various types. It is also popular with anglers in many coastal areas.

Arctic Flounder *Liopsetta glacialis*

Size 15–25cm; maximum 35cm. **Distinctive features** flattened asymmetrically with both eyes on the same side; no bony tubercles or platelets on body; 10–14 gill rakers on 1st arch. **Distribution** found only in Arctic coastal waters including estuaries and the lower reaches of some rivers. **Reproduction** February–May, in the sea. **Food** benthic invertebrates, especially molluscs. **Value** of local commercial value to coastal net fisheries. Of no sporting value.

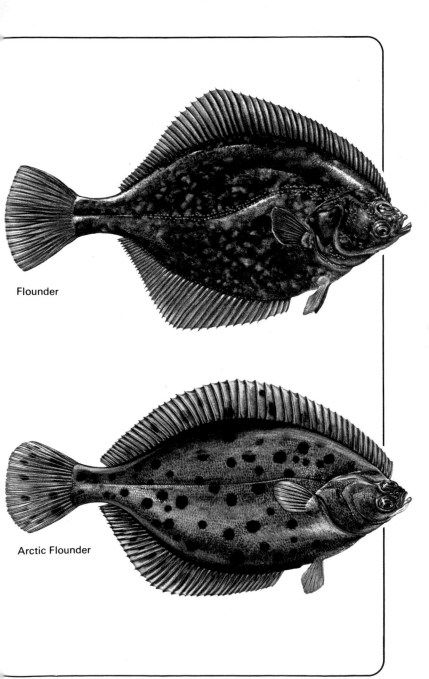

Flounder

Arctic Flounder

Age/length curves of some representative species

The curves below give typical age/length information for one typical species within each family of European freshwater fishes, except for a few cases where no information is available. In addition to giving a comparison of the growth rates of these species, they may be used to give an estimate of length if only the age is known, or vice versa. In use the known value (length or age) is plotted on the curve and the unknown read off the corresponding axis.

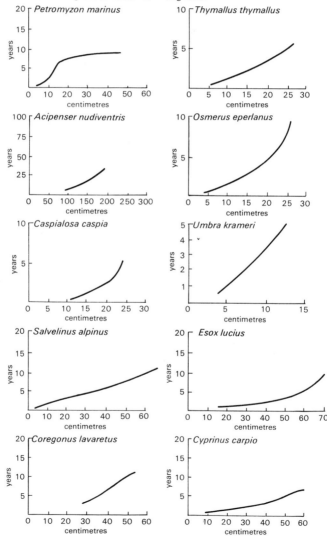

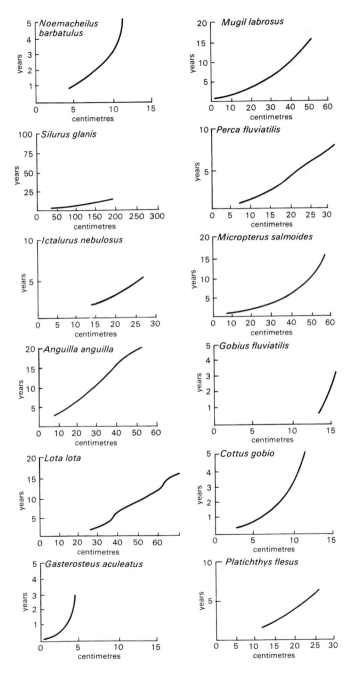

247

Bibliography

Albuquerque, R. M. 1956. Peixes de Portugal e ilhas adjacentes. *Port. Acta biol.*, B, 5, 1–1164.

Banaresch, P., Blanc, M., Gaudet, J. L. & Hureau, J. C. 1971. *European inland water fish: a multilingual catalogue*. Fishing News, London.

Bauch, G. 1953. *Die einheimischen Susswasserfische*. Neumann, Berlin.

Berg, L. 1947. *Classification of fishes both recent and fossil*. Edwards, Ann Arbor.

Berg, L. S. 1962. *Freshwater fishes of the USSR and adjacent countries*. Israel Program of Scientific Translation, Jerusalem.

Bini, G. 1962. *I pesci delle aque interne d'Italia*. Garzanti, Rome.

Von Brandt, A. 1975. *Fish catching methods of the world*. Fishing News Books, Farnham.

Cabo, F. L. 1964. *Los peces de las aguas continentales espanolas*. SNPFC, Madrid.

Falkus, H. & Buller, F. 1975. *Freshwater fishing*. MacDonald & Jane, London.

Greenwood, P. H., Miles, R. S., & Patterson, C. 1973. *Interrelationships of fishes*. Academic Press, New York.

Hervey, G. F. & Hems, J. 1973. *A guide to freshwater aquarium fishes*. Hamlyn, London.

Hoar, W. S. & Randall, D. J. 1971. *Fish physiology*. Academic Press, New York.

Huet, M. 1971. *Textbook of fish culture: breeding and cultivation of fish*. Fishing News, London.

Hutchinson, G. E. 1975. *A treatise on limnology*. Wiley, New York.

Innes, W. T. 1959. *Exotic aquarium fishes*. Innes, Philadelphia.

Ladiges, W. & Vogt, D. 1965. *Die Susswasserfische Europas*. Parey, Hamburg.

Lagler, K. F., Bardach, J. E., & Miller, R. R. 1967. *Ichthyology*. Wiley, New York.

Maitland, P. S. 1972. A key to the freshwater fishes of the British Isles with notes on their distribution and ecology. *Sci. Publ. Freshw. Biol. Ass.*, 27, 1–139.

Marshall, N. B. 1965. *The life of fishes*. Weidenfeld & Nicolson, London.

Michaelson, J. 1974. *Tackle angling*. Paul Stanley, London.

Muus, B. J. & Dahlstrom, P. 1967. *The freshwater fishes of Britain and Europe*. Collins, London.

Nikolsky, G. V. 1963. *The ecology of fishes*. Academic Press, London.

Norman, J. R. & Greenwood, P. H. 1975. *A history of fishes*. Benn, London.

Perry, F. 1951. *The garden pool*. Collingridge, London.

Pratt, M. M. 1975. *Better angling with simpler science*. Fishing News Books, Farnham.

Reid, G. K. 1961. *Ecology of inland waters and estuaries*. Reinhold, New York.

Rounsefell, G. A. & Everhart, W. H. 1953. *Fishery science: its methods and applications*. Wiley, New York.

Schindler, O. 1957. *Freshwater fishes*. Thames & Hudson, London.

Scott, W. B. & Crossman, E. J. 1973. Freshwater fishes of Canada. *Bull. Fish. Res. Bd. Canada*, 184, 1–966.

Spillman, C. J. 1961. *Poissons d'eau douce*. Lechevalier, Paris.

Sterba, G. 1973. *Freshwater fishes of the world*. Studio Vista, London.

Van Duijn, C. 1967. *Diseases of fishes*. Iliffe, London.

Welch, P. S. 1951. *Limnology*. McGraw-Hill, New York.

Wheeler, A. 1969. *The fishes of the British Isles and north-west Europe*. Macmillan, London.

Willock, C. 1975. *The anglers encyclopedia*. Pelham Books, London.

Glossary

adipose fin modified rayless posterior dorsal fin found in the Salmonidae and a few other families (see page 91).

alevin recently hatched stage of a salmonid fish when the yolk sac still protrudes externally.

anadromous maturing in salt water but migrating into fresh water to spawn.

axillary process pointed structure growing from the base of a fin.

benthic bottom living.

bifid forked.

biota flora and fauna of an area.

branchial of the gills.

branchiostegal of the gill covers.

buccal of the mouth or cheek.

catadromous maturing in fresh water but migrating into salt water to spawn.

caudal peduncle base of tail.

chromatophore pigment cell which can be altered in shape to produce colour change (see fig. 40).

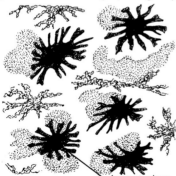

Fig. 40 chromatophore

circuli ring-like ridges on fish scales (see fig. 32).

ctenoid having a comb-like margin (see fig. 38).

cusp sharp point or prominence.

cycloid having an evenly curved free border (see fig. 32).

denticle small tooth-like process.

dentiform tooth-like.

diatom unicellular type of alga with silica walls.

dichotomous repeatedly forking or dividing.

dorso-ventral stretching from dorsal to ventral surface.

emarginate having a notched margin.

epithelial of a covering or enveloping tissue.

erythrocyte red blood corpuscle.

eutrophication increasing in chemical richness.

fimbria delicate fringing processes as found on the barbels of sturgeons.

freshet sudden but temporary increase in flow down a river, often due to heavy rain.

fusiform tapering gradually at both ends.

gene the unit of heredity found in living cells.

gene pool total hereditary material available within a population of animals or plants.

heterocercal tail fin in which the upper lobe is larger than the lower, and contains the upturned termination of the vertebral column (see page 77).

holocercal tail fin in which the upper and lower lobes are the same size (see page 91).

hyoid bone lying at the base of the tongue in fishes.

inferior below.

infra-oral below the mouth.

interorbital between the eye sockets.

isthmus narrow piece of tissue connecting two larger structures (see fig. 41).

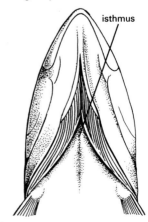

isthmus

Fig. 41

keeled having a single ventral ridge.

labial referring to structures which are part of the lips or mouth.

lamella thin plate-like structure.

lateral situated on the side.

lateral band strip of colour along the side of the body.

leucocyte colourless blood corpuscle.

lingual of the tongue.

littoral zone of shallow water around the edges of lakes and seas.

lobule small lobe or projection of an organ.

lymphocyte small colourless blood corpuscle.

mandibular of the lower jaw.

maxillary of the upper jaw (see fig. 45).

medio-lateral along the middle of a side.

occipital of the back part of the head.

operculum gill cover (see fig. 8).

otolith calcareous particle found in the inner ears of fishes (see fig. 10).

palatine occurring in the region of the palate (see fig. 45).

papilla small projection from the body surface (see fig. 42).

pharyngeal of the gullet, or anterior part of the alimentary canal.

photosynthesis the process in green plants where, under the action of light, carbohydrates are synthesized from carbon dioxide and water.

phytoplankton microscopic plants (mainly algae) which drift free in the water.

platelet small flattened disc.

postorbital behind the eye sockets.

preopercular anterior to the gill cover.

preorbital in front of the eye sockets.

pyloric caeca small blind-ending pouches opening to the posterior part of the stomach (see fig. 43).

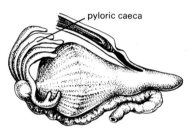

pyloric caeca

Fig. 43

redd depression in gravel dug out by a female salmonid fish in which to lay her eggs.

scute bony scale-like structure (see page 79).

smolt immature stage of a salmonid fish following the parr stage when the whole fish becomes completely silver in colour.

suborbital below the eye sockets.

subterminal situated almost, but not quite, at the end of a structure.

superior above.

supra-oral above the mouth.

taxa definite units in the classification of plants and animals.

taxonomist a scientist involved in the classification of plants and animals.

terminal situated at the end of a structure.

tricuspid having three tapering points.

trifid divided to form three lobes.

triserial arranged in three rows.

truncated terminating abruptly.

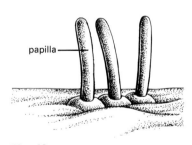

papilla

Fig. 42

parietal in fishes, usually referring to paired bones on the roof of the skull (see fig. 45).

parr immature stage of a salmonid fish between fry and smolt when a row of distinct dark marks are present along each side.

pelagic zone zone of open water away from the edges and bottom of a lake or sea.

peristalsis movement by means of successive waves of muscular contraction.

tubercle small rounded swelling
(see fig. 44).
tubule any small hollow cylindrical
organ.
turbid cloudy with suspended
matter.
unicuspid having one tapering
point.
uniserial arranged in one row.
vermiculate marked with
numerous bending lines of colour
(see *Salvelinus fontinalis*, page 97).
vomer bone in the nasal region
(see fig. 3a).
zooplankton microscopic animals
which drift free in the water.

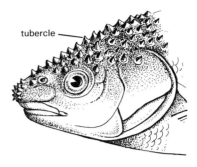

Fig. 44

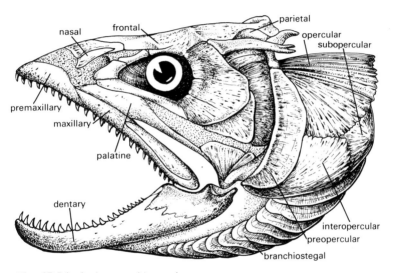

Fig. 45 Principal external bones in
the head of a fish (*Salmo*)

Index